بسم الله الرحمن الرحيم

An Introduction to Methodology of Islamic Jurisprudence
(Uşūl al-Fiqh)
A Shiite Approach

An Introduction to Methodology of Islamic Jurisprudence

(Uṣūl al-Fiqh)

A Shiite Approach

Alireza Hodaee

British Library Cataloguing-in-Publication Data
A catalogue record for this book is available from the British Library.

ISBN: 978-1-911361-30-5 (pbk)

This English edition first published in 2016

Islam and West Research Center Ltd
3, Research Center, Golders Green
London NW11 8ED

CONTENTS

Preface	XIII
Transliteration	XV
Introductory Discussions	1
Definition of the Science of *Uṣūl al-Fiqh*	1
Subject-Matter of the Science of *Uṣūl al-Fiqh*	2
Benefit of the Science of *Uṣūl al-Fiqh*	2
Parts of the Science of *Uṣūl al-Fiqh*	2
Convention (*al-Waḍʿ*)	3
Varieties of Convention	4
Signs of Literal and Figurative Meanings	5
Literal Principles	6
Usage of One Term in More than One Meaning	7
The Juristic-Literal Meaning *(al-Ḥaqīqa al-Sharʿiyya)*	8
The Sound (*al-Ṣaḥīḥ*) and What Incorporates Both (*al- Aʿamm*)	9
Part I : Discussions of Terms	11
Chapter 1 : The derived *(al-Mushtaqq)*	13
Chapter 2 : The commands *(al-Awāmir)*	15
Appearance of the Command	15
Varieties of Mandatory Acts	16
Absolute (*al-Muṭlaq*) and Conditional (*al-Mashrūṭ*)	16
Suspended (*al-Muʿallaq*) and Definite (*al-Munadjdjaz*)	17
Determinate (*al-Taʿyīnī*) and Optional (*al-Takhyīrī*)	18
Individual (*al-ʿAynī*) and Collective (*al-Kifāʾī*)	18
Extended (*al-Muwassaʿ*) and Constricted (*al-Muḍayyaq*)	19

Religiously (*al-Ta'abbudī*) and Instrumental (*al-Tawaṣṣulī*) 21
Varieties of Mandatory Acts and the Absoluteness of the Mode (*al-Ṣīgha*) 21
Promptitude (*al-Fawr*) or Belatedness (*al-Tarakhī*) 24
Once (*al-Marra*) or Repetition (*al-Takrār*) 25
To Command Something Twice 26
Denotation of "Command to Command" 27
Chapter 3 : The prohibitions (*al-Nawāhī)* 29
The Desired in the Prohibition 29
Denotation of the Prohibition as to Permanence (*al-Dawām*) and Repetition (*al-Takrār*) 30
Chapter 4 : Implicatures of sentences (*al-Mafāhīm*) 31
Varieties of *Mafhūm* 32
1. *Mafhūm* of the Condition (*al-Sharṭ*) 33
The Criterion for *Mafhūm* of the Condition 34
Conditions Being Multiple While Consequents Being One 36
2. *Mafhūm* of the Qualifier (*al-Waṣf*) 39
The Justifiable Opinion on *Mafhūm* of the Qualifier 39
3. *Mafhūm* of the Termination (*al-Ghāya*) 42
4. *Mafhūm* of the Exclusivity (*al-Ḥaṣr*) 42
5. *Mafhūm* of the Number (*al-'Adad*) 43
6. *Mafhūm* of the Designation (*al-Laqab*) 43
Three Important Denotations Not of Kind of *Mafhūm* or *Manṭūq*: Necessitation (*al-Iqtiḍā'*), Hint (*al-Tanbīh*), and Implicit Conveyance (*al-Ishāra*) 44
Chapter 5 : General (*al-'Āmm)* And Particular (*al-Khāṣṣ*) 47
Varieties of Generality 47
Terms of Generality 48
The Joint Restrictor (*al-Mukhaṣṣiṣ al-Muttaṣil*) and the Separate Restrictor (*al-Mukhaṣṣiṣ al-Munfaṣil*) 49
Usage of the General in the Restricted (*al-Mukhaṣṣaṣ*) 50

Authority or Otherwise of the Restricted General in the Remaining (*al-Bāqī*) 51
Penetration or Otherwise of Ambiguity of the Restrictor into to the General 52
1. The Dubiety concerning the Concept 53
2. The Dubiety concerning the Instance 54
Unlawfulness of Implication of the General before the Quest for the Restrictor 55
A General Preceding a Pronoun which Refers to Some Instances of the General 56
An Exception Preceded by Multiple Sentences 56
Restriction of the General by *Mafhūm* 57
Restriction of the Book by Single Tradition 58
Chapter 6 : Absolute (*al-Muṭlaq)* And Qualified (*al-Muqayyad*) 61
Is Absoluteness by Convention? 61
Premises of Wisdom (*Muqaddimāt al-Ĥikma*) 62
Contradictory Absolute and Qualified 63
Chapter 7 : Ambiguous (*al-Mudjmal)* and Clear (*al-Mubayyan*) 65
Part II: Intellectual Implications 67
Chapter 8 : Replacement (*al-Idjzā'*) 69
1. The Compelling Command 70
2. The Apparent Command 71
2.1. The Replacement with Respect to the Authorized Conjectural Proof When the Error Is Revealed with Certainty 72
2.1.1. In the precepts 72
2.1.2. In the objects 73
2.2. The Replacement with respect to the Practical Principles When the Error Is Revealed with Certainty 73
2.3. The Replacement with respect to Both Authorized Conjectural Proof and Practical Principle When the Error Is Revealed by an Authoritative Proof 74
Change in the Certitude 76
Chapter 9 : The Preliminary of the Mandatory Act (*Muqaddima al-Wādjib*) 77

Chapter 10 : The Problem of the Opposite (*Mas'ala al-Đidd*) 79
1. The General Opposite 79
2. The Particular Opposite 80
2.1. The Way of Implication 80
2.2. The Way of Being Preliminary 81
The Outcome of This Discussion 83
Chapter 11 : Conjunction of the Command and
the Prohibition (*Idjtimā' al-Amr Wa'l Nahy*) 85
Conjunction of the Command and the Prohibition with a Way Out 88
The Argument for Impossibility 89
The Argument for Possibility 91
The Outcome of This Discussion 91
Conjunction of the Command and the Prohibition without a Way Out 93
Not Preceded by Free Will 93
Preceded by Misuse of Free Will 94
Chapter 12 : Denotation of Prohibition As To Annulment (*Dalalā al-Nahy ala'l Fasād*) 99
Prohibition of Act of Worship 99
Prohibition of Transaction 100
Part III: Discussions of Authority (*al-Ĥudjdja*) 103
Introductory Discussions of the Tird Part 105
The Meaning of *al-Ĥudjdja* 105
Amāra and *al-Żann al-Mu'tabar* 106
Amāra and the Practical Principle 106
The Criterion for Proving Authority of *Amāra* 107
Essentiality of Authority of Certitude (Knowledge, *'Ilm*) 109
The Position of Authority of *Amāra* 109
The Particular Conjecture and the Absolute Conjecture 110

Preliminaries of the Closure Proof (*Dalīl al-Insidād*) 110
Commonness of Precepts between the Knowledgeable and the Ignorant 112
Why Is *Amāra* an Absolutely Authoritative Proof? 113
Amāra Being a Path (*Ṭarīq*) or a Cause (*Sabab*) 115
Chapter 13 : The Book (*al-Kitāb*) 117
Abolishment of the Book 117
Possibility of Abolishment of the Qur'ān 118
Principality of Non-Abolishment 120
Chapter 14 : *Sunna* 121
Denotation of Act of the Infallible-Innocent Personality 122
Denotation of Acknowledgment (*Taqrīr*) of the Infallible-Innocent Personality 123
The Massive Report (*al-Khabar al-Mutawātir*) 124
The Single Report (*Khabar al-Wāḥid*) 125
Proofs of Authority of Single Report from the Book 126
Proofs of Authority of Single Report from *Sunna* 129
Proofs of Authority of Single Report from Consensus 130
Proofs of Authority of Single Report from the Conduct of the Wise 131
Chapter 15 : Consensus (*Idjmā'*) 133
Sunnī Approach to the Consensus 134
Shiite Approach to the Consensus 135
Chapter16 : The Intellectual Proof (*al-Dalīl al-'Aqlī*) 137
Justification of Authority of the Intellect 138
Chapter 17 : Authority of Appearances (Ḥudjdjiyya al-Żawāhir) 139
Justification of the Authority of Appearance 141
Authority of the Appearance with regard to Those Whose Communication Is Not Meant 142
Authority of Appearances of the Book 144
Chapter 18 : The Celebrity (*al-Shuhra*) 147
Chapter 19 : The Custom (*al-Sīra*) 151

Authority of the Conduct of the Wise 151
Authority of the Custom of the People of the Religion 153
Chapter 20 : The (Juristic) Analogy *(al- Qiyās)* 155
Definition of *Qiyās* 155
Pillars of *Qiyās* 156
Authority of *Qiyās* 156
Provoking Knowledge 156
Definite Proofs Proving Authority of *Qiyās* 157
Shiite Position on *Qiyās* 157
Chapter 21 : Equilibrium and Prefrences (*al-Ta'ādul wa'l Tarādjīḥ*) 159
Contradiction (*al-Ta'āruḍ*) 159
Conditions of Contradiction 159
Primary Principle as to Contradictory Proofs 160
Secondary Principle as to Contradictory Proofs 160
Customary Gathering (*al-Djam' al-'Urfī*) 161
Preferrers 161
Interference (*al-Tazāḥum*) 162
Sovereignty (*al-Ḥukūma*) and Entry (*al-Wurūd)* 163
Part IV: The Practical Principles (al-Usūl al-'Amaliyya) 165
Chapter 22 : The Principle of Clearance *(Aṣāla al-Barā'a)* 169
1. The Dubiety concerning the Precept as to Unlawfulness Because of Lack of the Proof 169
1.1. *Uṣūlīs'* Proofs of Clearance 170
1.1.1. The Book 170
1.1.2. *Sunna* 171
1.1.3. Consensus 174
1.1.4. The Intellect 175
1.2. *Akhbārīs'* Proofs of Precaution 176

1.2.1. The Book 176
1.2.2. *Sunna* 177
1.2.3. The Intellect 178
2. The Dubiety concerning the Precept as to Unlawfulness Because of Ambiguity of the Proof 178
3. The Dubiety concerning the Precept as to Unlawfulness Because of Contradiction of Proofs 179
4. The Dubiety concerning the Object as to Unlawfulness 179
5. The Dubiety as to Obligation concerning the Precept Because of Lack of the Proof, Because of Ambiguity of the Proof, Because of Contradiction of Proofs, and concerning the Object 179
Chapter 23 : The Principle of Option (*Aṣāla al-Takhyīr*) 181
Chapter 24 : The Principle of Liability (Precaution)(*Aṣāla al-Iḥtiyāṭ or Ishtighāl)* 185
1. The Dubiety Being over Two Divergent Things 187
1.1. The Dubiety concerning Unlawfulness 187
1.1.1. The Dubiety concerning the Object 187
1.1.1.1. The Small-Scale Dubiety (al-Shubha al-Maḥṣūra) 187
1.1.1.2. The Large-Scale Dubiety (al-Shubha Ghair al-Maḥṣūra) 189
1.1.2. The Dubiety concerning the Precept 191
1.2. The Dubiety concerning Obligation 191
1.2.1. The Dubiety concerning the Precept 191
1.2.1.1. Because of Lack of Proof 191
1.2.1.2. Because of Ambiguity of Proof 191
1.2.1.3. Because of Contradiction of Proofs 192
1.2.2. The Dubiety concerning the Object 192
2. The Dubiety Being over the Least and the Most of One Thing 192
2.1. The Independing Least and Most 193
2.2. The Relational Least and Most 193

2.2.1. The dubiety concerning the precept whether as to unlawfulness or obligation, caused by either lack of proof, ambiguity of proof, or contradiction of proofs 193
2.2.1.1. The dubiety over object of the duty 193
2.2.1.2. The dubiety over causes 194
2.2.2. The dubiety concerning the object whether as to unlawfulness or obligation 195
Chapter 25 : The Principle of Continuity of the Previous State (*Aṣāla al-Istiṣĥāb*) 197
Constituents of *Istiṣĥāb* 197
Proofs of Authority of *Istiṣĥāb* 198
1. The conduct of the wise 198
2. *Ĥadīṯh*s 199
Secondary Discussions of *Istiṣĥāb* 201
The Rule of Certainty (*Qā'ida al-Yaqīn*) 201
Continuity of the Previous State of the Universal (*Istiṣĥāb al-Kullī*) 201
Selected Bibliography 205
Index 207

PREFACE

Uṣūl al-Fiqh, the methodology of jurisprudence, which is usually – and inaccurately, if not incorrectly – translated "principles of jurisprudence," is an Islamic science which is developed by Shiite scholars in two recent centuries into an unparalleled intellectual, logical system of thought and a comprehensive branch of knowledge which not only serves as the logic of jurisprudence but as an independent science dealing with some hermeneutical problems.

Lack of precise English equivalents to expressions and terms of this complicated science indicates the least difficulties of preparing the first English version of Shiite *uṣūl al-fiqh*. Relying on the Almighty's constant grace, however, I did my best to present this unique Shiite science to the western world in its best fashion; and I pray to the Almighty to have been successful in doing such a difficult job. Nonetheless, it should be noted that most of complicated arguments of such profound science cannot be presented in an introductory work; they should be pursued in detailed books written by great Shiite *Uṣūlīs*. I have to express my gratitude to my dearest friend, Dr. Seyyed Mohsen Miri, head of Islam and West Research Center of al-Mustafa International Research Institute (M.I.R.I), who prepared the ground for constitution of this work.

Alireza Hodaee
Tehran, April, 2015

TRANSLITERATION KEY

Arab./Pers Letter	Roman Equivalent	Arab./Pers Letter	Roman Equivalent
ء	’ (except when initial)	ض	đ
ا	a	ط	ţ
ب	b	ظ	ż
پ	p	ع	‘
ت	t	غ	gh
ث	th	ف	f
ج	dj	ق	q
ح	ĥ	ک	k
خ	kh	ل	l
د	d	م	m
ذ	dh	ن	n
ر	r	ه	h
ز	z	و	w
س	s	ی	y
ش	sh	ة	h *or* t
ص	ş		

Short Vowels	
ـَ	a
ـُ	u
ـِ	i

Long Vowels	
ىٰ or آ	ā
ـُو	ū
ـِي	ī

Diphthongs	
ـَو	aw
ـَي	ay
ـِيّ	iyy (final form: ī)
ـُوّ	uww (final form:ū)
ـِيا	iyā
ّ	the letter is doubled

Introductory Discussions

Definition of the Science of *Uṣūl al-Fiqh*

The science of *uṣūl al-fiqh* is a science in which such rules whose results are placed in ways of deduction of juristic precepts are discussed. For instance, performing the prayers (*ṣalāt*) is mandatory in Islam, and this Qur'ānic verse proves that obligation: "And that perform the prayers." (6:72) However, denotation of the verse is dependent upon the imperative, like "perform" in that verse, being apparent in the obligation on the one hand and Qur'ānic apparent meanings being authoritative proofs on the other. Those two issues are dealt with in the science of *uṣūl al-fiqh*. Now, when the jurist learns through this science that the imperative is apparent in the obligation and that the Qur'ānic apparent meanings are authoritative proofs, he can infer from the said verse that the prayers is mandatory.

In the same way, deduction of every juristic precept inferred from any juristic or intellectual proof must be dependent upon one or more issues of this science.

It should be known that precepts are of two kinds:

1. The precept is directed to something *per se* as it is an act; such as the prayers, since the obligation is directed to the prayers as it is prayers and an act *per se* without consideration of anything else. Such precept is called "the actual precept" (*al-ḥukm al-wāqi'ī*) and the proof proving it "the persuasive proof" (*al-dalīl al-idjtihādī*).
2. The precept is directed to something as its actual precept is unknown; such as the dispute among jurists whether or not smoking is unlawful. Here, where there is no proof to support any of the existing opinions, the jurist doubts the primary, actual precept of the disputed matter, and since he is not supposed to remain perplexed practically there must exist another

precept, though intellectual, for him, such as obligation of precaution, clearance from obligation, or ignoring the doubt. Such a secondary precept is called "the apparent precept" (*al-ḥukm al-ẓāhirī*) and the proof proving it "the juristic proof" (*al-dalīl al-faqāhatī*) or "the practical principle" (*al-aṣl al-ʿamalī*).

Discussions of the science of *uṣūl al-fiqh* cover both of such precepts.

Subject-Matter of the Science of *Uṣūl al-Fiqh*

Different things are said by various *Uṣūlī*s to be the subject matter of this science. However, there is no need to treat them as true and, as later *Uṣūlī*s have said, this science has no specific subject-matter. It discusses various subjects which are all common in its purpose, which is inferring juristic precepts. Detailed discussions on this topic can be found in detailed works of *uṣūl al-fiqh*.

Benefit of the Science of *Uṣūl al-Fiqh*

Since it is clearly known that any human voluntarily act has a precept in Islam, whether obligation, unlawfulness, or any of the five-fold burdensome precepts, on the one side, it is known that not all those precepts are known to everyone by self-evident knowledge but most of them are in need of survey and proof, i.e., they are deductive on the second, and *uṣūl al-fiqh* is the only science formulated for proving juristic precepts on the third, the benefit of this science would be seeking assistance for deducing precepts from their proofs.

Parts of the Science of *Uṣūl al-Fiqh*

Discussions of this science are presented in various parts in the works of *uṣūl al-fiqh*. However, the best division is presented by al-Muḥaqqiq al-Iṣfahānī (d. 1940) in his last course of teaching (as narrated by his great student Muḥammad Riḍā al-Muẓaffar in his *Uṣūl al-Fiqh*, p. 11) according to which all *uṣūlī* topics are discussed in the four following parts: Discussions of "terms" (*mabāḥith al-alfāẓ*), those of "intellectual implications" (*mabāḥith al-mulāzamāt al-ʿaqliyya*), those of "the authority" (*mabāḥith al-ḥudjdja*), and those of "practical principles" (*mabāḥith al-uṣūl al-ʿamaliyya*).

Discussions of terms deal with denotations and appearances of terms from a general aspect, such as appearance of the imperative in the obligation, that of the prohibition in the unlawfulness, and the like.

Discussions of intellectual implications survey implications of precepts even though such precepts may not be inferred from terms, such as discussing truthfulness of mutual implication of intellectual judgments and juristic precepts, of obligation of something necessitating obligation of its preliminaries (known as "the problem of preliminary of the mandatory act"), of obligation of something necessitating unlawfulness of its opposite (known as "the problem of the opposite"), of possibility of conjunction of the command and the prohibition, and so on.

Discussions of the authority investigate whether some specific thing is juristically treated as a proof; for instance, whether report of a single transmitter, appearances, appearances of the Qur'ān, *Sunna*, consensus, intellect, and the like are authoritative proofs.

Discussions of practical principles deal with what the jurist refers to when he cannot find a persuasive proof, such as the principle of clearance from obligation, that of precaution, and so forth.

Convention (*al-Waḍʿ*)

A smoke essentially denotes a fire; but the case is not the same with denotation of words – whatever the language may be – for in that case all people throughout the world should have been speaking the same language. Thus, denotation of words is just through convention. That convention, however, is not made by a specific person, otherwise that person should have been named in the history of every language; rather, it is the human nature that invents a specific word when man wishes to denote a specific meaning and communicate others. Others, in turn, do the same; and with the passage of time the structure of a language takes shape, and then its vocabulary and grammar gradually develop. Convention of a word, therefore, means to make that word for a meaning and to designate it to that meaning.

Words normally denote their meanings by making (*al-dja'l*) and specification, and this kind of convention is called "convention by specification (*al-waḍʿ al-taʿyīnī*)." However, that denotation is sometimes caused by specification of a word to a meaning by repetition in the usage which makes minds familiar with it in such a way that as soon as one hears the word one refers to the meaning. This kind of convention is called "convention by determination (*al-waḍʿ al-taʿayyunī*)."

Varieties of Convention

In the convention, the term and the meaning must necessarily be conceived; for convention is a judgment on the meaning and the term, and making judgment on something is not acceptable unless it is conceived and known – even though in an undifferentiated mode, for any given thing can be conceived either by itself (*bi-nafsih*), or by its general facet (*bi-wadjhih*). For instance, when you see a white object from a distance you can judge that it is white while you do not know what exactly it is; this judgment is acceptable because you have somehow conceived it – as a thing, an animal, or the like – and that is not like an absolutely unknown object which in no way can be judged.

Now, since the meaning must be conceived on the one side, its conception is of two kinds on the second, and it is particular or general on the third, the convention can be divided into the four following varieties:

1. The conceived meaning is particular and the object of convention is the very particular, i.e., the object of convention is a particular meaning conceived by itself and not by its general facet. This kind is called "the convention particular and the object of convention particular (*al-waḍ‘ khāṣṣ wa'l mawḍū‘ lah khāṣṣ*)."
2. The conceived meaning is general and the object of convention is the very general, i.e., the object of convention is a general meaning conceived by itself and not by a general facet. This kind is called "the convention general and the object of convention general (*al-waḍ‘ ‘āmm wa'l mawḍū‘ lah ‘āmm*)."
3. The conceived meaning is general and the object of convention is an instance of that general and not itself, i.e., the object of convention is a particular meaning conceived not by itself but by its general facet. This kind is called "the convention general and the object of convention particular (*al-waḍ‘ ‘āmm wa'l mawḍū‘ lah khāṣṣ*)."
4. The conceived meaning is particular and the object of convention is a general facet of that particular. This kind is called "the convention particular and the object of convention general (*al-waḍ khāṣṣ wa'l mawḍū‘ lah ‘āmm*)."

There is no dispute among *Uṣūlīs* that the first three varieties are possible, and the first two varieties have occurred _ the first like proper nouns, and the second like common nouns such as water, heaven, star, and the like. Dispute is over the possibility of the fourth as well as the occurrence of the third. Referring the reader to detailed works on the Shiite *uṣūl al-fiqh*, here we just mention that the fourth is impossible – for the particular cannot be a facet of the general;

rather, the case is vice versa, i.e., the general is a facet and aspect of the particular – and the third has occurred and its instances are prepositions, demonstrative pronouns, pronouns, and the like.

What we discussed was concerning the meaning. That discussion can somehow be pursued with regard to the term as well. If the term is specified for the meaning while it is conceived by itself, as is the normal procedure, the convention is called personal (*al-shakhṣī*), and if it is conceived by its general facet it is called typical (*al-naw'ī*) – like dispositions in typical phrases and sentences, as the disposition in conditional clauses to denote that the consequence is dependent upon the antecedent.

Signs of Literal and Figurative Meanings

Usage of a term in its designated meaning is literally correct, in another meaning with which it has some pertinence along with some contextual evidence is figuratively correct, and in another meaning without any pertinence is wrong. Therefore, usage of a term literally and figuratively is correct and "the usage" cannot specify whether a term is designated for a meaning or it is used figuratively.

Now, should one know, through assertion of philologists, that a term is designated for a meaning it would obviously be clear that such word is to be used literally in that meaning and figuratively in other pertinent meanings. However, the case is not that clear sometimes and one may wonder how to treat the usage. What can one do in that case in order to find out whether such a usage is literally correct or it is figuratively so and hence one should use it with some contextual evidence?

Uṣūlīs have mentioned some signs of recognition of the literal meaning the most important of which being preceding (*al-tabādur*) and incorrectness of divesting(*'adam ṣiĥĥat al-salb*). By *tabādur* is meant that when one thinks of a term, a specific meaning comes to one's mind first – from the very term without there being any contextual evidence – and precedes other meanings. This clearly proves that the term indicates its meaning merely because of convention and nothing else. By *'adam ṣiĥĥat al-salb* is meant that divesting a term of a meaning is not correct. To exercise both of these signs, let us consider the example of the term "lion." We know that this term is used for a specific animal literally and for a brave man figuratively. Now, when you hear the term "lion" it is the meaning of that animal which comes to your mind first and not a brave man, and this is *tabādur*. Also, you cannot divest "lion" of that animal while you can do that of a brave man, and this is *'adam ṣiĥĥat al-salb*. Thus, *tabādur* and *'adam ṣiḥḥat al-salb* are two signs which indicate the literal meaning of a term.

Literal Principles

When a doubt occurs concerning a term it can be of two kinds: a doubt concerning convention whether that term is specified for a certain meaning, and a doubt concerning intention of a speaker whether he has meant the literal or figurative meaning. Presenting two signs of recognition of the literal meaning, the pervious discussion dealt with the first kind of doubt. However, that is not enough for the removal of the second doubt, for those signs cannot determine speaker's intention. What can we do, then? *Uṣūlīs* have presented some principles in this connection, called "literal principles (*al-uṣūl al-lafẓiyya*)," their most important ones being the following:

1. *The Principle of Literalness (Aṣāla al-Ḥaqīqa).* This principle is used when one doubts whether a certain speaker has intended the literal or the figurative meaning, where there is no contextual evidence while its existence is probable. In that case, it is said that "the principle is the literalness," i.e., one should principally treat the term as being used in its literal and not figurative meaning, for to use a word figuratively needs contextual evidence which does not exist.
2. *The Principle of Generality(Aṣāla al-'Umūm).* This principle is used when a speaker has used a general term and one doubts whether it is still general or it has been restricted. In that case, it is said that "the principle is the generality," i.e., one should principally treat the term as being used in its general meaning without being restricted.
3. *The Principle of Absoluteness(Aṣāla al-Iṭlāq).* This principle is used when a speaker has used an absolute term which has some states and conditions and one doubts whether its absolute meaning is intended by the speaker or he may have intended some of those states or conditions. In that case, it is said that "the principle is the absoluteness," i.e., one should principally treat the term as being used in its absolute meaning without being limited to some states or conditions.
4. *The Principle of Appearance(Aṣāla al-Żuhūr).* When a term is explicitly used in a meaning in such a way that no other meaning is probable it is called *naṣṣ*, and when it is used in a meaning not in such an explicit way, i.e., some other meaning is also probable though that probability is not considerable and people usually ignore it, it is called *żāhir* (apparent). Now,

when a speaker uses a term in the second way and one doubts whether some other meaning is meant, it is said that "the principle is the appearance," i.e., one should principally treat the term as being used in its main meaning and not the less probable one.
In fact, all literal principles refer to this one; for the term is apparent in its literal, general, absolute (when it is general or absolute) meaning and not vice versa.

As for the authority of such principles, they are all based on "the conduct of the wise (*binā' al-'uqalā'*)"— which is to be discussed in the third part in detail. According to that conduct, we see that the wise practically consider the apparent meaning of terms in their communications and ignore other inconsiderable probable meanings – as they ignore the probability of heedlessness, fault, jest, ambiguousness, and the like – and since the divine lawgiver has not prohibited us from that conduct and has not declared another specific way in His communications, we lawfully conclude that He has indorsed and confirmed that conduct having treated apparent meanings as authoritative proofs – precisely as the wise do.

Usage of One Term in More than One Meaning

Doubtless usage of a homonym in one of its meanings along with contextual evidence is allowed, and in case no such evidence is provided the term will become ambiguous having no indication. Also, there is no doubt that such term can be used in all of its meanings as such – although figuratively and in need of contextual evidence inasmuch as it is an unconventional usage. The dispute is over veraciousness of using a homonym and intending more than one meaning in the same usage in such a way that every meaning is separately meant by the term as if it is uttered to denote it alone. Ignoring details and different opinions, we should say that such usage is incorrect and not allowed; for using a term to denote a meaning means creation of that meaning by that term – although not by its real but rather its conventional, secondary existence (since there is only one existence which is attributed to the term in a primary, essential and to the meaning in a secondary, accidental manner, existence of the term is secondarily existence of the meaning). Hence, when a speaker utters a term in order to use it in a meaning he indeed utters the very meaning and not the term, and delivers the meaning to the hearer. In this way, the term is considered by the speaker, and even for the hearer, secondarily and as an instrument for and a way to the meaning. The term is annihilated in the meaning. Thus, what is considered primarily and independently is the meaning and not the term. The case is like an image in the mirror; the image exists by the existence of the mirror. The real, essential existence belongs to the mirror and that very existence is secondarily and accidentally attributed to the image. When one looks at the image in the mirror one is in fact looking at it through the mirror in one look. That one look is primarily and independently at the image and secondarily and dependently at the mirror. Consideration of the mirror, therefore, is secondarily with regard to that of image – as was the case with the term.

That is why one term cannot be used except in one meaning. For if it is used in two meanings independently in such a way that both of them are meant by the term, as in the case where any of them is used alone, it necessitates that every one of them should be considered primarily, which, in turn, necessitates that the term should be used secondarily twice at once. This is obviously impossible, for one thing can have only one existence in the soul at any given moment.

What we said is not true only as to two, or more, literal meanings. It is true even where one uses a literal and a figurative meaning at once, for the problem is the same: attachment of two considerations to one object at one moment.

The Juristic-Literal Meaning *(al-Ĥaqīqa al-Shar'iyya)*

Doubtless all Muslims understand specific juristic meanings from such words as *ṣalāt* (the prayers), *ṣawm*(fasting), *ĥadjdj* (pilgrimage to Mecca), and the like, while we know that such meanings were unknown to Arabs before Islam and were transferred to those new juristic meanings after the Islamic era. Now, the question is that whether such transfer has happened in the holy Prophet's time so that we may have the juristic-literal meaning or it has occurred after him and therefore what we have in hand is Muslims' literal meaning (*al-ĥaqīqa al-mutasharri'iyya*).

The answer to that question would make a difference in the process of inferring juristic precepts from the Qur'ān and *Sunna*. Should there exist the juristic-literal meaning, any such term without contextual evidence would be predicated to its juristic meaning, while it must be interpreted as its usual meaning if such a juristic-literal meaning does not exist.

It is obviously clear that those new meanings were not made through convention by specification, for in that case it should have been narrated to us in one way or another. As for the convention by determination, it must be said that it had doubtlessly happened in Imām Ali's time, for by that time all

Muslims have been using such terms in their new juristic meanings for a long time. Hence, since in Shiite jurisprudence only such prophetic *ḥadīths* that are narrated by holy Imāms are treated as valuable, all such terms in their words should be predicated to their new juristic meanings where they are void of any contextual evidence. As for the holy Qur'ān, there is no room for such a dispute, since almost all such words are used in it along with contextual evidence and convey their new juristic meanings.

The Sound (*al-Ṣaḥīḥ*) and What Incorporates Both (*al- A'amm*)

There is a dispute among *Uṣūlīs* whether terms of acts of worship and transactions are designations specified for sound meanings (i.e., perfect in terms of parts and conditions) or for what incorporates imperfect (*al-fāsid*) ones as well. In other words, when such term is used, should it be predicated only to perfect instances or could it be predicated to imperfect ones too (the latter being termed "what incorporates both" in this discussion)?

The outcome of this discussion is that when it is doubted whether or not a condition is considered in a specific act of worship or transaction, one who believes in the latter (who is called *al-a'ammī*) can refer to the principle of absoluteness in order to negate consideration of that condition while one who believes in the former (who is called *al-ṣaḥīḥī*) cannot.

To explain this, let us take an example. When the Lord commands us to actualize something and we are doubtful whether that thing would be realized by bringing about a specific external instance, such case can have two states:

1. It is known that designation of the commanded holds true for that instance, but it is probable that an additional condition is taken into consideration in the Lord's purpose which does not exist in that instance. For example, when the Lord commands to free a slave, it is known that "slave" does hold true for an unbelieving one, but we are doubtful whether or not the condition of "faith" is considered in the purpose of the Lord and therefore it becomes probable that being faithful is a condition of the commanded. In such case, one is principally supposed to refer to the principle of absoluteness in order to negate consideration of the probable condition. Hence, acquiring that condition would not be mandatory and one can content oneself in the position of obedience with actualizing the doubtful instance (i.e., freeing an unbeliever slave in the given example).
2. It is doubted whether designation of the commanded holds true for that

external instance. For example, the Lord has commanded to perform dry ablution with *al-ṣaʿīd* in case of lack of water and we wonder whether *ṣaʿīd* means soil alone or it includes stone and whatsoever lies on the ground as well. Here, the doubt is over *ṣaʿīd* holding true for other than soil. In such case, one cannot refer to the principle of absoluteness in order to enter the doubtful instance in the designation of the commanded so that one can content oneself with it in the position of obedience. Rather, one should refer to such practical principles as precaution or clearance in accordance with the situation.

Now, when the Lord commands us to perform *ṣalāt* (the prayers) and we doubt whether *sūra*, for example, is part of *ṣalāt*, the case would be an example of the first state should we hold that *ṣalāt* is designation of what incorporates both, and would be an example of the second one should we hold that it is designation of the sound. The reason for the former is that we know that designation of *ṣalāt* holds true for the one which lacks *sūra* and we only doubt whether or not an additional condition is taken into consideration. In that case one may refer to the absoluteness of the Lord's speech, negate consideration of the additional condition, and content oneself in the position of obedience with performing *ṣalāt* without *sūra*. The reason for the latter is that when consideration of *sūra* is doubted, it is in fact doubted whether or not designation of *ṣalāt* holds true for the one which lacks *sūra*. For, designation of the commanded is the sound and the sound is designation of the commanded; therefore, what is not sound is not *ṣalāt*. Thus, what lacks the doubtful part is both doubted whether it is veracious and whether designation of the commanded holds true for it. In this case, it is not allowed to refer to the principle of absoluteness in order to negate consideration of *sūra* as part of *ṣalāt* so that one can content oneself in the position of obedience with the instance lacking *sūra*. Rather, one should refer to either the principle of precaution or that of clearance – on the basis of what will be explained in the fourth part.

What is the justifiable opinion, then? It is the second one, i.e., terms being specified for what incorporates both, since it is the denotation of preceding (*al-tabādur*) and incorrectness of divesting (*ʿadam ṣiḥḥat al-salb*) which are two signs of literalness – as explained earlier. When we think of a term, what incorporates both comes to the mind first and precedes the sound, and also it is not veracious to divest the term of the imperfect instance.

Part I

Discussions of Terms

The purpose of this part is to recognize appearance of terms from a general view, whether by convention or by absoluteness of the speech, to result in universal rules which clarify minor premises of "the Principle of Appearance" – a general principle to be discussed in detail in the third part. Such discussions are concerned with doubted, disputed dispositions of speech, either dispositions of terms such as command and prohibition or those of sentences such as implicatures of sentences (*al-mafāhīm*) and the like. As for specific terms and their convention as well as appearances, since there can be no general rule in this connection, they are not to be discussed in this science and it is dictionaries and the like that are supposed to deal with such issues.

CHAPTER 1

THE DERIVED *(AL-MUSHTAQQ)*

Since there is no precise word in English to convey the meaning of *al-mushtaqq* in its *uṣūlī* usage, we have no choice but to use the closest term to it and just rely on its explanation in our discussion. For the purpose of clarification of this complicatedly presented discussion, let us take an example. Suppose that Ali has finished the high school, he is now studying law at a university, and he will definitely become a judge when he is graduated.

A. If we say, "Ali *was* a student," "Ali *is* a university student," and "Ali *will be* a judge" we are literally correct. In those examples we are using exactly the time when "student," "university student," and "judge" are attributed to Ali. That time is called "the time of possession (*ḥāl al-talabbus*)." Thus, when we attribute something to somebody or something else in the time when the former possesses the latter, we are *literally* correct and there is no dispute over this among *Uṣūlīs*.
B. If we say, "Ali *is* a judge" we are attributing something to Ali when he has not possessed it yet, i.e., the time of attribution (*ḥāl al-isnād*) is different from that of possession (*ḥāl al-talabbus*) which will be in the future. In this case, we are *figuratively* correct, since Ali will be a judge in the future; and this point is also not a matter of dispute among *Uṣūlīs*.
C. Now, suppose that Ali finished the university course, was appointed as a judge, finished his thirty years of duty, and became retired having no position in the juristic system. In this case, if we say, "Ali *was* a judge" we are literally correct, since we used the time of possession, and there is no dispute over this. But how would be the case if we would say, "Ali *is* a judge"? Is this usage correct literally or figuratively? Such case, i.e., when something is attributed to somebody or something else because he, or it, has possessed it in the past, is the matter of dispute among *Uṣūlīs*: some consider it as being literally and others as being figuratively correct.

The justifiable opinion is that it is used figuratively in such case, for it does not precede other meanings in coming to our mind on the one hand and it is correct to divest it of someone who is no longer in that position on the other. In other words, signs of literalness do not exist; hence, such usage is figurative.

So far the problem is clarified in a simple way. However, we need to explain some specific terms used in this discussion by *Uṣūlīs* to become able to present this discussion in its normal scholarly way.

In this discussion, somebody or something that may or may not possess a quality while in both cases he or it permanently exists is addressed as *al-dhāt* (like Ali in the example),that quality as *al-mabda'* (like being a judge),to possess that quality as *al-talabbus* (like actually being a judge), to lose that quality as *inqiḍā' al-talabbus* (like being retired and no longer being an actual judge), and what is abstracted and derived from the quality as *al-mushtaqq* (like the "judge").

To sum up what was explained in a simple way in its specific scholarly way, note the following:

1. To use *al-mushtaqq* with regard to *ḥāl al-talabbus* is absolutely a literal usage, whether the time used is past, present, or future (as explained in A) – without there being any dispute among *Uṣūlīs.*
2. To attribute *al-mushtaqq* to the *dhāt* presently, i.e., with regard to *ḥāl al-isnād* before the time of *al-talabbus* because the *dhāt* will possess it later on (as explained in B), is a figurative usage – without there being any dispute among *Uṣūlīs.*
3. To attribute *al-mushtaqq* to the *dhāt* presently, i.e., with regard to *ḥāl al-isnād* when it no longer possesses the *mabda'* merely because it has had it in the past (as in the second example in (3)), is the matter of dispute among *Uṣūlīs* whether it is a literal or a figurative usage.

This dispute manifests its result in some juristic precepts. For instance, according to some *ḥadīth*s performing minor ablution with some water warmed by the sun is disapproved. "The water warmed by the sun" is a *mushtaqq.* Suppose that such water has now become cold. A jurist who holds that calling that water "warmed by the sun" is literally correct gives verdict that performing minor ablution with that water is still disapproved, while the one who maintains that such calling is a figurative usage does not treat such an ablution as being disapproved.

CHAPTER 2

THE COMMANDS (*AL-AWĀMIR*)

By *command* is meant *wish* (in the sense that one wants something to be done: *al-*ṭalab) which, in turn, means to express will (*al-irāda*) and desire through speech, writing, pointing, or the like; whether by such terms as "I command you" or by an imperative. Thus, the sheer will and desire without being expressed in some way is not called *wish*. However, any wish is not called command, but a specific one, that is, wish of superior from inferior. Hence, superiority is considered in the command, whether the superior demonstrates his superiority or not, and whether he uses an imperative (or uses the verb "command") or not – the only point is that he should somehow express his wish. On the other hand, wish of the one who is not superior, whether he is inferior or coequal, is not a command, even though he pretends superiority or uses an imperative.

Appearance of the Command

The important point, however, is the denotation of the command, which is a matter of dispute among *Uṣūlīs*. There are a variety of opinions in this connection the most important of which being obligation (*al-wudjūb*), preference (*al-istiḥbāb*), and the common point between obligation and preference. The truth, however, is that the command is apparent in the obligation – not conventionally, but because of judgment of the intellect. It is intellect's judgment that when the Lord commands us we must obey Him and must be provoked in order to fulfill our duty as servants, unless He declares that His command is not a matter of must and we are free not to do it. Thus, this appearance is not a literal appearance and this denotation is not a lingual one, for the imperative is neither literally nor figuratively used in the concept of obligation, since obligation is something out of the reality of its object of denotation and also it is not among its qualities or states.

Concerning appearance of the command, however, there remain two secondary discussions:

1. Should a declarative sentence be used as configuration, it denotes obligation exactly as the imperative does, for the criterion, which is the intellect's judgment to obey the Lord's provoking, exists in both of them – no matter in what way that provoking is declared. An example of this is the case where the holy Imām was asked about occurrence of a problem in the prayers and he said, "He repeats his prayers." One may even say that indication of obligation is definitely emphasized in this kind, for it is assumed that the duty-bound will surely do it.
2. When a command is preceded by an actual or an assumed prohibition, there is a dispute among *Uṣūlīs* whether it is apparent in the obligation, permissibility, or merely permission, i.e., removal of prohibition without dealing with any of the five-fold burdensome precepts, or it returns to its previous precept before the prohibition.

The justifiable opinion is the third one, for we said earlier that indication of obligation by the command is because of intellect's necessitation of being provoked where there is no permission to relinquish. Nonetheless, there is no provoking here; it is just permission to do and nothing more. For instance, when the Almighty God says, "...Do not profane God's Way marks [when you are in pilgrim sanctity]... but when you have quit your pilgrim sanctity, then hunt," (5:1-2) it clearly does not mean that hunting is mandatory, but rather permitted.

Of course, if there is contextual evidence that such a command is issued to provoke the duty-bound to perform something, or with the intention of allowing him to do it, it will definitely denote obligation and permissibility respectively, and cannot be a matter of dispute. Wherever there is a dispute, it is about a case where no contextual evidence exists.

Varieties of Mandatory Acts

Mandatory acts are of some varieties some of which being as follows:

Absolute (*al-Muṭlaq*) and Conditional (*al-Mashrūṭ*)

Should a mandatory act be compared with something external, it can only be of the two following kinds:

1. If its obligation is dependent upon that thing and that thing is considered

in the obligation of the mandatory act as a condition, such as pilgrimage to Mecca (*al-ḥadjdj*) with regard to financial capability (*al-istiṭā'a*), it is called "conditional mandatory act," since its obligation is conditional upon actualization of that external thing; and that is why the pilgrimage will not become mandatory unless financial capability is actualized.

2. If its obligation is not dependent upon actualization of that thing, such as the pilgrimage with regard to travelling to Mecca – even though its actualization is dependent upon the latter – it is called "absolute mandatory act," since its obligation is unconditional upon that external thing.

The example of pilgrimage indicates that the absolute and conditional are relative, since one mandatory act is absolute with regard to one thing and conditional with regard to another.

It should also be known that all mandatory acts are conditional with regard to general conditions of burden, i.e., puberty, power, and intellect. Hence, the minor, impotent, and insane have no burden in the actuality.

Suspended (*al-Mu'allaq*) and Definite (*al-Munadjdjaz*)

Doubtless when condition of the conditional mandatory act is realized its obligation becomes actual, like the absolute mandatory act, and the burden is actually directed to the duty-bound. However, actuality of the burden is conceivable in two ways:

1. If actuality of the obligation and the mandatory act is simultaneous, in the sense that the time of mandatory act is the very time of the obligation, the mandatory act is called "definite" (*al-munadjdjaz*); such as the prayers when its time comes, since its obligation is actual and the mandatory act, i.e., the prayers, is also actual.
2. If actuality of the obligation is prior to that of the mandatory act and therefore the time of mandatory act is later than that of obligation, it is called "suspended" (*al-mu'allaq*), since the act and not its obligation is suspended until a time not realized yet. An example of this is the pilgrimage, since when the financial capability is actualized the obligation of the pilgrimage becomes actual – as it is said – while the mandatory act is suspended until coming of the time of the ritual. Here, when the financial capability is actualized the pilgrimage becomes mandatory, and that is why it is mandatory for the

duty-bound to provide all preliminaries to become able to perform it in its specific, limited time.

In this connection, there are two disputes among *Uṣūlīs*:

First, whether *al-wādjib al-mu'allaq* is possible. Some believe in its possibility, while the majority of *Uṣūlīs* hold that it is impossible – a discussion beyond the level of an introductory work.

Secondly, whether appearance of the conditional sentence in such an example as "when the specified time comes perform the prayers" is that the condition is a condition for "the obligation" and hence the prayers will not become mandatory except when the time has come, or it is a condition for "the mandatory act" and hence the mandatory act itself is suspended until coming of the time while the obligation is actual and absolute. If the first, the mandatory act will be a conditional one and none of the preliminaries would be mandatory before actualization of the condition; and if the second, the mandatory act will be an absolute one in which the obligation is actual before actualization of the condition, and hence if one knows that the condition will become actualized later on one should provide all preliminaries. This dispute needs a detailed consideration to be observed in the respective discussion.

Determinate (*al-Ta'yīnī*) and Optional (*al-Takhyīrī*)

The determinate mandatory act is the one which is determinately wished and has no horizontal parallel in the position of obedience, such as prayers and fasting in Ramaḍān. To Add "horizontal" is necessary because there are some determinate mandatory acts that have some vertical parallels, such as ablution which has the vertical parallel, i.e., dry ablution (*al-tayammum*), since the latter is lawful only when the former is not possible.

The optional mandatory act is the one which is not determinately wished and has a horizontal parallel. In other words, what is wished is whether this one or another, in such a way that the duty-bound is free to choose each of them. An example of this kind is the penance when one does not observe fasting in Ramaḍān deliberately, sine he must either fast sixty days, or feed sixty needy people, or free a slave.

Individual (*al-'Aynī*) and Collective (*al-Kifā'ī*)

The individual mandatory act is the one which is obligatory for every duty-bound and cannot be substituted by obedience on the part of others, such as the prayers, fasting, pilgrimage, and so forth.

The collective mandatory act is the one in which what is desired is merely actualization of the act, no matter who has done it, such as burying a dead person, purifying the mosque, and the like. Hence, that affair is obligatory for all, but should it be done by some it is considered done and others will be exempted. However, if it is eschewed by all and left undone all will be punished, but in the case of being done by some only those who have participated will be rewarded.

Extended (*al-Muwassa'*) and Constricted (*al-Muḍayyaq*)

Considering the time, the mandatory act is divided into of specified time (*al-muwaqqat*) and of unspecified time (*ghayr al-muwaqqat*). The one of specified time, in turn, is divided into extended and constricted; and the one of unspecified time into urgent (*fawrī*) and non-urgent (*ghayr fawrī*).

The mandatory act of unspecified time is the one in which no specific time is considered juristically, though no act can be done without a time as its vessel, such as belated performing of the prayers, purification of the mosque, and the like. This kind, as was said, is in turn divided into the urgent which cannot be delayed from the first possible time, such as returning a greeting, and non-urgent which can be delayed, such as belated performing of the prayers, burial prayers, paying the fifth (*al-khums*) and so on.

The mandatory act of specified time is the one in which a specific time is considered juristically, such as the prayers, the pilgrimage, fasting, and the like. The relation between this kind and its specified time can logically be conceived only in three ways: when its performing takes more time than its specified time, when both times are equal, and when the former is less than the latter. The first is impossible, since it is charging with the impossible. The second is doubtlessly possible and has occurred in the *Sharī'a* as well, and that is the one called constricted, such as fasting whose specified time precisely covers its time of performing. And the third is the one which is called extended, since the duty-bound is free to perform it in the first, middle, or the last part of the time; such as daily prayers which cannot be left undone in the whole time but must be done once in its specified time.

Every Muslim knows that some mandatory acts of specified time, such as prayers, fasting, and the like, must be performed belatedly if they are not performed in their specified time. However, there is a dispute among *Uṣūlīs* whether such performing is principally a matter of must, in the sense that the very command to the mandatory act of specified time denotes that it must be belatedly performed if it is not performed in its specified time and hence obligation of belated performing is proved by the very proof of original performing, or it is not so and obligation of the belated performing needs a proof other than that of the original performing itself – the dispute being addressed by *Uṣūlīs* as whether the belated performing *follows* the timely one or not (*hal yatba' al-qaḍā' al-adā'?*).

There are three opinions in this connection: the belated performing absolutely following the timely, the former absolutely not following the latter, and distinguishing between the case where the proof of time appointing is mentioned in the proof of the mandatory act itself and the case where it is mentioned separately. According to the third opinion, in the first case the belated performing does not follow the timely one while in the second case it does.

It seems that the origin of the dispute is the disagreement among *Uṣūlīs* whether what is understood from the time appointing is unity of the desired, or its multiplicity; i.e., whether there is one desired affair in the mandatory act of specified time and it is the act qualified by the time as it is qualified or there are two desired affairs, i.e., the act itself and its being done in a specific time. If the first, when the command is not obeyed in its specified time there would remain no wish for the act itself and hence a new command to perform the act out of its time must be assumed; and if the second, when the command is not obeyed in its specified time only one desired affair is not obeyed, i.e., the one demanding its being in the specified time, while the wish for the act itself is still enduring – and that is why some have held the third opinion.

The justifiable opinion is the second one, i.e., the belated absolutely not following the timely; for the appearance of qualification is that the proviso is a pillar in the desired. Thus, if the Lord says, "Fast on Friday," only one desired for one purpose is understood, and it is particularly fasting on that day; it is not understood that fasting *per se* is one desired and its being on Friday is another one. The case is the same with the separate proof of time appointing. For instance, if the Lord says, "Fast," and then He says, "Observe the fasting on Friday," the absolute should be predicated upon the qualified – as is the rule in such cases. Predication of the absolute upon the qualified means confining the very first desired to the proviso; such qualification revealing that what was really meant by the absolute from the very beginning was just the qualified, and thereby both proofs become one due to taking both of them altogether. It does not mean that the qualified is a desired affair other than the absolute, otherwise it would mean that the absolute has remained absolute; and this is not predication and taking two proofs altogether (*djam' bayn al-dalīlayn*), but rather keeping each of them separately (*akhdh bi'l dalīlayn*).

Religiously (*al-Ta'abbudī*) and Instrumental (*al-Tawaṣṣulī*)

In the Islamic holy *Sharī'a*, there are obligations that are not considered sound and their commands are not obeyed unless they are performed with the intention of proximity to God, such as the prayers, fasting, and the like. Such obligations are called religiously obligations (*al-ta'abbudiyyāt*). On the other hand, there are other obligations whose commands are obeyed merely by being performed without having any divine intention, such as saving a drowning person, burying a dead person, purifying cloths and body for the prayers, and the like. Such obligations are called instrumental obligations (*al-tawaṣṣuliyyāt*).

Varieties of Mandatory Acts and the Absoluteness of the Mode (*al-Ṣīgha*)

When a command is issued, if there is a contextual evidence determining which variety of command is intended, e.g., extended or constricted, determinate or optional, etc., it is obviously clear that one must definitely obey the command in the way it is specified. However, if there is no such evidence, where the command is absolute and lacks any contextual evidence, what should the duty-bound do? Should he treat it as extended, or constricted; determinate, or optional, and so forth? Does absoluteness of the imperative necessitate that the command should be individual, or collective; determinate, or optional; extended, or constricted; suspended, or definite; and finally religiously, or instrumental?

The general criterion for such recognition is to find which variety is in need of more depiction; that is the one which must be dismissed, since it is the one which needs contextual evidence – something missing as was assumed. For instance, when the Lord commands, "Perform the prayers," it can be considered collective only if He adds in His command "unless others should have done it." This is an additional proviso which He has not added, while He could do so. Hence, from this lack of depiction we can logically conclude that He had not wished that proviso, and thereby we treat that command as being individual. Thus, absoluteness of the imperative necessitates that the command should be individual, determinate, extended, and definite; since these varieties are not in need of more depiction.

The case with the religiously and instrumental, however, is not that simple;

it is somehow complicated if one specific meaning of intention of proximity to God is taken into consideration. It is clearly known that the intention of proximity to God can be actualized in some different ways. One is to intend that the commanded act is essentially liked and desired by the Lord. Another is to intend merely the Lord's pleasure. Should such meanings of intention of proximity to God be meant, there would be no doubt that absoluteness of the imperative would necessitate that the command should be treated as instrumental if there were no contextual evidence, for what is in need of more depiction is the religiously mandatory act inasmuch as its command is supposed to include an additional proviso, i.e., being performed with the intention of proximity to God – something missing. In such case, the duty-bound can refer to the principle of absoluteness in order to negate that proviso.

However, one kind of intention of proximity to God is that of "obeying the commandment." Since it is impossible to consider this proviso in the commanded act, whose reason will be explained below, should this meaning of intention of proximity to God be considered one could not refer to the principle of absoluteness in order to negate this proviso and conclude that since the Lord has not uttered that proviso He has not considered it in His commandment. For this non-utterance may have two reasons: He has not wished it, or He has wished it but He has not uttered it because of impossibility of that utterance. That is why one cannot conclude in such case that absoluteness of the imperative necessitates that the command should be instrumental. Rather, since consideration of that impossibility is probable in that non-utterance, the intellect judges that one must perform the act with that proviso in order to make sure that he has obeyed the Lord's command as such; and should that act be done without that proviso, the intellect would judge that the duty-bound has not performed his divinely duty as he was supposed to and deserves punishment in the hereafter. The principal rule in such cases is that when one definitely knows that the Lord has commanded something, since one is sure that such a command has been issued, one must obey the command in such a way that one could definitely be certain of observing the Lord's command – whatever the case may be in the actuality – and this necessitates observing all probable provisos.

In order to explain that impossibility, we should mention that there are two kinds of division with regard to the mandatory acts: *primary*, and *secondary*.

Primary Divisions. Such divisions are those which are considered in a mandatory act *per se* apart from consideration of attachment of anything to it. For instance, prayers can be divided in itself, without consideration that a command is directed to it, into "with ablution and without it," "with *sūra* and without it," and so forth. In such divisions, the mandatory act can be of one of the following three states with regard to any proviso:

1. If the mandatory act is conditional upon that thing, it is called "conditioned-by-something" (*bi-sharṭ shay'*); such as ablution, *sūra, rukū', sajda*, and other conditions of the prayers.
2. If the mandatory act is conditional upon non-existence of that thing, it is called "negatively conditioned" (*bi-sharṭ lā*); such as speaking, laughing, and other things which interrupt the prayers.
3. If the mandatory act is absolute with regard to that thing being conditional neither upon its existence nor its non-existence, it is called "unconditioned" (*lā bi-sharṭ*); such as the prayers with regard to *qunūt* (special prayer in the second *rak'a* before *rukū'*), color of the clothes worn, and so on.

Now, if the proof declaring obligation of something denotes that it is conditional upon existence or non-existence of something else, it must doubtlessly be followed in the way it is declared. However, if a condition is probable but neither positively nor negatively is mentioned in the proof, one may refer to the principle of absoluteness in order to negate that probable condition – if all "premises of wisdom" which allow one to refer to that principle are actualized, as will be explained in chapter 6 – and thereby discover that the speaker has really wished the absolute from the very beginning, which means that the mandatory act is not taken in relation to the proviso except in the unconditioned mode. In short, there is no problem with referring to the principle of absoluteness in order to negate probability of qualification in the primary divisions.

Secondary Divisions. From another view, mandatory act, if it is really commanded, is divided into what is externally done for the purpose of its command and what is done not for the purpose of its command, and the like. Such divisions are called *secondary divisions* as they are additional to the precept when a real obligation is assumed; for before actualization of a precept performing of the commanded for the purpose of its command is nonsensical, since it is assumed that it is not commanded in that state so that one can intend its command. Thus, in such divisions, qualification of the commanded act is impossible, for intending obedience of the command is subject to the existence of the command; how could it be plausible that the command is qualified by it, then? This necessitates that the command should be subject to intending the command while intending the command has been subject to the existence of the command, necessitating that the precedent should be subsequent and the subsequent be precedent – something impossible, since it is either self-contradiction or vicious circle. Now, should qualification be impossible, absoluteness would be impossible too; since contrariety of qualification and absoluteness is that of possession and privation; hence, absoluteness cannot be assumed except in a case that can be qualified. Thus, where qualification is impossible, one cannot infer from non-qualification that the absolute is willed; and this results, with regard to the topic in question, that the absoluteness of the imperative necessitates that the mandatory act should be treated as being religiously.

On the other hand, there is a way to conclude that even in the secondary divisions, in which qualification is impossible, absoluteness of the imperative principally necessitates that the mandatory act should be instrumental; and that is the "absoluteness of the position (*iṭlāq al-maqām*)." Although mentioning the condition in the command itself is impossible in such divisions, should one who commands wish that condition, one is not supposed to be heedless to that and should follow another way to attain one's purpose – even though by issuing two commands: one for the act itself without the proviso, and another for the proviso. These two commands are in fact one, for they are issued for one purpose and the second is a depiction for the first. Hence, should the second command not be obeyed, the first would not be considered obeyed if done without the proviso. Therefore, the second command joined to the first is common with the qualification in the result, even though it is terminologically not called qualification. Now, where the Lord commands something and He is in the position of depiction but He does not command for the second time that such command should be performed with the intention of obedience, it will be discovered that the intention of obedience has no role in His purpose; otherwise, He would have expounded it by another command. Therefore, the principle in mandatory acts is being instrumental except where it is proved by a proof that they are religiously.

Promptitude (*al-Fawr*) or Belatedness (*al-Tarā<u>kh</u>ī*)

There is a dispute among *Uṣūlīs* whether the imperative *per se* conventionally denotes promptitude, belatedness, both of them as homonymous, or none of them but rather it is the contextual evidence that designates any of them.

The justifiable is the last opinion; for, as mentioned earlier, the imperative denotes merely the wishful relation and hence has no indication of any of the promptitude or belatedness. Thus, should an imperative be void of any evidence, it could be performed either promptly or belatedly.

Once (*al-Marra*) or Repetition (*al-Takrār*)

There is another dispute among *Uṣūlīs* whether the imperative *per se* denotes conventionally once or repetition, and the justifiable opinion is the same with the previous problem. For, as was said there, the imperative denotes merely the wishful relation and nothing else. Of course, obedience to the command necessitates bringing about at least one instance of the nature of the act, for not doing that is equivalent to disobedience. However, the absoluteness of the mode necessitates that performing the mandatory act once is enough; for the Lord's desire can only be considered as one of the three following probabilities:

1. The desired is sheer existence of the thing without any proviso or condition, in the sense that He wishes that His desired should not remain non-existent but rather come out from darkness of non-existence into the light of existence – even though through one single instance. In such case, the desired would necessarily be actualized and obeyed by the first existent and doing the mandatory act more would merely be a vain performance; its example being daily prayers.
2. The desired is one existence with the proviso of unity, i.e., it is conditional upon not being more than the first existence. In such case, should the duty-bound perform it twice, he has absolutely not obeyed the command; its example being the inaugural *takbīr* (saying "God is the greatest") of daily prayers, since the second nullifies the first and becomes null itself.
3. The desired is the repeated existence; either conditional upon repetition, i.e., the desired being the whole as a whole and hence obedience not being actualized by doing the mandatory act once such as *rak'a*s of one prayers, or unconditioned with regard to its repetition, i.e., the desired being each of existences, such as fasting in days of Ramaḍān inasmuch as each day has its specific obedience.

Doubtless the two later facets are in need of more depiction. Thus, should the Lord, who is in the position of depiction, command in an absolute way and do not qualify His command to any of those two facets, it would be discovered that He has wished the first facet. Hence, the obedience, as was said earlier, would be actualized by the first existence and the second one would be considered neither disobedience nor obedience.

To Command Something Twice

If an act is commanded twice, this can be considered in two ways:

1. The second command is issued when the first one is already obeyed. In such case, it must doubtlessly be obeyed again.
2. The second command is issued when the first one has not been obeyed yet. In such case, one may doubt whether one must perform it twice or one performing would be enough. Should the second command be initiation (*ta'sīs*) of another obligation, it must be performed twice; but should it be an emphasis (*ta'kīd*) of the first, one performing would be enough. In order to find out the justifiable opinion, it should be noted that this assumption is of four states:
   2.1. Both commands are unconditional, e.g., the Lord says, "Perform the prayers" and again He says, "Perform the prayers". Here, the second command should be predicated to the emphasis, for directing two commands to one thing without existence of any distinctiveness is impossible. Had the second been initiation and not emphasis, the speaker would have been supposed to qualify its object even though by such a statement as "for the next time." Thus, from non-qualification on the one hand and the appearance that the object in both of them is one on the other, the command in the second becomes apparent in the emphasis – although appearance of a speech *per se* is principally initiation and not emphasis.
   2.2. Both commands are conditional upon one proviso, e.g., the Lord says, "Perform minor ablution for the new prayers if you have not performed it for the previous one" and then He repeats the same words. In this case, the second is predicated to the emphasis, for the same reason expounded in the previous state.
   2.3. One command is conditional while the other is not, e.g., the Lord says, "Perform the major ablution (*al-ghusl*)," and then He says, "Perform the major ablution if you have had sexual intercourse." The desired in this case is also one and the second is predicated to the emphasis, for the commanded act is apparently one and this prevents directing two commands to it – though here absoluteness of the absolute command, i.e., the unconditional, is predicated to the qualification through which the second qualifies absoluteness of the first and reveals what was intended by it.
   2.4. One command is conditional upon one proviso and the other upon

another, e.g., the Lord says, "Perform the major ablution if you have had sexual intercourse," and then He says, "Perform the major ablution if you have touched a dead body." In this case, the second is apparently predicated to the initiation, for the appearance is that the desired in either of them is different from the other. It is very unlikely that the desired in both of them would be one.

There are two other probabilities here: emphasis (*ta'kīd*), and intervention (*tadākhul*). Emphasis is nonsense here. As for the intervention, in the sense that one could content oneself with doing the commanded act once, although it is possible, it contradicts primary principles; that is why one can refer to it only where there is a specific proof revealing that. (The problem of *tadākhul* would be discussed in chapter 4 in detail.)

Denotation of "Command to Command"

Should the Lord command one of His servants to command another servant to do something, would it be a command to that act so that it would be mandatory for the second to do it? The case can be conceived in two ways:

1. The first commanded person is considered as an agent to deliver the Lord's command to the second one. Doubtless the act is mandatory for the second in this case, and all commands of prophets to duty-bounds are of this kind.
2. The second commanded person is not considered as an agent but rather he is commanded to direct the command to the second person independently for himself, such as the *ḥadīth* in which the holy Imām says, "Command your children to perform the prayers when they are seven years old." It is this kind that is a matter of dispute among *Uṣūlīs*. The case would be the same where it is not clear of which kind that command is.

The justifiable opinion is that the command to command is apparent in its obligation upon the second person. In order to explain this more, notice that the command to command not as an agent can be issued in two ways:

2.1. The Lord's purpose is performing of the act by the second commanded person and His command to command is a way to the actualization of His purpose. It is obviously clear that in such case His command to command is a command to the act itself.

2.2. The purpose of one who commands is merely issuance of the command by the commanded person, e.g., where a king commands his son to command his servant to do something while his purpose is not actualization of the act but rather to accustom his son to issue commands. It is clear that in such case the command is actually not directed to the second person and he would not be considered disobedient should he not perform the act.

Now, should there be a contextual evidence designating one of those two states, one would doubtlessly be supposed to consider it. However, if there is no such contextual evidence, appearance of commands is that they are ways for actualization of the act. Add to this that commands in the second way have no room in religiously commandments.

CHAPTER 3

THE PROHIBITIONS (*AL-NAWĀHĪ*)

By *prohibition* is meant wish of the superior from the inferior to eschew and not to do an act, whether by such terms as "I prohibit you" or by any other mode; or, to be more precise, the superior's dissuading and forbidding the inferior from doing an act whose requisite being wish of eschewing and not doing that act.

The prohibition is like the command in denoting necessity and obligation intellectually and not conventionally, precisely as we said and proved in the previous chapter. The only difference is that the purpose in the command is obligation of doing while in the prohibition is that of eschewing. Therefore, the prohibition is apparent in the unlawfulness as the command was apparent in the obligation.

It should be noted that by "act" in the definition of prohibition is meant what is conveyed by the infinitive, even though it may not be an existential affair. Thus, "Do not leave the prayers" is a prohibition while "Eschew drinking wine" is a command – though they mean "Perform the prayers" and "Do not drink wine" respectively.

The Desired in the Prohibition

There is a dispute among *Uṣūlīs* specifically in the discussion of the prohibition over this issue whether the desired in the prohibition is merely not to do (*nafs an lā tafʿal*) or continence (*kaff al-nafs*). The difference between the two is that the former is a sheer non-existential affair while the latter is an existential one inasmuch as continence is a psychic act.

The justifiable opinion is the first. What caused some to believe in the second is that they thought that "to eschew," whose meaning is to keep non-existence of the prohibited act as it is, is not possible for the duty-bound, since it is pre-eternal, out of reach of power, and cannot become an object of wish. However, it is quite plausible that the continence, which is a psychic act, would become an object of wish in the prohibition. The answer to this illusion is that impossibility of non-existence in the pre-eternity does not contradict its possibility in the continuity, for the power for existence implicates the power for non-existence. One can even say that the power for non-existence is based on the nature of the power for existence; otherwise, should non-existence be impossible in the continuity the existence would not be possible at all, since the free, powerful agent is the one who performs the act if he wishes and does not perform the act if he does not wish.

However, the truth is that such discussion is basically nonsense, for, as was said earlier, "wish" is not the meaning of prohibition so that it may be discussed whether the desired is eschewal or continence. The wish for eschewing is an implication of the prohibition; the meaning of prohibition is forbidding and dissuading – yea, to forbid an act implicates logically the wish for its eschewing. Thus, the prohibition is basically directed to the act itself and there is no room for doubting whether the wish in the prohibition is for eschewal or continence.

Denotation of the Prohibition as to Permanence (*al-Dawām*) and Repetition (*al-Takrār*)

Like the dispute over the command, there is a dispute among *Uṣūlīs* whether prohibition indicates once or repetition by the prohibition. The justifiable opinion is the same with the case of command; hence, the prohibition denotes neither repetition nor once – what is prohibited is the sheer nature of the act. However, there is a rational difference between those two in the position of obedience, for the prohibition is obeyed by eschewing the actualization of the nature of the act and that would be realized only when all instances of the act are left, since if the duty-bound do the act even once he will not be considered an obedient servant. On the other hand, obedience to the command will be actualized by bringing about the first existence of instances of the nature of the act; the nature of obedience is not dependent upon more than doing the commanded act once. That difference is not due to the convention and denotation of those two, but rather is the rational necessity of the nature of prohibition and command.

CHAPTER 4

IMPLICATURES OF SENTENCES (*AL-MAFĀHĪM*)

The Arabic term *mafhūm* (pl. *mafāhīm*) is used for three different expressions the third of which being meant in this discussion. The first is used to denote "meaning," and the second to denote "concept" as the opposite of instance (*miṣdāq*). The third, however, is used merely in *uṣūl al-fiqh* to convey a specific meaning equivalent to implicature of a sentence. This meaning is used in opposition to *manṭūq* (the uttered) which means what is denoted by the sentence *per se* in such a way that the uttered sentence is bearing that meaning and is a frame for it. By *mafhūm*, therefore, is meant what the sentence is not bearing and does not denote comprehensively; rather, it is an "obvious implicature in the most particular sense" of the sentence. (An implicating conceiving of whose implicated would implicate conceiving of itself is called "obvious implicating in the most particular sense," as in "two being twice as one" in which the very conceiving of two implicates immediate conceiving of its being twice as one.) Hence, *mafhūm* is specifically used for the implicative denotation (*al-dalāla al-iltizāmiyya*).

Let us take an example in order to give a clear insight of *manṭūq* and *mafhūm* at the beginning of our discussion. Suppose that the jurist has said, "If the water is pure, one can make ablution with it." In this sentence, *manṭūq* is the content of the sentence, i.e., lawfulness of making ablution with pure water, and *mafhūm*, should such a sentence have *mafhūm*, is unlawfulness of making ablution with impure water.

Hence, *manṭūq* can be defined as "a precept denoted by the word where it is uttered," and *mafhūm* as "a precept denoted by the word where it is not uttered." Here, by the precept is meant precept in the most general meaning and not one of the five-fold burdensome precepts. Sometimes the phrase "non-existence where non-existence" (*al-intifā' 'ind al-intifā'*) is used for *mafhūm*, meaning non-existence of the judgment where the condition, qualifier, and the like become non-existent.

As was seen, there is no single word to convey precisely that specific meaning of *mafhūm* in English; hence, we use the Arabic term in this connection emphasizing that wherever the Arabic term *mafhūm* is used in this book it is only this specific meaning which is intended. Although this is not exactly the case with *manṭūq* and it can be conveyed by the term "the uttered," we use the Arabic term in our discussion for the sake of consonance.

Before anything else, two important points should be borne in mind with regard to the discussion of *mafhūm*:

1. When the matter of dispute is entitled "dispute over authority of *mafhūm*" it questions whether a specific kind of sentence has *mafhūm* or not. It does not question whether or not *mafhūm* of a specific kind of sentence which has *mafhūm* is authorized– as is the case with authority of *ḥadīṯḫ*s. For instance, where *mafhūm* of condition is disputed it means that whether such sentence has *mafhūm* and denotes preclusion of precepts when the condition is precluded or not; it does not mean that such sentence has *mafhūm* but *Uṣūlīs* dispute whether or not that *mafhūm* is an authoritative proof.

2. The dispute is over cases where no contextual evidence exits. Should there be any contextual evidence the sentence would doubtlessly be treated the way the evidence designates. Thus, the dispute is over whether the *type* of conditional sentence, for instance, has *mafhūm* when it is void of any specific evidence or not.

Varieties of *Mafhūm*

Mafhūm is generally divided into two types: accordant (*al-mafhūm al-muwāfiq* or *mafhūm al-muwāfaqa*), and disaccording (*al-mafhūm al-mukhālif* or *mafhūm al-mukhālafa*).

1. Accordant is the one in which the type of precept accords with the precept in the *manṭūq*, i.e., if the precept in the *manṭūq* is obligation it is obligation in the *mafhūm*, if it is unlawfulness in the former it is unlawfulness in the latter, and so forth – as in the Qur'ānic verse: "Do not say to them (your parents) Fie," (17: 23) that denotes prohibition of assault and battery which are more insulting and painful than to say "Fie" which is explicitly declared unlawful in the verse.

There is no dispute over authority of accordant *mafhūm* in the sense that the precept transmits to that which has priority in terms of motive of the

precept.
2. Disaccording is the one in which the type of precept disaccords with the precept in the *manṭūq*. There are six instances of this kind with which we should deal separately and in detail.

1. *Mafhūm* of the Condition (*al-Sharṭ*)

Doubtless *manṭūq* of the conditional sentence conventionally denotes that the consequent is dependent upon the antecedent. However, conditional sentences are of two kinds:

1.1. That which is made to depict the object of judgment. In this kind, the antecedent is the very object of the judgment; the judgment in the consequent is dependent upon the condition in the antecedent in such a way that consideration of the judgment without condition is implausible. For instance, in this Qur'ānic verse: "And do not constrain your slave-girls to prostitution if they desire to live in chastity," (23: 33) supposition of constraining to prostitution is implausible unless when the desire of slave-girls to live in chastity is assumed.
All *Uṣūlīs* are in agreement that such conditional sentences have no *mafhūm*, since non-existence of the condition means non-existence of the judgment; hence, to judge that the consequent does not exist is nonsensical except in the way of "negative by non-existence of the object": it is not to judge that consequent does not exist, it is non-existence of the judgment. Thus, there is no *mafhūm* for the verse in question and it cannot be said that if your slave-girls did not desire to live in chastity you should constrain them to prostitution.
1.2. That which is not made to depict the object of the judgment. In this kind, the antecedent is not the very object of the judgment and the judgment in the consequent is dependent upon the condition in the antecedent in such a way that its consideration without condition is plausible. For instance, when one says, "If your friend did you a favor, do him a favor," to do one's friend a favor is not logically dependent upon one's friend's doing one a favor, since one can do one's friend a favor whether the latter does the former a favor or not.

It is this kind of conditional sentence that is a matter of dispute in this discussion. It refers to the dispute whether or not the conditional sentence denotes non-existence of the judgment where the condition becomes non-existent, in the sense that whether or not it is understood from the nature of making the judgment conditional upon the condition that the *type* of precept, obligation for instance, would become non-existent should the condition become non-existent.

Concerning *mafhūm* of the condition, there are two opinions: having *mafhūm* and not having *mafhūm*, and the justifiable one is the former. Before dealing with arguments, we have to discover the criterion for *mafhūm* of the condition.

The Criterion for *Mafhūm* of the Condition

In order to have *mafhūm*, conditional sentence needs to denote three subsequent affairs, whether conventionally or by absoluteness, as follows:

1. To denote that there is a relation and implication between the antecedent (*al-muqaddam*) and the consequent (*al-tālī*).
2. To denote that, in addition to relation and implication, the consequent is dependent upon, subsequent to, and subject to the antecedent; hence, the antecedent is a cause for the consequent.
3. To denote that, in addition to those two, the antecedent is the exclusive cause, in the sense that there is no parallel cause upon which the consequent can be dependent.

That the *mafhūm* of the conditional sentence is dependent upon those three affairs is obviously clear; for should the sentence be occasional, or the consequent not be dependent upon the antecedent, or be dependent but not in an exclusive way, the consequent would not become non-existent where the antecedent does not exist. The only thing to be proved is that the sentence is apparent in those three-fold affairs, whether conventionally or by absoluteness, so that it can have *mafhūm*.

The truth is that the conditional sentence is apparent in those affairs, conventionally in some and by absoluteness in others:

1. As for the relation and existence of necessary connection between the two, it appears that it is conventional – because of *tabādur*. It should be noted, however, that it is not because of articles of condition being specified to that so that one may deny it; it is necessitated by the compound disposition of the conditional sentence as a whole.

2. As for the consequent being dependent upon the antecedent, no matter what kind of dependence it might be, it is also conventional; but not in the sense that the sentence is specified twice – one for the implication and another for the dependence – but rather in the sense that it is specified once for the specific relation which is dependence of the consequent upon the antecedent. Again, the reason is *tabādur* of dependence of the consequent upon its antecedent, as the conditional sentence denotes that the antecedent is situated in the position of supposition and in case of its actualization the consequent will be actualized secondarily, i.e., consequent follows the antecedent in the actualization. In other words, what immediately comes to the mind from the conditional sentence is that its consequent would necessarily be actualized should its condition be actualized. This is obviously clear and cannot be denied, except by someone who is obstinate or negligent, for it is the meaning of dependent-making of something – which is the content of conditional sentence. The conditional sentence has no content other than that; that is why its first clause is called subordinate clause and antecedent and its second clause principle clause and consequence.
3. As for exclusiveness of the condition, it is by absoluteness; for had there been another condition to substitute that one or to be added to it so that they may both make one compound condition, there would have necessarily been an additional depiction either by "or" in the first state or "and" in the second. Now, where dependent-making of the consequent upon the condition is left absolute, it reveals that the condition is independent and inclusive; it has neither a partner nor a substitute or parallel. Otherwise, the wise speaker was mandatorily supposed to depict that where he was in the position of depiction.

In short, there is no doubt that the conditional sentence is apparent in having *mafhūm*, except in cases where it is made to depict the object of the judgment or there is contradictory contextual evidence. This can clearly been proved by the following *ḥadīth* of the sixth Imām:

> Abū Baṣīr asked, "A lamb is slaughtered and blood came out, but no part of its body moved."
> Imām replied, "Do not eat. Ali said, 'If the leg jerked or the eye blinked, eat.'"
> It is clear that Imām's appeal to Imām Ali's words cannot be justified except when the conditional sentence has *mafhūm*, i.e., "If the leg did not jerk or the eye did not blink, do not eat."

Conditions Being Multiple While Consequents Being One

What should one do where there are two or more conditional sentences in which conditions are multiple but consequents are one? The case in question may be of two kinds:

1.The consequent is religiously unrepeatable, as in two *ĥadīths* concerning the prayers when one is travelling: "If the call to prayers (*adhān*) is not heard, perform your prayers shortened," and "If ramparts are not seen, perform your prayers shortened."
2.The consequent is religiously repeatable, as in: "If you had sexual intercourse, make major ablution," and "If you touched a dead body, make major ablution."

Since the discussion in either of these two kinds differs from the other, we will discuss them separately:

1. In this kind, contradiction between proofs would appear should the conditional sentence have *mafhūm* – though between *mafhūm* of each and *manṭūq* of the other. For instance, if one is in a place where one does not hear the call to prayers but sees the ramparts, according to *manṭūq* of the first one should perform one's prayers shortened while according to *mafhūm* of the second one should not do so. To solve this problem, one may take one of the two following ways:
1.1. To qualify both conditions with respect to their appearance in "independence in the causality" – an appearance caused by that absoluteness which is contrary to qualification with "and." Hence, the condition would, in fact, become a compound of two conditions each of them being part of the cause. Thus, the two sentences will be like one whose antecedent is the compound of two conditions: "If the call to prayers is not heard *and* ramparts are not seen, perform your prayers shortened." In that case, the two sentences may have one *mafhūm* which is non-existence of both conditions or one of them – as if they were one sentence.
1.2. To qualify both conditions with respect to their appearance in "exclusiveness" – an appearance caused by that absoluteness which is contrary to qualification with "or." Hence, the condition would be either of them, or, if possible, an inclusive affair covering both of them either of

them being its instance.

Now, the question is that which of those two ways is more justifiable. There are two opinions in this connection. The more justifiable one is to take the second way; for the contradiction is originated by appearance of two conditional sentences in exclusiveness which necessitates their appearance in *mafhūm* – something, in turn, causing contradiction of *manṭūq* of each to *mafhūm* of the other, as explained earlier. Therefore, one should abandon appearance of each of them in the exclusiveness – of course, to the extent denoted by *manṭūq* of the other, since appearance of *manṭūq* is stronger. As for the appearance of each sentence in the independence, it has no contradictory side so that one should abandon it.

Now that the second opinion is preferred, each condition will be independent in the efficacy. Thus, should one condition be actualized singly the judgment will be proved by it; and should both conditions be actualized, if they are actualized subsequently the judgment will be proved by the first, and if they are actualized simultaneously the judgment will be proved by both of them and they are treated as one condition – since it is assumed that the consequent cannot be repeated.

2. This kind is, in turn, of two kinds:

2.1. It is proved that each condition is part of the cause. Doubtless, the consequent is one and will be actualized when both conditions are realized.

2.2. It is proved, either by another proof or by the appearance of the same proof, that each condition is an independent cause. Here, whether or not the conditional sentence has *mafhūm*, it is disputed whether the rule to which one is supposed to refer to in such cases necessitates intervention of causes so that they may have one consequence, or necessitates non-intervention of causes so that the consequence should be repeated by repetition of conditions. Doubtless, as we have frequently stressed, the specific proof should be followed in this respect should there be one, as in the case with intervention of causes of ablution such as urine, sleep, and the like and non-intervention of causes of obligation of prayers such as coming of the time of daily prayers, eclipse of the sun or moon, and so forth. The dispute is over the problem where no specific proof exists and one wonders what one is principally supposed to do – a problem known as the problem of "intervention of causes."

2.2.1. The problem of intervention of causes (*tadākhul al-asbāb*). The justifiable opinion concerning this problem is non-intervention of causes. The reason is that every conditional sentence has two appearances: appearance of the condition in independence in the causality, and appearance of the consequence in that the object of the judgment is the sheer being. As for the former, the appearance necessitates that the consequence should be multiple in the conditional sentences; hence, causes do not intervene. As for the latter, since the sheer being of something cannot be object of two judgments, it is necessitated that all causes should have one consequence and judgment when their conjunction is assumed; hence, the causes intervene.

Thus, those two appearances contradict one another. If the first appearance is preferred, we should believe in non-intervention, and if the second, in intervention. Now, which one is more justifiable to be preferred?

The justifiable idea is to give the appearance of condition priority over that of consequence. Since the consequence is dependent upon the condition it is subject to the latter both in realization and demonstration: if the latter is one it is one, and if the latter is multiple it is multiple. Now that the antecedent is multiple, because of appearance of two conditional sentences, the consequent, which is subject to it, is not apparent in the unity of the desired. Thus, there would be no contradiction between the two appearances; rather, the appearance in the multiplicity removes the appearance in the unity, since the latter cannot exist unless when it is assumed that the appearance in the multiplicity is removed or that there is no such appearance, while there is such appearance here. The principle in such case, therefore, is non-intervention.

2.2.2. The problem of intervention of the caused (*tadākhul al-musabbabāt*). Should one believe that causes intervene, one would not be in need of discussing whether or not the caused intervene. That discussion, however, is necessary for those who hold the contrary opinion, for they should find out whether or not is it acceptable to content oneself with one obedience where the caused are common in the designation and reality, such as major ablutions. In other words, they should find out whether or not the caused intervene.

The principle here is also non-intervention. The reason is that obedience of multiple mandatory acts by one act, even though where all of them are intended, needs a specific proof; otherwise, every obligation necessitates a specific obedience incapable of substitution by any other obedience – even in cases where mandatory acts share the same designation and reality.

2. *Mafhūm* of the Qualifier (*al-Waṣf*)

By *waṣf* (the qualifier) in this discussion is meant whatsoever can be a condition, in its broadest sense, for the object of burden.

The qualifier here should have an object of qualification, for a case where the qualifier itself is the object of judgment – like this verse: "And the thief, male and female, cut off the hands of both" (5: 38) – is called designation (*al-laqab*) and should be discussed in the *mafhūm* of designation. The reason is that there must be a constant object of the judgment which can be both qualified and not qualified by the qualifier so that the negation of judgment can be assumed.

The qualifier here should also be more particular than the qualified either absolutely or in some aspect, since should it be equal or absolute general, it would make no constriction in the qualified so that one can assume negation of the judgment from the qualified where the qualifier is negated. However, the more particular in some respect is considered only with respect to the separation of the qualified from the qualifier and not to that of the qualifier from the qualified, for the object, i.e., the qualifier, should be preserved in the *mafhūm*; a given object neither proves nor negates any other object. Thus, *mafhūm* of "there is *zakāt* in the pastured sheep" – should there be *mafhūm* for such sentence – would be "there is not *zakāt* in the fed sheep," and not "there is not *zakāt* in other than the pastured sheep" nor "there is not *zakāt* in other than the pastured, such as camel."

The Justifiable Opinion on *Mafhūm* of the Qualifier

Should there be contextual evidence that a qualifier has or does not have *mafhūm*, the denotation would doubtlessly be in accordance with the evidence. An instance of the qualifier having no *mafhūm* is this verse: "Forbidden to you are… and your stepdaughters who are in your care" (4: 23) in which the quality of stepdaughters being in one's care is declared because it has been the prevalent situation – the qualifier alludes implicitly to the cause of the judgment, since those girls who are in one's care are like one's own daughters. Such sentences have absolutely no *mafhūm*, since it is clearly understood that neither in existence nor in non-existence is the judgment made dependent upon the qualifier.

The dispute is, then, whether the sheer qualification by the qualifier, without there being any contextual evidence, denotes *mafhūm*, i.e., denotes non-existence of the judgment of the qualified where the qualifier does not exist. There are two opinions in this connection, the prominent one being that such sentence has no *mafhūm*. The problem in this discussion is that whether the qualification understood from the qualifier is the qualification of the judgment which means that the judgment is made dependent upon the qualifier, or it is the qualification of the object of the judgment – or the object of the object (*muta'allaq al-mawḍu'*), due to difference of cases –the object or the object of the object being the combination of the qualified and the qualifier altogether.

If the first, the qualification by the qualifier is apparent in non-existence of the judgment where the qualifier does not exist; because of absoluteness, for absoluteness necessitates that when dependence of the judgment upon the qualifier is assumed the qualifier should be exclusive – as explained in the qualification by the condition.

If the second, however, the qualification by the qualifier is not apparent in non-existence of the judgment when the qualifier does not exist, for this case is included in *mafhūm* of designation. Here, the qualifier and the qualified are merely uttered to limit the object of judgment; the case is not that the object is the essence of the qualified and the qualifier being a condition for judging it. For instance, if the teacher says, "Draw a quadrilateral, perpendicular, equilateral shape," it is clearly understood that what he desires is a square and he has expressed his wish by using those terms to allude to that. In this case, the object is the total meaning denoted by the statement, which is a compound of the qualified and the qualifier, i.e., "a quadrilateral, perpendicular, equilateral shape" in the example which is in place of square. Thus, as the sentence "draw a square" does not denote non-existence where non-existence, what is in its place does not denote either, for it is in fact like a qualifier which is not dependent upon a qualified.

Now, it is time to determine the justifiable opinion. The appearance of the qualifier *per se* and without any contextual evidence is the second, i.e., it is a condition for the object and not the judgment. Thus, the judgment is absolute with regard to it; hence, there is no *mafhūm* for the qualifier. This presentation, however, is not enough to convince the opponents and we have to deal with doubts raised by them in this connection – and they are as follows:

1. Should the qualifier not denote non-existence where non-existence, there would be no benefit in using it.

The answer is that the benefit is not exclusively its reference to the judgment.

Suffice it to say that it limits and qualifies the object of the judgment.
2. Conditions are principally supposed to be constrictive (*iḥtirāzī*).
The answer is that although this is undeniable, it means to constrict the realm of the object and to expel other than the condition from being covered by the *person* of the judgment; and this is something we believe in too. However, it has no relation to *mafhūm*, since to prove a judgment for an object does not negate affirmation of the *type* of the judgment for others – as is the case with *mafhūm* of designation. In short, the condition being constrictive does not necessitate its playing the role of condition for the judgment.
3. The qualifier adumbrates causality, i.e., it adumbrates that the qualifier is the cause for the judgment; hence, it necessitates that the judgment should be dependent upon it.
The answer is that although that adumbration is undeniable, it does not denote *mafhūm* so long as it has not reached the state of explicit-definite denotation. The explanation is that there are three states of denotation where a sentence is uttered by someone. If the term one utters leaves no probability for any other meaning but what is uttered, it is called *naṣṣ* (explicit, definite). If it leaves some probability for other meanings but that probability is so scanty that the wise do not take it into consideration and ignore it, it is called *ẓāhir* (apparent). Finally, if it leaves a notable room for other meanings in such a way that the wise take other probabilities into consideration as well, this transmission of meaning is called *i<u>sh</u>'ār* (adumbration). *Naṣṣ* is essentially an authoritative proof, and *ẓāhir* is made an authoritative proof by the conduct of the wise – something to be discussed in the third part in detail – but there is no proof of authority of *i<u>sh</u>'ār*; hence, it cannot be useful for proving *mafhūm* of the qualifier.
4. There are some sentences whose having *mafhūm* is absolutely clear, such as the prophetic *ḥadī<u>th</u>*: "Procrastination of the wealthy man [in paying his debt] is injustice."
The answer is that there is contextual evidence in that sentence, since the conformity between judgment and object declares that procrastination of a rich debtor in payment of his debt is injustice, contrary to the poor one who has no money to pay his debt and if he procrastinates he will not be considered an unjust person. As was frequently repeated, should there be any contextual evidence in any kind of sentences it is the evidence that should be followed, even though it is against primary principles. The problem in the discussion of *mafhūm* is that whether a specific kind of sentence *per se* has or does not have *mafhūm* without there being any contextual evidence.

3. *Mafhūm* of the Termination (*al-Ghāya*)

In the sentences where a termination occurs, such as the Qur'ānic verse: "Then complete the Fast *unto* the night," (2, 187) and the *ḥadīth*: "Everything is lawful *until* you know that it, itself, is unlawful," there is a dispute among *Uṣūlīs* over two problems: one over *manṭūq* and the other over *mafhūm*.

1. As for *manṭūq*, it is disputed whether or not the termination is included in *manṭūq*, i.e., in the judgment of the terminated first; and secondly, whether the termination, i.e., what comes after the article of termination such as to, unto, until, and the like, is included in the terminated with regard to judgment or not and its role is only terminating the terminated in terms of object and judgment.

   Ignoring details of opinions in this connection, we merely state that the justifiable opinion is that the very qualification by the termination neither makes the termination included in nor excluded from the terminated; it is the contextual evidence that determines the situation. However, there is no doubt that the termination is not included where it is a termination for the precept, as in the *ḥadīth*: "Everything is lawful...," since inclusion of knowledge of unlawful in the precept of lawful is nonsensical.

2. As for *mafhūm*, it is disputed whether or not qualification by termination denotes negation of *type* of the judgment from other than termination as well as from termination itself should it not be included in the terminated.

The criterion for *mafhūm* of the termination is the very criterion for that of condition and qualifier. Should the termination be condition for the judgment it would have *mafhūm* and would denote negation of the judgment from other things, and should it be condition for the object or the predicate only it would not denote *mafhūm*. Now, the question is that which of those two probabilities can be justified.

What seems to be more justifiable is to hold that the termination is apparent in referring to the judgment and to be a termination for its preceding relation; it is its reference to the object itself or the predicate itself is the one which is in need of depiction and evidence. Hence, the termination has *mafhūm*.

4. *Mafhūm* of the Exclusivity (*al-Ḥaṣr*)

There are some different words in Arabic alluding to exclusivity; that is why they are all supposed to be discussed separately in order to determine whether they denote *mafhūm* or not. However, as the case is not the same in English, we simply assert that whatsoever denotes exclusivity will definitely denote *mafhūm*, since such structure is merely made to convey non-existence where non-existence, otherwise there would be no need to use such structure with such terms and one could simply convey one's desire by using simple words in simple sentences. What we said in this connection is enough and leaves no room for any further discussion.

5. *Mafhūm* of the Number (*al-'Adad*)

Limitation of an object to a specific number will doubtlessly not denote negation of the judgment from others. Thus, this command: "Fast three days of every lunar month" does not mean that fasting other than the three days is not recommended; hence, it does not contradict another proof which commands fasting some other days of every month.

Of course, should the precept be obligation, for instance, and limitation by the maximum number be for determination of the highest level– such as the proof that makes fasting thirty days of Ramaḍān obligatory – it would doubtlessly denote that the more is not mandatory. However, this is not due to the limitation by number having *mafhūm*, but rather because of peculiarities of the case. Thus, limitation by number has no *mafhūm*.

6. *Mafhūm* of the Designation (*al-Laqab*)

By *al-laqab* is meant any noun used as an object of the judgment, such as the thief in this Qur'ānic verse: "And the *thief*, male and female, cut off the hands of both." (5: 38) *Mafhūm* of the designation means that the judgment does not cover what is not covered by the noun in general.

Since we did not accept that the qualifier denotes *mafhūm*, it is more plausible to hold that the designation does not have such denotation, for the very object of the judgment does not even allude to the judgment being dependent upon the designation, let alone any appearance in the exclusiveness. The ultimate thing understood from the designation is that the *person* of the judgment does not cover what is not generally covered by the noun, but this is far from negation of the *type* of the judgment from another object. It is even said that should the designation have *mafhūm*, it would be the weakest one.

Three Important Denotations Not of Kind of *Mafhūm* or *Manṭūq*: Necessitation (*al-Iqtiḍā'*), Hint (*al-Tanbīh*), and Implicit Conveyance (*al-Is̲h̲āra*)

It was said that *manṭūq* is what is denoted by the essence of a sentence and *mafhūm* is what is denoted by a sentence through an obvious implicature of *manṭūq* in the most particular sense.

However, there are some denotations that are included neither in *mafhūm* nor in *manṭūq*, such as the case where the speech denotes implicatively a single word or a single meaning not mentioned in the *manṭūq*, or it denotes contents of a sentence which is an implicature of *manṭūq* but not obviously in the most particular sense. Those are all called neither *mafhūm* nor *manṭūq*.

To address those denotations in a general way, a good number of *Uṣūlīs* have called them contextual denotation (*al-dalāla al-siyāqiyya*) meaning that the context of a speech denotes a single or compound meaning, or an omitted word. Such denotations are divided into the three following varieties:

1. ***Denotation of necessitation.*** In this denotation, two criteria are taken into consideration: the denotation being conventionally meant by the speaker, and the truth or correctness of the speech being logically, juristically, lexically, or conventionally dependent upon the denotation. Numerous examples can be found for such denotation two of which being as follows:

In the verse 82 of *sūra* 12 of the holy Qur'ān, parts of words of Joseph's brothers to their father when they returned from their journey to Egypt are narrated in this way: "Question the city wherein we were," and it is clear that the city cannot be questioned. Thus, the sentence can rationally be correct only if the word "people" is considered omitted in it, so that the sentence should be "Question people of the city… ."

There is a *ḥadīt̲h̲* saying, "There are no prayers for the mosque's neighbor except in the mosque," while we know that should such a person say his prayers in his home it will be juristically acceptable. Thus, the truth and correctness of the sentence is dependent upon the word "perfect" being omitted so that what is negated should be perfection of the prayers and not the prayers itself.

Generally speaking, all implicative denotations to single meanings and all figurative meanings refer to the denotation of necessitation.

2. ***Denotation of hint.*** In this denotation, only the first criterion, i.e., the denotation being conventionally meant by the speaker, is taken into consideration. Here, the truth or correctness of the speech is not dependent upon the denotation; it is the context of the speech that causes certainty that such requisite is meant or makes its non-consideration unlikely. This denotation has also numerous instances the most important of which being classified as follows:

a) The speaker whishes to depict something but expresses its logical or conventional requisite. For example, one addresses his friend saying, "It is ten o'clock" in order to remind him that the time they had agreed upon to go somewhere has come.
b) The speech is associated with some word which conveys that something is a cause, condition, impediment, or part of the judgment. To mention the judgment is thereby a hint that the thing mentioned is a cause, condition, impediment, part of the judgment or it is not so. For instance, if the jurist says, "Repeat your prayers," where he is asked about the doubt concerning numbers of *rak'a*s of a two-*rak'a* prayers, it is understood that the said doubt is a cause for annulment of the prayers and the obligation of repetition.
c) The speech is associated with some word which determines some objects of the act. For instance, when someone says, "I reached the river and drank," it is understood that what was drunk was water and it was from the river.

3. ***Denotation of implicit conveyance.*** In this denotation, neither of the two criteria is taken into consideration and what is denoted is only an unclear implicature of the speech or an obvious implicature of the speech in the most general sense – no matter the object of denotation is understood from a single sentence or from a couple of sentences.
An instance of this is denotation of two Qur'ānic verses as to the minimum time of pregnancy: the verse 15 of the *sūra* 46 "And painfully she gave birth to him his bearing and his weaning being thirty months," and the verse 233 of the *sūra* 2 "Mothers will suckle their children two complete years completely for such as desire to complete the suckling," since to subtract two years, i.e., twenty four months, from thirty months is six and thereby it becomes clear that the minimum time for pregnancy is six months. It is also of this kind the question of obligation of something necessitating obligation of its preliminary, since it is an obvious implicature of the obligation of

the thing in the most general sense. That is why they consider obligation of the preliminary of a mandatory act a secondary and not a primary one; for it is not a denotation of the speech by intention and is only understood secondarily, i.e., by the denotation of implicit conveyance.

Authority of Such Denotations

As for denotations of necessitation and hint, they would undoubtedly be an authoritative proof should there be a denotation and appearance, because of authority of appearances.

Denotation of implicit conveyance, however, cannot be treated as an authoritative proof because of authority of appearances, for there is no appearance where it is assumed that such thing is not intended – it is obviously clear that denotation is subject to the intention. Therefore, implicit conveyance should only be called adumbration and implicit conveyance without using the term denotation; hence, it is clear that such conveyance is not included in the appearances so that it can be an authoritative proof from that aspect. Of course, it would definitely be an authoritative proof should there be an intellectual implication through which its requisites, whether judgment or otherwise, could be discovered, such as taking requisites of one's confession into consideration even though he claims that he has not intended them or he denies existence of any implication there.

CHAPTER 5

GENERAL (*AL-ʿĀMM*) AND PARTICULAR (*AL-KH*ĀṢṢ)

General and particular are among clear, self evident concepts which need no definition but lexical explanation for the sake of bringing the meaning closer to the mind. By *general* is meant a term whose concept covers whatsoever capable of being conformable to its designation in realization of the judgment. A judgment, too, is sometimes called general due to its covering all instances of the object, the object of burden, or duty-bound. On the contrary, by *particular* is meant a term, or a judgment, which covers only some instances of its object, object of burden, or duty-bound.

In the discussion of general and particular, there are two frequently used expressions whose definition seems necessary: *al-takhṣīṣ* (restriction), and *al-takhaṣṣuṣ* (non-inclusion). The former means to *expel* some instances from being covered by the *judgment*, and the latter means *not being included* from the very beginning in the *object*. In order to clarify that, let us take an example. Suppose that John is a teacher in the school while Joshua is not. Now, the principal orders his deputy to pay salaries of all teachers except John's. Should there not be such exclusion in the principal's order, John should be paid too, since he was a teacher; but the case is not the same with Joshua, since he is not a teacher at all. In the first case it is exclusion, while in the second it is non-inclusion; and that is the difference between *takhṣīṣ* and *takhaṣṣuṣ*.

Varieties of Generality

With regard to direction of a judgment to a general, generality is divided into three kinds:

1. The encompassing generality (*al-ʿumūm al-istighrāqī*), such as "respect

every scholar." In this kind, the judgment covers every single instance in such a way that every instance is singly an object of the judgment and every judgment of every instance has its own specific obedience or disobedience.
2. The total generality (*al-'umūm al-madjmū'ī*), such as "believe in the holy Imāms." In this kind, the judgment is for the total as such and the total is treated as one object. Hence, the obedience in the example will not be actualized unless one believes in the all twelve Imāms and not even in the eleven. Thus, in this kind there would only be a single obedience, i.e., obedience of the total, and disobedience even in one instance will be considered an absolute disobedience.
3. The substitutional generality (*al-'umūm al-badalī*), such as "respect any scholar you wish." In this kind, the judgment is directed to one instance in a substitutional way. Hence, only one instance, in a substitutional way, is the object of the judgment and should one instance be obeyed the burden would absolutely be treated as being obeyed.

Should it strike you that this third kind cannot be treated as generality, since to be substitutional, in which the object is not but one, contradicts generality, we would remind you that the meaning of generality in this kind is generality in the substitution, i.e., capability of every instance to be an object. Of course, should the generality in this kind be understood because of absoluteness, it would be included in the absolute and not the general.

Generally speaking, generality of the object of the judgment with regard to its states and instances, if it is an object of a mandatory or a recommended command, is mostly of the kind of substitutional generality.

Terms of Generality

Doubtless there are some terms specifically used for generality either by convention, or by absoluteness through Premises of Wisdom (*Muqaddimāt al-Ḥikma*,) something to be explained in detail in the sixth chapter). Such terms are either single words like "every," "all," "any," "ever," and so forth, or lexical dispositions like occurrence of an indefinite noun in a negative or prohibitive context. There are some discussions in this connection with regard to some terms in the Arabic language, as the language of *Kitāb* (the holy Qur'ān) and *Sunna*, but as they make no sense in the English language we refer readers to Arabic texts on *uṣūl al-fiqh* for further, detailed studies.

The Joint Restrictor (*al-Mukhaṣṣiṣ al-Muttaṣil*) and the Separate Restrictor (*al-Mukhaṣṣiṣ al-Munfaṣil*)

Qualification of a general can be made in two ways:

1. The restrictor is depicted in the same single utterance delivered by the speaker, such as "perform your prayers completely except when travelling." This restrictor is called *joint* and denotes that by general is meant other than the particular. The case is the same with the circumstantial evidence denoting peculiarity in such a way that the speaker can count on it in depicting his will.
2. The restrictor is not uttered in the same speech, but rather in an independent utterance before or after that. This restrictor is called *separate* and like the first denotes that by general is meant other than the particular.

These two types have no differences with regard to being evidence for the real intent of the speaker. The difference appears with regard to formation of the appearance in generality; as in the joint restrictor the appearance is not formed but in peculiarity while in the separate restrictor the appearance is initially formed in generality but since the appearance of the particular is stronger it is given precedence over the general – and this is due to the principle of giving the more apparent (*al-aẓhar*) or the explicit-definite (*al-naṣṣ*) precedence over the apparent.

The reason is that no appearance for any kind of speech, general or otherwise, would be formed unless when that speech is customarily ended and terminated in such a way that there would customarily remain no room for addition of any supplement as an evidence of changing the speech's primary, initial appearance. Hence, the appearance of the speech is suspended while the speech is customarily not terminated. Should the speech be ended without addition of any contrary evidence, its primary appearance would become established and the appearance of the speech would be formed upon that. However, should contrary evidence be added the primary appearance of the speech would change into another, on the basis of denotation of the evidence, and the appearance of speech would be formed upon that evidence. That is why if the evidence is ambiguous or there exists something that can probably be evidence the primary appearance is not formed; and since there is no other appearance the speech as a whole becomes ambiguous.

Now, since the restrictor is contrary evidence: if it is separate, it will not harm the primary appearance of the speech, as the appearance had been formed before it intervened; and if it is joint, it will change the primary appearance of the general and will form its appearance in accordance with the joint restrictor. However, where a separate restrictor occurs, it intervenes in the appearance of the general, and as it is evidence revealing the real intent of the speaker it should be given precedence over the general.

Usage of the General in the Restricted (*al-Mukhaṣṣaṣ*)

As was said, both kinds of restrictors reveal that by the general is meant other than the particular; hence, what is meant by the general is some of the objects covered by its appearance. However, there is a dispute among *Uṣūlīs* whether such usage is literal or figurative. Opinions in this connection are various the most notable of which being as follows: (1) it is absolutely figurative, (2) it is absolutely literal, and (3) the case differs with regard to the joint and separate restrictors.

Investigate of the reason presented by those who believe in the first reveals the truth and proves that the justifiable opinion is the second, i.e., such usage is absolutely literal. Holders of the first opinion argue that since the particle of generality is conventionally made to denote extensiveness of its posterior term as well as its inclusiveness with regard to all of its instances, it would have been used in other than what it is specified for had by that be meant some and not all instances – and this is a figurative usage.

This is an illusion, however, and would be removed by simple deliberation. Since the explanation will be somehow different with regard to the joint and the separate restrictors, we will deal with them separately:

1. In the restriction by a joint restrictor, such as "perform all your prayers completely except when travelling," the particle of generality, i.e., all, is not used but in its meaning, i.e., inclusion of all instances of its posterior term. However, the meaning of restriction is that the term next to does not cover whatsoever the term prayers holds true for, but rather the home-performed prayers in particular. As for the term "all," it still has its signification of generality and inclusion; for it denotes inclusion of every home-performed prayers. That is why changing it with "some" and saying "Perform some of your prayers completely except when travelling" is not correct and makes no sense. It also makes no sense if one says, "Perform completely some of the home-performed prayers," since it does not denote limitation of the object

as in the case where both "all" and "exception" exist.

2. The case would be the same with the restriction by a separate restrictor, for the meaning of restriction by a separate restrictor is to make the particular a separate evidence for allocation of the term next to "all" to other than the particular. Thus, neither in the particle of the generality nor in its posterior term has a change been made; in the process of restriction, the particular reveals what the speaker has really meant by the general.

Authority or Otherwise of the Restricted General in the Remaining (*al-Bāqī*)

In case where it is doubted whether some remaining instances of a restricted general are included in that general or not, it is disputed whether or not the general is an authoritative proof in that portion so that one can or cannot appeal to the appearance of the generality in order to include it in the judgment of the general. For instance, if the Lord says, "Every water is pure," and then excepts from that general, whether by a joint or a separate proof, the water polluted by a juristically impure object, and at the same time it is probable that the scant water (*al-mā' al-qalīl*) touched by a juristically impure object without being polluted is excepted. Now, should we hold that the restricted general is an authoritative proof in the remaining, we would reject that probability by the appearance of the generality of the general in the whole remaining, judging thereby that the touched, unpolluted water is juristically pure. However, if we believe in the contrary view, that probability remains suspended without there being any proof from the very general as to it. Hence, we should look for another proof to prove its juristic purity or impurity.

Opinions in this connection are multiple some of which differentiating between the joint and the separate restrictors. To find the justifiable opinion, however, is not that difficult; for this problem is secondary to the previous one, and since we held there that the restricted general is literally, and not figuratively, applied to the remaining, we should hold here that it is absolutely an authoritative proof, no matter of what kind the restrictor is. The reason is that, as we said, the particle of the generality still holds its meaning of encompassing all instances of its posterior term. Now, when some of its instances are excepted by restriction, no matter of which kind the restrictor is, its indication of the generality still remains established and it is only the scope of its posterior term that has become limited by the restriction. Thus, there is no difference between the restricted and the unrestricted general in being apparent in encompassing whatsoever may possibly be included in them.

As for those who believe that the restricted general is figuratively applied to the remaining, they encounter a problem concerning the appearance of the general and its authority in the whole remaining. For it is assumed that usage of the general in the whole remaining is one figurative application and its usage in some of the remaining is another; hence, it is disputed whether the first figurative application is closer to the literalness making the general become apparent in it or both of applications are equal in this connection and the general has no appearance in neither of them. If the first, the general is an authoritative proof in the whole remaining, and if the second, it is not an authoritative proof. Thus, it is not true that those who believe in the figurative application believe absolutely in non-authority of the restricted general.

Penetration or Otherwise of Ambiguity of the Restrictor to the General

The previous discussion was based on the presumption that the particular was clear without having any ambiguity. The matter doubted there was whether something, other than the particular, which was clearly known that it was not included in the particular, is restricted or not. The present discussion, however, deals with the authority of the general in the case of ambiguity of the particular.

First of all, we should bear in mind that the ambiguity in question is of two types:

1. The dubiety concerning the concept (*al-s̲h̲ubha al-mafhūmiyya*). Here, the doubt is about the concept of the particular *per se*, i.e., the particular is ambiguous; such as this *ḥadīt̲h̲*: "Every water is juristically pure except what its taste, color, or smell is polluted [by a juristically impure object]," in which it is doubted whether by pollution is meant the sheer sensory pollution or it includes the assumed pollution as well. Or this order, for instance, by the commander: "Trust soldiers of the squadron except John," in which it is doubted whether John refers to John Smith or John Cooper.
2. The dubiety concerning the instance (*al-s̲h̲ubha al-miṣdāqiyya*). Here, the doubt is about the inclusion of an instance of the general in the particular while the concept of the particular is clear without any ambiguity. For instance, we doubt whether specific water has been polluted by something juristically impure and has been included in the precept of the particular or not and still holds its purity.

Another thing to be mentioned before dealing with the problem in detail is the meaning of penetration of ambiguity of the restrictor into the general. Whenever it is said that the ambiguity of the restrictor penetrates into the general it means that one cannot refer to the principality of generality in order to include the doubtful instance in the precept of the general.

1. The Dubiety concerning the Concept

The dubiety in this type is sometimes over the least (*al-aqall*) and the most (*al-akṯẖar*), like the first example in which it was doubted whether the sheer sensory pollution is excepted or the restriction includes the assumed change as well (the least being the sensory pollution, and the most being what incorporates the assumed as well), and sometimes over two divergent things (*al-mutabāyinayn*), such as the second example in which the restriction is doubted whether it addresses John Smith or John Cooper. On the other hand, the restrictor can be joint or separate – something influential in the case in question. For the sake of comprehensiveness, therefore, we will discuss the problem in the following separate states:

> 1 & 2. Where the restrictor is joint, whether the dubiety is over the least and the most or over two divergent things. Here, the ambiguity of the restrictor penetrates into the general. For, as was said earlier, the joint restrictor is of kind of joint evidence of the speech; hence, no appearance takes form for the general except in other than the particular. Therefore, should the particular be ambiguous, its ambiguity would penetrate into the general; since other than the particular is unknown, and it is clear that no appearance will take form for the general in something whose exclusion of the designation of the particular is not known.
>
> 3. Where the restrictor is separate while the dubiety is over two divergent things. In this state, too, the ambiguity of the restrictor penetrates into the general. For it is known in summary fashion that the restriction has actually occurred, though between two things in a doubtful manner, and this will cause non-authority of the general in either of them.

The difference between this and the previous state is that in the latter the very *appearance* of the speech in the generality is eliminated while in the former the *authority of appearance* is eliminated – though the primary appearance is still remaining – and one cannot refer to the principality of generality in either of the two doubtful things.

4. Where the restrictor is separate while the dubiety is over the least and the most. Contrary to all previous states, the ambiguity of the restrictor does not penetrate into the general in this state. For in a general restricted by a separate restrictor, the appearance takes form in the generality, as was said earlier in the second chapter, and the particular is given precedence over the general only because it is stronger. Thus, should the restrictor be ambiguous with regard to the additional to the definite amount, it would not be an authoritative proof in that additional; for it is assumed that the restrictor is ambiguous having no appearance in that additional and is an authoritative proof exclusively in the definite amount, which is the least. Therefore, it cannot interfere with the general whose appearance in encompassing all of its instances, among which being the definite amount of the particular as well as the additional to the definite amount whose inclusion in the particular is doubtful, has been established. Now, should the definite amount be excluded by an authoritative proof stronger than the general, the additional to the definite amount would remain included without interference of anything with the appearance as well as authority of the general in it.

2. The Dubiety concerning the Instance

Although it is sometimes said that the prominent opinion among the earliest jurists has been that the ambiguity of the restrictor does not penetrate into the general in the dubiety concerning the instance and one can refer to the principality of generality in order to include the doubtful instance in the precept of the general, the justifiable opinion is contrary to that with regard to both joint and separate restrictors. The reason is that since the particular is a stronger authoritative proof than the general, it causes allocation of the precept of the general to its remaining instances and removes the authority of the general from some of its objects of denotation. In the case in question, it is doubted whether the doubtful instance is included in or excluded from what the general is an authoritative proof in, while the general does not denote its inclusion in what it is an authoritative proof in. Therefore, the general is not an authoritative proof in the doubtful instance without encountering any interference – as argued by those who believe in the contrary opinion.

In other words, there are two known, authoritative affairs here: the general which is an authoritative proof in other than the particular, and the restrictor which is an authoritative proof in its object of denotation; the doubtful instance is doubted whether it is included in this authoritative affair or that one.

What we said clarifies the difference between "the dubiety concerning the instance," and "the dubiety concerning the concept where the restrictor is separate while the dubiety is over the least and the most" in which the ambiguity of the restrictor does not penetrate into the general. For in the latter the particular is not an authoritative proof except in the least, and it is not the doubtful additional which is doubted to be included in what the particular is clearly an authoritative proof in; rather, it is the particular which is doubted whether it is made an authoritative proof as to the doubtful additional or not – and, as will be proved in the third part, something whose authority in something else is doubtful is definitely not an authoritative proof in that thing. The general, however, is authoritative proof except in what the particular is authoritative proof in. Thus, the most is not doubted whether to be included in this or that authoritative proof, as was the case with the doubtful instance; on the contrary, it is known that the particular is not an authoritative proof in the most – because of the doubt – and therefore the particular does not interfere with the authority of the general in it.

Unlawfulness of Implication of the General before the Quest for the Restrictor

Doubtless a good number of general precepts in the Qur'ān and *Sunna* are restricted by separate restrictors which describe what is meant by them, and this is so clearly known from the conduct of the holy Prophet and holy Imāms that a sentence has constantly been prevalent: "there is no general except it is restricted." This fact necessitates that the jurist should not hasten to implicate the general before a thorough quest for the restrictor, since that general may be among those which are restricted by a separate restrictor existing in the Book or *Sunna* not known by the one who received the general. The reason is simple: when we know that the Divine Lawgiver's conduct is to count on separate evidence in expounding His objectives, there will remain no confidence in the appearance of the general in its generality – as it is a primary appearance. That is why the Divine Lawgiver (*al-Shāri'*) has the right to punish the duty-bound if he shirks his duty of questing for the restrictor. However, should the duty-bound do his level best and make a thorough quest for the restrictor where it is supposed to exist in such a way that he becomes confident that there exists no restrictor, he would have the right to take the appearance of the general and implement it. Thus, should there actually exist a restrictor but in such a way that the duty-bound could not attain it through his quest, he would be excused for implementation of the general.

What we said concerning divine laws applies to all other kinds of appearances too, for one is not allowed to take them except after one has made a quest for the separate evidence. This is summed up in a rule: "the principality of appearance will not be an authoritative proof except after one has made a thorough quest for the evidence and one has despaired of finding it."

A General Preceding a Pronoun Which Refers to Some Instances of the General

In the verse 228 of *sūra* 2: "Divorced women will wait by themselves for three periods...in such time their mates have better right to restore them..." "divorced women" is general covering both revocable and irrevocable divorcées while by pronoun in "their mates" is merely meant revocable divorcées. In such cases, one has to oppose either the appearance of the general in generality restricting it to those to which the pronoun refers, or that of reference of the pronoun to what has preceded it referring it to some of them (something called *istikhdām* in Arabic rhetoric) which leaves no room for the generality.

There are different views in this connection the justifiable one being that there is no problem with reference to the principality of generality. The reason is that the reference of pronoun to some instances of the general makes no changes in the appearance of the general, for determination of some instances because of reference of the pronoun due to some evidence does not necessitate that some instances are determined by the general's precept *per se*; as the precept in the sentence containing pronoun is different from the precept in the sentence containing general and there is no connection between the two sentences. Thus, reference of the pronoun to some instances of the general is not such evidence capable of necessitating change in general's appearance in the generality.

An Exception Preceded by Multiple Sentences

In verses 4-5 of *sūra* 24: "And those who cast it up on women in wedlock and then do not bring four witnesses, scourge them with eighty stripes, do not accept any testimony of theirs ever, and they are the ungodly; save such as repent thereafter and make amends...," there are three general precepts followed by an exception in the end. In such cases, one doubts whether the exception is made to the last sentence or to all sentences.

There are four opinions in this connection:

1. The speech is apparent in reference of the exception to the last sentence.

Although its reference to other than the last is possible, it needs evidence.
2. The speech is apparent in its reference to all sentences, and it is its reference to the last sentence that needs proof.
3. The speech is apparent in neither of them – though its reference to the last sentence is something for sure. As for other sentences, they remain ambiguous, because of existence of some potential evidence; hence, no appearance in generality takes form for them and one cannot refer to the principle of generality in this connection.
4. Differentiation should be made between the case where the object of sentences is repeated in every sentence, like the verse mentioned, and the case where the object of sentences is one and is just mentioned in the first sentence, like: "do people good, respect them, and satisfy their needs, except evildoers." In the latter, the object, i.e., people, is mentioned only in the first sentence and is not repeated in others – what is repeated is a pronoun referring to it – while in the verse in question the object of all precepts is a pronoun which refers to a word mentioned in the beginning without being accompanied by a judgment.

According to this opinion, in cases where the object of sentences is not repeated, the exception is apparent in referring to all sentences. For the exception is to be made from the object with the consideration of the judgment, and the object is only mentioned in the beginning; hence, it refers to all. However, in cases where the object of sentences is repeated, the exception is apparent in referring to the last sentence. For the object is mentioned in the last sentence independently and the exception has found its reference. Restriction of previous sentences is in need of another proof which, as was assumed, is missing; that is why one may refer to their principality of generality with regard to them.

The fourth opinion can bring all opinions together, since one may make any of them conformable to a case mentioned in this view.

Restriction of the General by *Mafhūm*

As explained earlier in chapter 4, implicatures of sentences (*mafāhīm*) are divided into accordant and disaccording. There is no dispute among *Uṣūlīs* that a general can be restricted by an accordant *mafhūm*. For instance, according to the general ruling of the verse 40 of *sūra* 42 "the recompense of evil is evil the like of it," if one is beaten by another one is allowed to beat him. On the other hand, the verse 23 of the *sūra* 17 declares that: "Your Lord has decreed you … to be good to parents … and do not say to them Fie," according to whose accordant *mafhūm* one is not allowed to beat one's parents. The general ruling of that verse is restricted by accordant *mafhūm* of this verse, then.

As for disaccording *mafhūm*, it is a matter of dispute among *Uṣūlīs*. For instance, according to the general ruling of the verse 36 of *sūra* 10 "indeed conjecture is no substitute for the truth," no conjecture may be treated as an authoritative proof even though it is caused by report of a righteous-trustworthy transmitter, while according to the disaccording *mafhūm* of the verse 6 of *sūra* 49 "O believers, if an evildoer bring you some news you should verify it," it is allowed to treat a report by a righteous-trustworthy person as valid without verifying it. Since the appearance of the disaccording *mafhūm* is not as strong as the appearance of *Manṭūq* or that of the accordant *mafhūm*, it is disputed whether it is stronger than the appearance of the general and should be given precedence over it, the general is stronger and it is the general that should be given precedence, they are equal in the appearance and none of them should be given precedence, or the case differs in various states.

Since it is assumed that *mafhūm* is more particular than the general, the former is conventionally treated as evidence for what is intended by the latter; and it is the rule that evidence should principally be given precedence over that which has evidence, no matter its appearance is stronger or not. Of course, if the general is explicit-definite, it is the general that should be considered as evidence for what is intended by the sentence containing *mafhūm*, and in this case the sentence will not have *mafhūm*.

Restriction of the Book by Single Tradition

Since issuance of the holy Qur'ān is for certain while that of single tradition (*khabar al-wāḥid*) is doubtful, to restrict the Qur'ān by single tradition seems problematic. However, there has always been consensus that the latter should be given precedence over the former. The reason is that definite proofs have proved that single tradition, where it is valid because of certain evidence, is an authoritative proof though its issuance is not for certain. Now, should theme of a single tradition be more particular than a general Qur'ānic verse, one should either reject the tradition and treat its transmitter as a liar, or make some change in the appearance of the Qur'ān; for one can neither change the theme of a tradition, as it is explicit-definite (*naṣṣ*) or more apparent (*aẓhar*), nor reject the transmission of the Qur'ān since it is for certain. In other words, one should oppose either the conjecture for the truth of tradition or the conjecture for the generality of the Qur'ānic verse.

Doubtless the tradition can be evidence for changing the appearance of the

Book, for it is assumed that it has an eye for the appearance of the Book and comments on it. On the contrary, the appearance of the Book is not capable of rejecting the proof of authority of the tradition, for it is assumed that it has no relation with the latter in this respect so that it can have an eye for it or comment on it. The language of the tradition is that of commenting on the Book; hence, it should be given precedence over the latter. The appearance of the Book, however, does not intend to comment on the proof of authority of the tradition so that it may be given precedence over it. In other words, it is assumed that the tradition is evidence for the Book and the principle as to the evidence, i.e., the principle of truthfulness of the transmitter, should be given precedence over the principle as to that which has evidence, which is the principle of generality.

CHAPTER 6

ABSOLUTE (*AL-MUṬLAQ*) AND QUALIFIED (*AL-MUQAYYAD*)

By absoluteness is meant encompassment and extensiveness of a term with regard to its meaning and states without the term being used in encompassment in the way understood from an indefinite noun in a negative context – since in that case the term would be considered general and not absolute.

As was said earlier, the contrariety of absolute and qualified is that of possession and privation, for absoluteness is lack of qualification in that which can be qualified. Thus, absoluteness follows qualification in the possibility, in the sense that if qualification is possible in the speech or proof the absoluteness is possible and if it is impossible the absoluteness is impossible. Hence, in a case where qualification is not possible, one cannot discover absoluteness from the speech of speaker; that speech is neither absolute nor qualified – though in fact one of them is necessarily intended by the speaker. In such cases, however, one can discover absoluteness from absoluteness of the position (*iṭlāq al-maqām* or *al-iṭlāq al-maqāmī*) and not from that of speech. By absoluteness of the position is meant that although the speaker cannot qualify his words in one sentence, he can qualify it by adding another sentence after finishing his first sentence and utter the condition he intends.

Is Absoluteness by Convention?

Doubtless absoluteness of proper nouns with regard to their states as well as that of sentences is not by convention, but rather by premises of wisdom (*muqaddimāt al-ḥikma*). However, there is a dispute among *Uṣūlīs* whether absoluteness of generic nouns (*asmā' al-ajnās*) and the like is by convention or by premises of wisdom. In other words, are generic nouns (such as star, mountain, water, etc.) designated by convention for their meanings as they are extensive and encompassing in such a way that encompassment, i.e., absoluteness, is taken into consideration in the meaning of the term, or are they designated for their very meanings *per se* and absoluteness is understood from another indicator, i.e., the very term's voidance of the condition where premises of wisdom exist?

The justifiable opinion is the second one. Its explanation, however, is beyond the boundaries of an introductory work and should be found in detailed works.

Premises of Wisdom (*Muqaddimāt al-Ĥikma*)

Now that terms are designated for the essence of meanings and not for the meanings as they are absolute, there must be particular or general evidence which make the speech *per se* apparent in the absoluteness in order to prove that by the term is intended the absolute and to make the judgment penetrate into all instances. Such general evidence will exist only if the three following premises exist:

1. Possibility of absoluteness and qualification. This exists where the object of judgment is capable of division before being judged, since if it is capable of division only after being judged the qualification will be impossible – as was explained earlier in chapter 2 where secondary divisions were explained.
2. Lack of any evidence, neither joint nor separate. The joint evidence forms the appearance of the speech only in the qualified. As for the separate evidence, although an appearance in the absoluteness takes form for the speech, that appearance is not an authoritative proof – because of existence of the evidence, which should be given precedence. That appearance, therefore, is a primary one leaving no room for the principality of absoluteness.
3. The speaker being in the position of depiction. Should the speaker not be in the position of depiction, but in the position of law-making only or in that of depicting another precept, no appearance in the absoluteness would take form for the speech. For instance, in the verse 4 of *sūra* 5: "and such hunting dogs as you teach…eat what they catch for you," the Almighty is in the position of depiction of lawfulness of what hunting dogs catch and not in that of purity of parts bitten by dogs so that one can refer to the absoluteness of the speech and judge that such parts are juristically pure and they need not to be purified by water.

What should one do if one doubts whether or not the speaker is in the position of depiction? The principle in such cases is that the speaker is in the position of depiction, for as the wise treat the speaker as being attentive not unconscious and serious not joking when they doubt that, they treat him as being in the position of depiction and explanation not in that of negligence and ambiguousness.

The conclusion is that any speech capable of being qualified but not being qualified by a speaker who is wise, attentive, serious, and in the position of depiction is apparent and an authoritative proof in the absoluteness, in such a way that both the speaker and the listener can refer to its absoluteness in the position of argumentation.

Contradictory Absolute and Qualified

By contradiction between absolute and qualified is meant that one cannot take the duty in the absolute and that in the qualified altogether if one wishes to keep appearances of both; i.e., they contradict one another in their appearances. Contradiction appears only where both causes and judgments are the same. Hence, there would be no contradiction where (a) causes are different, for instance: "If you break your fasting deliberately, then free a slave," and "If you commit injurious assimilation, then free a slave," (b) judgments are different, for instance: "If you break your fasting deliberately, then free a slave," and "If you break your fasting deliberately, then fast sixty days," (c) judgment in the absolute is mandatory while it is recommended in the qualified, and (d) it is understood from the duty in the qualified that it is another duty to be performed.

Now, should one find contradictory absolute and qualified in a juristic statement, one would have no choice but to either change the appearance of the absolute and predicate it upon the qualified or to change the qualified in such a way that it does not contradict the absolute leaving it to keep its absoluteness. Which of those change-makings is preferable, then? Since absolute and qualified agree or disagree in affirmation or negation on the one hand and absoluteness is either substitutional (when the noun is indefinite) or inclusive (when the noun is definite) on the other, we have to discuss the problem in some different states. Before dealing with the problem, however, it should be noted that whenever it is said that the absolute is predicated upon the qualified it means that one should take the qualified, and not the absolute, into consideration; since it is the qualified that is the real, serious intent of the speaker.

> 1 & 2. Absolute and qualified disagree in affirmation or negation, no matter the absoluteness is substitutional (*badalī*, such as "Free a slave," and "Do not free an unbeliever slave") or inclusive (*s͟humūlī*, such as "In the sheep there is *zakāt*" and "In the fed sheep there is not *zakāt*"). Doubtless the absolute should be predicated upon the qualified in such case, for the qualified is evidence for what is intended by the absolute. Thus, the conclusion in the

former is "free a believer slave" and in the latter is "in the pastured sheep there is *zakāt.*"

3. Absolute and qualified agree in affirmation or negation, and the absoluteness is substitutional. For instance, the two following commands by the divine lawgiver: "Free a slave," and "Free a believer slave." Here, though to predicate the qualified upon the absolute is possible, the appearance of the qualified in the determinate obligation should be given precedence over that of the absolute in the absoluteness, for the qualified can be evidence for the absolute and it is quite possible that the speaker has taken this into consideration.

4. Absolute and qualified agree in affirmation or negation, and the absoluteness is inclusive. For instance, the two following statements by the divine lawgiver: "In the sheep, there is *zakāt*" and "In the pastured sheep, there is *zakāt.*" This case is the only one in which the absolute should not be predicated upon the qualified, as there is no contradiction between those statements except if one believes that the qualifier denotes *mafhūm* – and we proved that the qualifier has no such denotation.

CHAPTER 7

AMBIGUOUS (*AL-MUDJMAL*) AND CLEAR (*AL-MUBAYYAN*)

By "ambiguous" is meant what whose denotation is not clear. In other words, ambiguous is the word or act by which it is not clear what the speaker or doer has meant. Thus, ambiguous is the word or act which has no appearance, contrary to the "clear" which has an appearance denoting what is meant by the speaker or doer in the way of conjecture or certitude. Hence, clear covers both the apparent (*ẓāhir*) and the explicit-definite (*naṣṣ*).

As for the ambiguous *act*, its mode of occurrence is not understood; for instance, when the holy Imām performs ablution in circumstances of possibility of dissimulation in which it is not understood whether he had dissimulated (so that it would not denote lawfulness of such performing) or he had performed it in the manner of actual ablution (so that it would denote its lawfulness), or when the holy Imām performs an act in his prayers and it is not understood whether it is done as a mandatory or a recommended act and hence it becomes ambiguous in this respect – though it is clear with respect to its denotation that such an act is lawful and not forbidden.

As for the ambiguous *word*, there are so many things that cause ambiguity in words. For example, where the word is homonymous but used without evidence, where the word is used in a figurative manner but without evidence, where it is not clear to what the pronoun refers, where the sentence suffers from incorrect arrangement, where the speaker is in the position of ambiguity and negligence, and so forth.

Ambiguity and clarity are not absolute, since something may be ambiguous for someone but clear for someone else, and a clear affair may be so by itself and may become so by another affair which clarifies it.

Numerous examples of ambiguous and clear can be found in the Qur'ān and *Sunna*. On the other hand, there are some examples doubted whether they are ambiguous or clear some of which being discussed by *Uṣūlīs* for the sake of training beginners. However, since they are mostly based on Arabic grammatical rules, we do not deal with them in this book.

Part II

Intellectual Implications

Among the four-fold sources of juristic precepts in Shiite *uṣūl al-fiqh* is intellect – the other three being the Book, *Sunna*, and consensus. The authority of these, including intellect, will be discussed in the third part. However, we need to discuss some minor premises of the authority of the intellect in this part in order to find out whether or not the intellect can discover from something being essentially good or evil that it is so with the divine lawgiver as well.

Generally speaking, intellectual proof is divided into independent and dependent. Independent intellectual proofs (*al-mustaqillāt al-'aqliyya*) are those whose both minor and major premises are intellectual, such as "justice is intellectually good," and "whatsoever is intellectually good is juristically good," which results that "justice is juristically good." This kind is usually discussed in the science of theology (*kalām*) and not *uṣūl al-fiqh*, as it is the major dispute between *Ashā'ira* and *'Adliyya* (including both *Mu'tazila* and *Shī'a*).

Dependent intellectual proofs (*ghayr al-mustaqillāt al-'aqliyya*) are those whose major premises are intellectual while their minor premises are juristic, such as "this act is juristically mandatory," and "whatsoever is juristically mandatory it is intellectually necessitated that its preliminary should juristically be mandatory," or "whatsoever is juristically mandatory it is intellectually necessitated that its opposite should juristically be forbidden," and so forth. As clearly seen, minor premises of such syllogisms are proved in the science of *fiqh*, so they are juristic, while their major premises are intellectual, i.e., it is the intellect's judgment that there exists an intellectual implication between the precept in the first premise and another juristic precept. The consequence of such minor and major premises becomes a minor premise of a syllogism whose major premise is authority of intellect – something to be discussed in the discussions of authority.

In this part, we will deal with independent intellectual proofs in 5 chapters.

CHAPTER 8

REPLACEMENT (*AL-IDJZĀ'*)

Idjzā' is infinitive, meaning that something has replaced something else in doing its job. Hence, "replacement" necessitates that the act done should not be repeated.

Doubtless when the duty-bound performs what the Lord has commanded him in its desired way, i.e., he performs the desired in accordance with what he is commanded observing all juristic and intellectual conditions, that act is considered obedience to that command no matter the command is voluntary-actual (*ikhtiyārī*), compelling (*idṭirārī*), or apparent (*żāhirī*). This neither is nor can be a matter of dispute.

There is also neither doubt nor dispute over that such an obedience of such characteristic is considered enough and need not be replaced by any other obedience – for it is assumed that the duty-bound has performed his duty in the desired manner, and that is enough. In this case, the command directed to the duty-bound will be removed, for that which was urged by the command has been actualized and its time has terminated. It is impossible for the command to remain after its purpose has been actualized – unless if one holds that the impossible, i.e., actualization of the effect without the cause, is possible.

The only case which can be disputed is where two commands exist: one primary, actual which is not obeyed by the duty-bound either because it has become impossible for him or because of his ignorance of it, and one secondary which is "compelling" in case of impossibility of the first or "apparent" in case of ignorance of the first. Now, should the duty-bound obey that secondary compelling or apparent command and then the compulsion or ignorance should be removed, it would be plausible to dispute whether or not what was performed in obedience to the second command is enough and replaces the first without any need for the first command to be repeated within the time or performed belatedly out of the time. This discussion is, in fact, to inquire whether there exists an intellectual implication between performing the commanded act by a compelling or apparent command and contenting oneself with it without obeying the primary, voluntary, actual command.

Since the type of discussion differs with regard to the compelling and apparent commands, we have to discuss them separately.

1. The Compelling Command

There are numerous commands in the Islamic law which are peculiar to the state of compulsion, i.e., impossibility or difficulty of obeying primary commands, such as dry ablution, minor or major ablution on the bandage, prayers of the one who is not able to stand, that of a drawing person, and so on. Doubtless compulsion removes the actuality of the duty, for the Almighty charges no soul save to its capacity (2:286), and the holy prophet has said in a very well-known authoritative *ḥadīth*, "Nine things are removed from my followers: …..what they are compelled to do… ." Such compelling, secondary commands are actual endowed with obligatory good – like primary commands.

However, one may ask if such compelling, secondary state was removed and the duty-bound returned to his normal situation in which he is able to perform the command in its usual manner, could what he has done in the state of compulsion be considered enough and replace the command in the state of volition, or should he repeat it within the time – if the compulsion is removed before ending the time on the one hand and hastening to perform the command in such case is allowed on the other – or perform it belatedly out of the time? This question is plausible because what has been performed in the state of compulsion is incomplete in comparison with the commanded act in the state of volition, and there would be no rational problem should the duty-bound be commanded to perform it again in order to acquire the complete good. Nevertheless, it is quite well-known that jurists give verdict that such performing in the state of compulsion is absolutely enough, and there is no need for repetition neither within nor out of the time.

Thus, there should be a secret in giving such a verdict. The secret can be one, or all, of the following points:

1. It is clear that precepts for the state of compulsion are legalized for the sake of alleviation and convenience of duty-bounds ("God desires ease for you, and does not desire hardship for you." Qur., 2: 185), and this would be contradicted should God command them to perform the duty again within or out of the time – even though the incomplete cannot replace the complete in acquiring its whole obligatory good.
2. Most of proofs as to compelling duties are absolute – such as: "… and you can find no water,then have recourse to pure soil,"(Qur4:43) – and their

absolute appearances necessitate that one can content oneself with the second duty for the state of compulsion, that the duty is restricted to that one, and that there is no other duty. Hence, had repetition within or out of the time been mandatory it should have explicitly been depicted. Now that the Almighty has not made such a depiction, it becomes clear that the incomplete does replace the complete both within and out of the time – especially when we find that in a *ḥadīth* the holy Imām has said, "Soil will be sufficient for you even for ten years."

3. Repetition out of the time will become obligatory only when *missing* holds true, while it can be said that in this case it does not hold true; for repetition out of the time can be assumed only when the compulsion continues in the whole time, and in that case there would be no command to the complete in the time. When there is no command, no missing of the mandatory act will hold true, for there is no mandatory act at all.

As for the repetition within the time, it can be assumed only when hastening is allowed, and in such case the duty-bound has hastened to perform the incomplete in early parts of the time while the compulsion is removed before the end of the time. The very permission for hastening, should it be proved, alludes to forbearance of the divine lawgiver with regard to acquiring the complete when one can acquire it, otherwise he would have made it obligatory for the duty-bound to wait and not to hasten in order to acquire the complete.

4. When we doubt whether repetition within or out of the time is mandatory while it is assumed that we have not negated their obligation by absoluteness or the like, we doubt the very existence of the duty; and the principle in such cases is that of clearance from obligation which declares non-obligation.

2. The Apparent Command

As mentioned in the preliminary discussions, the apparent precept has two meanings; one is used for practical principles, and the other for those precepts which are proved apparently when the actual precept with God is unknown. The second expression is more inclusive and covers precepts proved by authorized conjectural proofs (*al-amārāt*, sing. *al-amāra*) and practical principles both. In this discussion, by apparent command is meant the second expression.

Doubtless the actual command is not incontrovertibly directed to the duty-bound in cases of practical principles and authorized conjectural proofs both, i.e., there would be no punishment should practical principles or authorized conjectural proofs oppose the actual precept; for it is clearly evident that any duty which has not reached the duty-bound, after he has quested for and has become desperate to find it, is not incontrovertible. It is self-evident that the duty becomes incontrovertible (*munadjdjaz*) only when it reaches the duty-bound, even though in the form of knowledge in summary fashion (*al-'ilm al-idjmālī*). All those are definitely accepted, and they will be discussed in detail in the third part.

The only point to be discussed here is that if error of practical principle or authorized conjectural proof is revealed later while the duty-bound has opposed the actual precept by following the errant authorized conjectural proof or practical principle, is it obligatory for the duty-bound to obey the actual precept by repeating it within or out of the time or is it not so and he can content himself with what he has done in accordance with the practical principle or the authorized conjectural proof? It is well-known among Shī'a scholars that there is no replacement, neither in precepts nor in objects. In order to deal with the problem, however, we have to consider some different states, for acting in opposition to the actuality is sometimes because of authorized conjectural proof and sometimes because of practical principle on the one hand and the error is either revealed with certainty or by an authoritative proof on the other.

2.1. The Replacement with respect to the Authorized Conjectural Proof When the Error Is Revealed with Certainty

The authorized conjectural proof concerns either precepts, such as an authorized conjectural proof denoting obligation of *djumu'a* prayers on Friday instead of *żuhr* in The Occultation Time (the time when the twelfth Imām is in occultation), or objects, such as evidence denoting juristic purity of a cloth in which one has performed his prayers while it is revealed later that it has not been so.

2.1.1. In the Precepts.

There is no replacement in precepts because of consensus of Shiites on *takhṭi'a,* i.e., the belief that the jurist *may* or *may not* attain the actuality (opp. *taṣwīb*, i.e., to hold that the jurist *always* attains the actuality). For Shiites, there are constant precepts with God in respect of which both scholar and ignorant are common. In other words, such precepts are directed to the ignorant people as they are directed to scholars. However, they are not incontrovertible with respect to the incapable ignorant (*al-djāhil al-qāṣir*) while he is ignorant, i.e., he would be excused should he oppose the actual precept because of following the authorized conjectural proof. For according to Shīʿa, the authorized conjectural proof is a sheer way to acquire the actuality playing no other role. Thus, in case of error revelation there will remain no excuse, but rather the actuality will become incontrovertible without the duty-bound having done anything which can replace it.

There is only one way to the belief in the replacement: if one holds that the authorized conjectural proof of obligation of something creates an obligatory good in that thing in such a way that such good attains the good of the actuality and compensates for the good of the actual mandatory act. According to this, the authorized conjectural proof is considered as something principal by itself and not a way to acquire the precept. This means *taṣwīb* as attributed to *Muʿtazila*, i.e., to hold that although there are actual precepts with God, His precepts are subject to opinions of jurists and any opinion declared by a jurist He has already made a precept in accordance with it. This idea is nullified by Shiite scholars, though its detailed discussion is beyond the level of an introductory work.

2.1.2. In the Objects.

For Shiites, the authorized conjectural proof is taken as sheer way with regard to objects too. Hence, should the authorized conjectural proof not attain the actuality, the actuality would still be there without occurring any good to compensate for the good of actuality. The only point here is that the duty-bound will be excused in case of error – as was the case with the authorized conjectural proof. The reason why the authorized conjectural proof is taken as sheer way with regard to objects is not the problem of *taṣwīb*, since no *taṣwīb* occurs here, but rather is that the very proof which authorizes the authorized conjectural proof in precepts authorizes it in objects, without any difference in depiction.

2.2. The Replacement with respect to the Practical Principles When the Error Is Revealed with Certainty

Doubtless to act in accordance with the practical principle is allowed only where no persuasive proof of the precept is found by the duty-bound, and he has to refer to it as a duty considered for an ignorant person in order to escape from perplexity. Thus, as will be explained in the fourth chapter, the practical principle is in fact a duty in the position of action for an ignorant, doubtful person in order to remove his perplexity.

Generally speaking, practical principles are of two kinds: intellectual, and juristic. Intellectual principles are those which are judged by the intellect without inclusion of any apparent juristic precept, such as the principle of precaution (*iḥtiyāṭ*), that of option (*takhyīr*), and that of intellectual clearance (*al-barā'a al-'aqliyya*). Juristic principles are those which are made by the divine lawgiver for the state of doubt and perplexity, such as the principle of continuity of the previous state (*istiṣḥāb*) and that of juristic clearance (*al-barā'a al-shar'iyya*).

As for the principle of precaution, whether intellectual or juristic, discussion of replacement is nonsense, for it is assumed in this principle that the duty-bound has acted in a way that the actual precept, whatever it may be, is acquired.

The case is the same with other intellectual principles, for it is assumed that they do not include any apparent precept so that one may inquire whether or not they replace the actual precept. Theme of such principles is merely removal of the punishment and excusing duty-bounds.

The dispute, therefore, can be assumed only over juristic principles other than precaution, such as the principle of clearance (*barā'a*), that of continuity of the previous state (*istiṣḥāb*), that of lawfulness (*ḥilliyya*), and that of purity (*ṭahāra*). When no replacement can be assumed with regard to authorized conjectural proofs, it becomes clear that no replacement will be plausible with regard to those principles; since they are merely temporal, practical duties for the ignorant, doubtful duty-bound in order to remove his perplexity – they bear no relation to the actuality. Thus, the actual precept is still there; and when that precept becomes known through the error revelation, it becomes incontrovertible. To follow the practical principle has no good but that of removal of the perplexity; hence, it has no good to compensate for the good of the actuality so that it can replace it.

2.3. The Replacement with respect to Both Authorized Conjectural Proof and Practical Principle When the Error Is Revealed by an Authoritative Proof

This is the major problem in this discussion, since many times jurists change their opinions according to which the previous acts become apparently nullified, and laymen encounter the same problem because of following them. Also, laymen sometimes change their minds and refer to another jurist whose opinions sometimes oppose those of the first jurist, and the problem again occurs.

Before discussing the problem, we should bear in mind that there are three kinds of acts in this connection: coming acts with no relation to the past, passed acts with no effect in the future, and coming acts related to the past. Doubtless both jurist and layman should follow the newly established authoritative proof in the first case. As for the second case, there is no doubt that acts done in the past are over without any need to be repeated. The problem is concerning the third case; for instance, the error is revealed within the time of a mandatory act or out of the time but repetition of the act is obligatory, such as the prayers, or one has married without pronouncing the respective formula in Arabic and now the newly established authoritative proof necessitates that while his wife is still with him.

Now, let us deal with the problem:

In the objects, it is quite well-known that there is no replacement and what has been done previously should be repeated in accordance with the new proof.

As for the precepts, it is claimed that there is a consensus on the replacement, especially with regard to juristic duties such as the prayers. This alleged consensus, however, is not in accordance with the principle in such cases, since what is principally necessitated is non-replacement.

The only argument supporting the replacement is that although it is true that the duty-bound should follow the newly established authoritative proof in the future, his previous acts have been done in accordance with some authoritative proof in that time and hence they should not be repeated.

That argument is not sound, however, for the change occurred is either a change in the actual precept or in what has been an authoritative proof of the duty-bound and nothing else. Annulment of the first state is absolutely clear, since it clearly necessitates *taṣwīb*. As for the second, if by that is meant that the first authoritative proof has been authoritative with regard to previous acts in their own time it has nothing to do with the coming acts as well as effects of previous ones; and if it is meant that the first authoritative proof is absolutely authoritative even with regard to the coming acts as well as effects of previous ones it is absolutely null and void, for in the change of opinion of a jurist it is revealed that the previous proof has not absolutely been authoritative even with regard to the coming acts, or that the jurist thought it was authoritative proof while it was not so, and not that the first proof has absolutely been authoritative and the second one is another authoritative proof. The case is the same with the layman's following another jurist, for what is necessitated by following the second jurist is revelation of annulment of acts done in accordance with opinions of the first. Since on the one hand the previous authoritative proof, i.e., the first following, is not authoritative with regard to the coming effects, though it has been authoritative in its time, and on the other hand it is assumed that the actual precept is not changed, it becomes mandatory for the layman to act in accordance with the actual authoritative proof and what it necessitates.

Thus, should there really be a consensus on the replacement it would definitely be followed; otherwise, there is principally no room for the replacement in the precepts.

Change in the Certitude

Should the duty-bound become certain of something and act in accordance with it and should the error of his certitude become certainly revealed later, doubtless there would be no replacement. For, he has done nothing, in no way, to attain the good of actuality in his first certitude; so, how can the actual precept be removed? In fact, there has been no command directed to the duty-bound; he has just been thinking so. Thus, he should obey the actuality within or out of the time.

CHAPTER 9

THE PRELIMINARY OF THE MANDATORY ACT (*MUQADDIMA AL-WĀDJIB*)

It is absolutely clear for every wise man that if something is mandatory while its actualization is dependent upon some preliminaries it is necessary for him to acquire those preliminaries in order to actualize that act through them. This is for certain. The only thing which is a matter of doubt and dispute among *Uṣūlīs* is that whether or not this intellectual necessity reveals a juristic necessity as well, i.e., whether juristic obligation of something necessitates intellectually the juristic obligation of its preliminaries. In other words, the intellect doubtlessly judges that preliminaries of a mandatory act are mandatory. Now, does it judge that they are mandatory with the divine lawgiver as well? Thus, the intellectual implication between intellectual judgment and juristic obligation is the matter of dispute here.

The outcome of this discussion is deduction of juristic obligation of preliminaries in addition to their intellectual obligation, and this is enough as an outcome of a problem in *uṣūl al-fiqh*. However, this is not a practical outcome, for when preliminaries are intellectually mandatory the duty-bound has no way to leave them undone, and in such case to believe in their obligation or non-obligation is of no use. Nevertheless, there are a lot of scholarly outcomes for this discussion on the one hand and it is related to a good number of practical, juristic problems on the other – something that *Uṣūlīs* cannot ignore. That is why this discussion mostly deals with such problems as varieties of conditions and preliminaries, their possibility or otherwise, and the like; and discussing the very implication seems somehow a marginal issue. However, since such subtle, complicated discussions are higher than the level of an introductory work, we ignore them.

As for the opinions with regard to juristic obligation of the preliminary of the mandatory act, various differentiations are made by *Uṣūlīs*. The justifiable opinion, however, is that it is absolutely not mandatory. For, as proved in discussions of independent intellectual proofs, in cases where judgment of intellect for necessity of something exists in such a way that it calls the duty-bound to do that thing there will remain no room for the Lord's command as He is the Lord. The discussion in question is among such things with respect to the cause, for if the command to that which has preliminary calls the duty-bound to do the commanded act, that call will necessarily, due to the judgment of intellect, make him actualize whatever the commanded act is dependent upon in order to acquire that act. And with the assumption of existence of that motive in the duty-bound's soul there will remain no need for another motive from the Lord while He, as was assumed, knows that such motive exists; for the Lord as He is the Lord commands only for the sake of motivating the duty-bound to do the commanded act and establishing motive in his soul where there is no motivation. Furthermore, to establish a second motive from the Lord in such case is impossible, for it is acquiring what is already acquired – something impossible.

In other words, if the command to that which has preliminary is not enough to call the duty-bound to do the preliminary, no command to the preliminary will be enough to call to the preliminary as it is preliminary; and if the command to that which has preliminary is enough to call and motive to the preliminary, no need will remain for the command from the Lord – rather it is in vain, or impossible, since it is acquiring what is already acquired. That is why commands to some preliminaries should be predicated upon being guides to consideration of such preliminaries as conditions for the mandatory act – as is the case with all commands where there exists an intellectual judgment.

CHAPTER 10

THE PROBLEM OF THE OPPOSITE (*MAS'ALA AL-ḌIDD*)

Uṣūlīs have disputed whether or not to command something necessitates prohibiting its opposite. By the opposite in this discussion is meant that which is incompatible, in its broadest sense, with something else; hence, it covers both the "opposite" and the "contradictory" in their philosophical senses – the former being an existential while the latter being a non-existential affair. That is why *Uṣūlīs* have divided the opposite into "the general opposite", i.e., eschewal which is non-existential, and "the particular opposite", i.e., the existential, incompatible affair – and we will deal with those two separately since opinions differ with regard to either of them.

The dispute is, then, whether or not something commanded by the Lord would necessitate, intellectually or literally, that He, as He is the Lord, has prohibited its general or particular opposite. If positive, there is another dispute over how this can be proved.

1. The General Opposite (*al-Ḍidd al-'Āmm*)

The dispute over the general opposite is not over the necessity in principle, for *Uṣūlīs* apparently agree about the necessity; they disagree only on its nature. They have declared various opinions in this connection. Some have said that the necessity is the sameness, i.e., to command something is the same with prohibiting its opposite. Some have said that since the command is composed of wish of something and prohibition of its eschewal, the prohibition of eschewal is analytical part of meaning of obligation. Some have said that there exists an obvious necessitation in the most particular sense; hence, the denotation is literal, but implicative. Others have said that there exists an obvious necessitation in the most general sense or an unclear necessitation; hence, the denotation is merely intellectual.

The justifiable opinion, however, is that there exists no necessity of any kind, i.e., there is no religious prohibition of eschewal necessitated by the very command in such a way that there exists a juristic prohibition beyond the very command to the act. The reason is that the obligation, whether it is denotation of the imperative or its intellectual implication – the latter being true – is not a composite concept; but rather it is a simple, single one which is necessity of the act. A requisite of obligation of something, of course, is prohibition of its eschewal. However, that prohibition is not a juristic prohibition made by the Lord as He is the Lord, but rather is an intellectual secondary prohibition without there being a prohibition from the divine lawgiver beyond the very obligation. The reason is obvious: the very command to do something in an obligatory mode is sufficient to prohibit its eschewal; so, there is no need for the divine lawgiver to prohibit eschewal of something in addition to commanding it.

2. The Particular Opposite (*al-Ḍidd al-Khāṣṣ*)

To hold that to command something necessitates prohibiting its particular opposite is dependent upon and secondary to the belief in its necessitation the prohibition of its general opposite; and since, as proved, there is no juristic prohibition of the general opposite, there is no juristic prohibition of the particular opposite either. Thus, to command something necessitates prohibiting neither its general nor its particular opposite.

The question, however, is that how to hold that to command something necessitates prohibiting its particular opposite is dependent upon and secondary to the belief in its necessitating the prohibition of its general opposite. The answer is that those who believe in the prohibition of the particular opposite have only two ways in this connection both of which being dependent upon and secondary to that:

2.1. The Way of Implication

According to this way, unlawfulness of one of two implicative affairs needs and necessitates unlawfulness of the other. Since it is assumed that doing the particular opposite, such as eating, implicates eschewal of the commanded act (which is the general opposite), such as the prayers, on the one hand and the general opposite, i.e., eschewal of the prayers, is unlawful on the other, the particular opposite, i.e., eating, should also be unlawful. It is clearly seen that prohibition of the particular opposite is dependent upon prohibition of the general opposite according to this way.

However, since we held that there is no juristic prohibition of the general opposite, there is nothing to make us hold that the particular opposite is juristically prohibited because of such alleged implication; for, according to what we proved, the other implicative affair is not prohibited.

Furthermore, this way is incorrect *per se* : its major premise, i.e.,unlawfulness of one of two implicative affairs necessitating unlawfulness of the other, is not acceptable. For it is not necessary that two implicative affairs should have the same precept, whether obligation, unlawfulness, or any other one, while the criterion of the precept of one of them does not exist in the other. Of course, they should not disagree in the obligation and unlawfulness in such a way that one of them is mandatory and the other is prohibited, since it becomes impossible for the duty-bound to obey both of them in such case and it thereby becomes impossible for the Lord to command both of them. In such case, either one of them is prohibited, or the other is mandatory.

2.2. The Way of Being Preliminary

According to this way, eschewal of the particular opposite is a preliminary (*muqaddima*) of doing the commanded act. The syllogism is like this, for example: eschewal of eating is a preliminary of performing the prayers, preliminary of the mandatory act is mandatory, therefore eschew of the particular opposite is mandatory. If eschewal of eating is mandatory, its eschewal, i.e., eschewal of eschewal of eating, is prohibited; for to command something necessitates prohibiting its general opposite. And if eschewal of eschewal of eating is prohibited, its doing is prohibited; for negation of negation is affirmation. Thus, the particular opposite is prohibited. It is clearly seen that prohibition of the particular opposite is dependent upon prohibition of the general opposite according to this way.

However, since we held that there is no juristic prohibition of the general opposite, eschewal of eschewal of the particular opposite will not be juristically prohibited, i.e., doing the particular opposite will not be prohibited.

Furthermore, this way is incorrect from two other aspects:

1. This way, as it is clearly seen, is dependent upon obligation of the preliminary of the mandatory act, while we proved that it is not juristically mandatory; therefore, eschewal of the particular opposite is not juristically mandatory so that its doing should be prohibited.
2. We do not accept that eschewal of the particular opposite is a preliminary of doing the commanded act. This that eschewal of the particular opposite is a preliminary of doing the commanded act has always been a matter of

lengthy, complicated discussion among later *Uṣūlīs*. Nevertheless, since its annulment is clear according to what we said, there is no need for us to deal with it. In order to eradicate that fallacy, however, we have to explain it briefly here:
The claim of one who holds that eschewal of the opposite is a preliminary of its opposite is dependent upon this that lack of opposite is an example of lack of impediment with regard to the other opposite – because of reciprocal prevention of two opposite affairs, i.e., impossibility of their conjunction – and doubtless lack of impediment is among preliminaries; for it is among supplements to the cause, since it is well-known that the complete cause consists of the origin (*al-muqtaḍī*) and lack of impediment (*al-māniʿ*). Thus, the minor premise here is "lack of the opposite is an example of lack of impediment to its opposite" (because of reciprocal prevention of two opposite affairs), and the major premise is "lack of impediment is among preliminaries," which concludes that "lack of opposite is among preliminaries of the other opposite."

The fallacy is caused by consideration of the term "impediment" in an absolute manner treating it as having the same meaning in both premises, while the truth is that it has two different meanings in each premise and the middle term is not repeated in order to form a correct syllogism. By reciprocal prevention is sometimes meant reciprocal prevention in the existence, i.e., impossibility of conjunction and incompatibility of two things; and this is the meaning intended in the minor premise, since two opposite things can have no conjunction in the existence and are incompatible with one another. Reciprocal prevention, however, is sometimes used in the sense of prevention in the influence even though there may exist no contradiction in the existence. This meaning exists in two origins of two effects which are incompatible with one another, for the object is capable of allowing only influence of one origin; hence, the two origins encounter reciprocal prevention, since each of them can influence only on the condition of lack of the other. This is the meaning intended in the major premise, for the impediment whose lack is a condition for the influence of the origin is the other origin which opposes the influence of the first. That lack of impediment is either because the origin does not exist at all, or because it exists but has not reached the level of overcoming the other in the influence.

Thus, we agree that lack of the opposite is an example of lack of impediment, but this is lack of impediment in the existence while that which is among preliminaries is lack of impediment in the influence. Hence, the middle term is not repeated, and that syllogism does not conclude that lack of the opposite is among preliminaries.

The Outcome of This Discussion

Outcomes of this discussion mentioned by *Uṣūlīs* are peculiar to the particular opposite the most important of which being veraciousness of that opposite which is an act of worship according to the opinion that to command something does not necessitate prohibiting its opposite and its annulment according to the contrary opinion.

Should there be a mandatory act (no matter it is an act of worship or not) whose opposite is an act of worship (which is, in turn, commanded) and the mandatory act is preferable to that opposite, the actual, incontrovertible command would be the former and not the latter; for objects of commands are opposite, this causing interference of commands, while the first is preferable in the divine lawgiver's view. Now, if we hold that to command something necessitates prohibiting its particular opposite, the opposite which is an act of worship will be prohibited, and prohibiting an act of worship necessitates its annulment; and if we believe that to command something does not necessitate prohibiting its particular opposite, the opposite which is an act of worship will not be prohibited and hence will not be annulled.

Preference of the mandatory act to its opposite which is an act of worship occurs in four cases:

1. Where the opposite which is an act of worship is recommended (and it is doubtlessly clear that the mandatory takes precedence over the recommended), such as conjunction of a mandatory and a recommended prayers. According to the opinion that to command something necessitates prohibiting its opposite, one cannot perform the recommended prayers if the time for the mandatory prayers has just begun, and should one do so one's recommended prayers would be annulled. According to this opinion, therefore, one who has not performed some of one's daily prayers is absolutely not allowed to perform recommended prayers and must first perform belatedly one's missed mandatory prayers. According to the contrary opinion, however, unlawfulness of performing recommended prayers in such case is in need of specific proof.
2. Where the opposite which is an act of worship is mandatory but it is less important than the first, such as conjunction of saving a life and performing the mandatory prayers.

3. Where the opposite which is an act of worship is mandatory but it is extended while the first is restricted (and it is doubtlessly clear that the restricted takes precedence over the extended even though the extended may be more important), such as conjunction of purifying the mosque and performing mandatory prayers when its time is extended.
4. Where the opposite which is an act of worship is mandatory but it is optional while the first is determinate (and it is doubtlessly clear that the determinate takes precedence over the optional even though the optional may be more important, since the optional has a substitute), such as conjunction of a travel which has become mandatory through a vow and fasting as a penance; for should the duty-bound not travel and fast instead, his fast would be prohibited and annulled according to the opinion that to command something necessitates prohibiting its opposite.

It should be added that such occurrences are not sufficient for the outcomes to appear, and we are in need of two more points in this connection:

a) To hold that prohibition of a mandatory act of worship necessitates its annulment; for it is clear that should it not be so, the opposite which is an act of worship would be veracious whether one holds that to command something necessitates prohibiting its opposite or not.
The truth is that prohibition of a mandatory act of worship necessitates its annulment, and this will be discussed in detail in chapter 12.
b) To hold that veraciousness of an act of worship and its capability to take the duty-bound closer to God is not dependent upon its being actually commanded, but rather its essential desirability for the Lord is sufficient for that purpose – even though there may not be an actual command, because of some impediment. It is clear that should we hold the contrary opinion, that outcome would never occur; for in that case the opposite which is an act of worship is not actually commanded, because of interference of two commands, and where there is no command the act of worship will not be veracious even though we hold that to command something does not necessitate prohibiting its opposite.

The justifiable opinion is the first, for it is sufficient for capability of an act to take the duty-bound closer to God to be related to the Lord and to be done by the duty-bound with the intention of getting closer to Him, while there exists no impediment to that such as its being prohibited or to do it being law-making.

CHAPTER 11

CONJUNCTION OF THE COMMAND AND THE PROHIBITION (*IDJTIMĀʿ AL-AMR WA'L NAHY*)

Uṣūlīs have disputed from a long time ago whether or not conjunction of command and prohibition in one act is possible. Since terms "conjunction" and "one" may seem confusing, we have to explain what is meant by them in this discussion.

Conjunction. By conjunction (*al-idjtimāʿ*) is meant accidental encounter between the commanded act and the prohibited act in one thing. This may occur only where the command is directed to a designation and the prohibition to another designation which has no relation to the first, but those designations encounter rarely in one thing – here, conjunction of the command and the prohibition occurs, i.e., they encounter one another.

Such conjunction of and encounter between two designations is of two kinds:

1. It is a case conjunction (*al-idjtimāʿ al-mawridī*), i.e., there is no one act which corresponds to both designations, but rather there are two acts which have become synchronous and simultaneous one of which corresponding to the designation of the mandatory act and the other to the designation of the prohibited act. For instance, when someone is performing the prayers and in the meantime looking at a woman whom looking at is religiously prohibited, looking does not correspond to designation of the prayers, the prayers do not correspond to designation of looking, and both of them do not conform to one act.

   Such case conjunction is neither impossible nor a matter of dispute in this discussion. Hence, should one look at a woman whom looking at is religiously prohibited while performing one's prayers, one would be both obedient and disobedient simultaneously without one's prayers being annulled.

2. It is a real conjunction (*al-idjtimāʿ al-ĥaqīqī*), even though at a glance and in a conventional view, i.e., there is one act which corresponds to both designations, such as the well-known example of performing the prayers in an expropriated space. In that example, which is the matter of dispute in this discussion, designation of the prayers, which is the commanded act, has no relation to that of expropriation, which is the prohibited act, but it accidentally happens that the duty-bound gathers them by performing the prayers in an expropriated space. Here, designation of the commanded, i.e., the prayers, encounters designation of the prohibited, i.e., expropriation, in that prayers performed in an expropriated space; hence, that single act corresponds to both designations of the prayers and expropriation. Thus, that single act is included in the commanded act from one aspect which necessitates treating the duty-bound as obedient while it is included in the prohibition from another aspect which necessitates treating him as disobedient.

One. By one is meant a single act, as it has one existence, which is a gathering of two designations – contrary to the multiple with respect to existence, such as case conjunction. Gathering of two designations in one act as it has one existence occurs either because of its personal nature or because of its universal nature; the latter such as the very "universal" being a gathering of two designations, like the universal "being" which corresponds to the prayers and expropriation. Thus, by one in this discussion is meant one in the existence; so, the dispute is not restricted to the personal "one." On the other hand, one in genus is not a matter of dispute. By one in genus is meant the case where the commanded act and the prohibited act are different with respect to the existence but they are included in one nature; such as bowing down to God and to an idol, since both of them are included in the designation of bowing down. As we said, that is not a matter of dispute, for should one bow down to both God and an idol once, one would definitely be considered disobedient.

Now, the matter of dispute in this discussion becomes clear: Is it possible that the command should remain directed to that designation which corresponds to that "one" and also the prohibition should remain directed to that designation which corresponds to that "one" and the duty-bound should be considered both obedient and disobedient in one act, or is it not possible and the gathering of the two designations is either commanded only or prohibited only, i.e., either only the command remains actual and the duty-bound is obedient alone or only the prohibition remains actual and he is disobedient alone?

One who believes in the possibility, who is called *idjtimāʿī*, should hold either of the following:

1. It is the designation (*ʿinwān*) itself that is the object of duty and the precept does not penetrate into the designated (*muʿanwan*). Hence, correspondence between two designations and one act does not necessitate that such one should be an object of two precepts. That it why conjunction of designation of the commanded act and that of the prohibited act in "one" is not impossible, since it does not necessitate conjunction of the very command and prohibition in one.
2. Should the designated be the real object of the precept and not the designation, the designated becomes multiple when the designation is multiple; for, in the precise philosophical view, multiplicity of designation causes multiplicity of designated. Thus, although one act has apparently become correspondent to two designations, there are in fact two designated affairs each of them being correspondent to one of designations. Conjunction of obligation and prohibition, therefore, refers through intellectual precision to the case conjunction, which is of no problem. According to that, there is, in fact, no "one" in terms of the existence which is a gathering of two designations, but rather that which is commanded in its existence is different from that which is prohibited in its existence. In such case, neither penetration of the command into what the prohibition is directed to nor that of prohibition into what the command is directed to will be necessitated; hence, the duty-bound is at once obedient and disobedient in his gathering two designations, like the one who looks at a woman whom looking at is religiously prohibited while one is performing the prayers.

Thus, to hold the possibility of conjunction of the command and the prohibition is not to believe in the conjunction of the command and the prohibition in one act, but rather refers to either the belief in the conjunction of designations of the commanded act and the prohibited act in one act without there being conjunction of the command and the prohibition, or to the case conjunction where there is neither conjunction of the command and the prohibition nor that of the commanded act and the prohibited act.

As for the one who believes in the impossibility, who is called *imtināʿī*, he should hold that the precept penetrates from the designation into the designated, and that multiplicity of the designation does not necessitate that of the designated. In such case, it would be impossible that both the command and the prohibition should remain and should be directed to the one designated in terms of existence, for it would necessitate conjunction of the very command and prohibition in one, which is impossible. Therefore, there either remains a command without a prohibition, or a prohibition without a command.

A very important point to be borne in mind is that the matter of dispute among *Uṣūlīs* over possibility or otherwise of conjunction of the command and the prohibition concerns where the duty-bound has a way out (*mandūḥa*), i.e., he is able to obey the command in another case other than the gathering; or, in other words, he has encountered the conjunction deliberately because of misuse of his free will. It is such case that is a matter of disagreement among *Uṣūlīs*: some believe in its possibility and others in its impossibility. There is no dispute among *Uṣūlīs* over the impossibility of conjunction where obedience to the command can be actualized exclusively through the gathering and the duty-bound has become compelled to encounter the conjunction; for it is clear that in case of exclusion, the actuality of two duties becomes impossible, since obedience of both is impossible: if the duty-bound does the commanded act he has disobeyed the prohibition, and if he eschews it he has disobeyed the command. Therefore, all *Uṣūlīs* agree that conjunction of the command and the prohibition in such case is impossible and either the command or the prohibition is actual. However, there is disagreement among them as to which of them is so.

Considering what we said, we have to discuss the problem in two states:

Conjunction of the Command and the Prohibition with a Way Out

The Argument for Impossibility

1. Doubtless the five-fold burdensome precepts are opposite to one another in the position of actuality and arousal, for there is a self-evident opposition and contradiction between arousing to something in a specific time and dissuading from it in the same time – even though there may be no opposition between them before that position.
2. Doubtless object of precepts is the act of duty-bound: that which is done by him in the external world and that which he is its doer and maker; it is neither its name nor its abstracted designation.
3. Multiplicity of aspect and designation does not cause multiplicity of designated and does not affect unity of designation, for multiple concepts

and designations may correspond to one thing that has no multiplicity, such as the Necessary Being for whom all attributes of perfection hold true without affecting His Oneness.

(d) The existent by one existence has but one quiddity and single reality which is the answer to the question "what is it?" Thus, neither of the two concepts which hold true for that thing is its quiddity and reality; hence, what is one in existence is necessarily one in quiddity and essence. Therefore, although objects of the command and the prohibition hold true for the gathering, as it is one in the existence it is one in the quiddity and essence.

It becomes clear from what we said that since the gathering is one in the existence and essence, directing the command and the prohibition to it is impossible, even though their direction is through two designations, for it was proved that it is the act done by the duty-bound by its reality, and not by its designations, that is the object of precepts.

The Argument for Possibility

1. The object of duty, whether it is command or prohibition, is not the designated, i.e., the external instance of the designation as it has an external existence, for it is impossible; rather, the object of duty is constantly and permanently the designation.

In order to clarify that better, let us take the example of avidity. It is impossible for the designated to become object of avidity; for it either becomes object while it does not exist or when it exists, and neither of them is possible. The former is impossible because it necessitates constitution of existent by non-existent and actualization of non-existent as it is non-existent (since the object of avidity has a kind of actualization by realization of avidity for it) and this is a very clear impossibility; and the latter is impossible because avidity for the designated when it exists is acquiring what is already acquired, and that is also a clear impossibility.

Furthermore, avidity is among psychic affairs and it is not plausible that a psychic affair, such as knowledge, imagination, illusion, wish, and the like, could be individuated without an object. On the other hand, it is not plausible that avidity could be individuated by an objective thing which is out of the horizon of the soul. Thus, it should be individuated by the object of avidity as it has an assumed, designative existence which is the object of avidity primarily and essentially; it should be existent by the existence of avidity and by no other existence beyond avidity. However, since designation is taken into consideration as it is an indicator and a mirror of what exists in the external world, i.e., the designated, the latter is the object of avidity secondarily and accidentally. The case is like knowledge; it is not plausible that knowledge could be individuated by an external thing. The essentially, primarily known is constantly and permanently the designation which is existent by the existence of knowledge, but as it is an indicator and mirror of the designated. As for the designated of that designation, it is accidentally and secondarily known by consideration of annihilation of designation in it. In fact, such thing can become an object of avidity that has an aspect of presence and an aspect of absence; neither a non-existent from all aspects nor an existent from all aspects can become an object of avidity. The aspect of presence in the object of avidity is the designation existent by the existence of avidity in the horizon of the soul as it has an assumed, designative existence; and the aspect of absence in the object of avidity is its real non-existence in the external world the meaning of avidity for it being the desire for bringing it out from the assumption to the actuality.

What we said concerning avidity holds true for wish and arousal too without any difference. Thus, the reality of wishing something is to direct the wish to the designation in order to bring it out from the assumption to the actuality.

2. When we say that the object of duty is the designation and not the designated we do not mean that the designation with its subjective existence is the object of wish. This is self-evidently null and void; for the object of purpose, what causes effects, and that which bears good or evils is the designated and not the designation. Rather, we mean that the object is the designation in its subjective existence not as it has a subjective existence or as it is a concept. The object being the designation in its subjective existence means that wish is directed to the designation itself as it is a mirror of the designated and is annihilated to it; hence, its emptiness of subjective existence is its very embellishment with it.

3. When we say that the object of duty is the designation as it is a mirror of the designated and is annihilated into it we do not mean that the real object of the duty is the designated and the duty penetrates from the designation into the designated because of its annihilation to it – as some have said – for this is also self-evidently null and void; for, as we said earlier, it is impossible for the designated to become the object of duty under any circumstances. This is impossible even with the mediation of the designation, for mediation of the designation cannot bring it out from such impossibility. What we

mean is that the sound idea is that the object of duty is the designation as it is a mirror of the designated and is annihilated to it in such a way that its annihilation to the designated is merely a corrective to the direction of duty to it, since the purpose can only be actualized by the designated in which the designation is annihilated; we do not mean that the annihilation makes the duty being directed to and penetrate into the designated. There is a huge difference between that which is a corrective to the direction of duty to something and that which is itself the object of duty. It is lack of differentiation between those two that made some *Uṣūlīs* believe that the duty penetrates into the designated because of annihilation of the designation in it. It is annihilation and instrumentality in the consideration that causes mistake and confusion so that one gives what belongs to the designation to the designated and vice versa.

Now, the meaning of possibility of conjunction becomes clear: should the duty bound gather in one act an obligation directed to a designation and a prohibition directed to another designation accidentally through misuse of his free will, that one act, which is the designated of both designations, would not be the object of obligation and prohibition except accidentally; and this is not impossible – what is impossible is that one thing becomes essentially the object of obligation and prohibition. Thus, it would be justifiable that one act should become obedience to the command from one aspect since the designation of the commanded act holds true for it and become disobedience to the prohibition from another aspect since the designation of the prohibited act corresponds to it; for that one act is not essentially and by itself the object of the command and the prohibition, rather, annihilated designations are objects of the command and the prohibition.

Finally, it becomes clear from what we said that to believe in the possibility is not dependent upon the belief that multiplicity of designation causes multiplicity of designated; for, according to what was proved, the designated never becomes the object of duty. Add to this that there is no general rule necessitating that multiplicity of designation causes multiplicity of designated – it may or may not cause that.

The Outcome of This Discussion

The outcome of this discussion manifests itself where an act of worship is involved. As was said earlier, according to those who believe in the impossibility, either the command remains actual or the prohibition. However, there is disagreement among them which of those two should be preferred:

1. Should the prohibition be preferred, as it is well-known, the act of worship would be annulled where the duty-bound is aware of prohibition and he has committed the conjunction deliberately; for there is no command where prohibition is preferred, and there is also nothing in the essence of what has been done that can be capable of taking the duty-bound closer to God, as it is impossible for something causing distance to cause proximity. The case is so even though the essence of what has been done contains an essential good and we hold that intending the essential good is enough for acceptance of the act of worship.

But how is the case where the duty-bound has committed the conjunction while he has been ignorant of the prohibition incapably and not negligently, or he has forgotten it, while he has done the act with the intention of getting closer to God? The prevailing opinion is that the act of worship is acceptable, for its essential preference and its containing essential good is enough to take the duty-bound closer to God – if this is intended – even though the command should not be actual. However, some hold that the act of worship is annulled, for proofs of obligation and prohibition become contradictory according to impossibility, though they are not essentially contradictory. Now that the prohibition is preferred, as there remains no command, existence of cause for command, i.e., the essential good, in the gathering becomes also uncertain; for restriction of the command to other than the gathering may be either because of an impediment in the gathering to be included in the command or because of non-existence of the cause for command; hence, existence of the cause for command is not for certain.

2. Should the command be preferred, the act of worship would doubtlessly be acceptable; for there is no prohibition to prevent its acceptability, especially if we hold that the two proofs contradict one another according to the impossibility, since in such case the essential evils in the gathering is not for certain.

Acceptability of the act of worship is clear according to the possibility, for as it is possible to direct the command and the prohibition to two different designations gathered in the gathering – and that is why we believed in the possibility of conjunction in the position of law-making – there is no problem with the conjunction in the position of obedience too, as was explained earlier that the designated itself cannot become the object of duty neither before nor after its existence.

Conjunction of the Command and the Prohibition without a Way Out

As said earlier, conjunction of the command and the prohibition without a way out occurs where the duty-bound has become compelled to encounter the conjunction. Compulsion to encounter the conjunction occurs in two forms:

Not Preceded by Free Will

An example of this is one who intends to save a drowning person but the only way to reach him passes through an expropriated space. Here, to take that way is mandatory because of saving the drowning person and is prohibited because of expropriation. In such case, interference of the mandatory act and the prohibited act in the position of obedience occurs. For it is assumed that the duty-bound has no way out; hence, there would remain no way to obey the command to saving a drowning person but the gathering, since the obedience can exclusively be actualized in that prohibited instance and the duty-bound has no choice but to either disobey the command or disobey the prohibition. Generally speaking, in case of interference, one is principally supposed to take into consideration the more important criterion; if the criterion for the command is stronger, as in the example mentioned, the command is given the priority and actuality of the prohibition is removed, and if the criterion for the prohibition is stronger, as where saving an animal can exclusively be actualized by death of a human being, the prohibition is given the priority and actuality of the command is removed.

Another example is one who is compelled to commit a prohibited act without misuse of his free will and then he is compelled to perform an act of worship in such a way that the said prohibited act becomes an instance of that act of worship. In other words, the duty-bound is compelled to perform the act of worship as it is gathered with that prohibited act to which he is compelled. For instance, one who is imprisoned in an expropriated space and he is compelled to perform his prayers there. The question is that is performing that act of worship mandatory in such case, and is it acceptable if performed so? The answer to both questions is positive; for in case of compulsion to committing the prohibited act no actuality will remain for the prohibition – since power is a condition in all duties. Thus, nothing interferes with the actuality of the command and this makes performing the prayers mandatory, and in such case the prayers must doubtlessly be acceptable.

Preceded by Misuse of Free Will

The example of this is one who has entered an expropriated space through misuse of his free will but one has become repentant wishing to get out of the place while the very getting out from the place is itself expropriation – since there is still no permission from the owner. Two problems are discussed here: (1) whether such exit is prohibited or mandatory, and (2) whether the prayers performed while exiting is acceptable.

> 1. There are different opinions in this connection: that the exit is prohibited, that it is mandatory but the duty-bound will be punished, that it is mandatory and the duty-bound will not be punished, that it is both prohibited and mandatory, and that it is neither prohibited nor mandatory but the duty-bound will be punished. In order to find out the justifiable opinion, we have to discuss the reason for the prohibition and that for the obligation.

The reason for the prohibition is that expropriation, of any kind, whether entry, stay, or exit, has been prohibited from the very beginning before the compulsion. Hence, the duty-bound has been prohibited from every kind of occupation even that exit, for he has been able to eschew it by not entering.

One who holds that it is not prohibited argues that this much occupation is necessary whether the expropriator exits or stays; hence, its eschewal is impossible for him, and when its eschewal is impossible it cannot remain prohibited. This is not correct, however, for it is he who had made himself compelled through misuse of his free will while he has been capable of eschewal by eschewing the entry, and impossibility through free will does not contradict free will. Thus, he is commanded from the very beginning to eschew the occupation until he exits; hence, the exit *per se* as it is occupation was from the very beginning included in the instances of the prohibited designation. In other words, the prohibited designation, i.e., occupying someone else's property without one's permission, encompasses in its generality all occupations whose eschewal is possible – even the exit – and impossibility of such occupation because of misuse of one's free will does not exclude it from generality of the designation.

As for the reason for obligation, some hold that the exit is mandatory for itself since it is designated by the designation of "release from the prohibited act" and release from the prohibited act is both good intellectually and mandatory religiously, while others hold that it is mandatory for something else since it is a preliminary for the release from the prohibited act, i.e., the additional expropriation which will be actualized if he does not exit.

However, the truth is that neither of those opinions is correct; the exit is (1.1) neither mandatory for itself (1.2) nor mandatory for something else.

1.1 It is not mandatory for itself because:

First, it is clear that the release from something, whatever its meaning may be, is a designation contrary to that of involvement in that thing; it is a substitute for that and their contrariety is that of possession and privation. Now, the question is that what they mean by the release which they say it is good. If by that is meant release from the very expropriation *per se*, it is not correct, for by exit he is involved in expropriation and not being released from it, as it is occupation and passing through an expropriated space without permission. And if by that is meant release from the additional expropriation which will be actualized if he does not exit, that does not correspond to the motions in the exit. For, since release is contrary to involvement and is a substitute for it, the time which can be a time for involvement must be the same with the time which holds true for designation of release, while the time of motions in the exit precedes the time of additional expropriation if he does not exit. Thus, in the motions of the exit he is neither involved in nor released from the additional expropriation; rather, the expropriator is involved in expropriation from his entry until his exit and he is only released from expropriation when he is out of the expropriated space.

Secondly, should release be a designation which holds true for the exit, by the exit should not be meant the very motions in the exit, but rather that for which motions in the exit are preliminaries or like preliminaries; and in such case designation of release does not correspond to the prohibited occupation of the expropriated space – that which the holder of this opinion wishes to prove. The reason is clear, for exit is contrary to entry, and since entry is a designation for being in the space preceded by non-existence, exit must be a designation for being out of the space preceded by non-existence due to contrariety. As for the very occupation of the expropriated space by motions in the exit one of which being the exit, it is a preliminary or pseudo preliminary for the exit and not the exit itself.

Thirdly, if we accept that release is a designation which corresponds to the motions in the exit, we will not accept that it is mandatory for itself; for to be released from the prohibited act is nothing but eschewal of the prohibited act, and eschewal of the prohibited act is not mandatory for itself in such a way that it has an essential good contrary to the essential evils of the act. Of course, it is desired secondarily to the prohibition from the act, as was said earlier in discussions of commands and prohibitions in the first and the problem of the opposite in the second part. Therefore, as commanding something does not necessitate prohibiting its general opposite, i.e., its contradictory which is eschewal, prohibiting something does not necessitate commanding its general opposite, i.e., its contradictory which is eschewal. There is but evils of the act in the prohibition and the good of the act in the command.

1.2 It is not mandatory for something else because:

First, even if we accept that the release is mandatory for itself, we have already proved that the preliminary of the mandatory act is not mandatory.

Secondly, exit, which is motions while exiting as meant by one who holds that opinion, is not a preliminary for the very being released from the prohibited act, but rather is a preliminary for being out of the expropriated space. Being out of the expropriated space implicates designation of being released from the prohibited act and is not the very being released from it, and assumption of obligation of release does not implicate obligation of its implicative; for, as explained earlier in the problem of the opposite, two implicative affairs are not necessarily common in the precept. Now that being out of the expropriated space is not mandatory, how can its preliminary be so?

Thirdly, even if we accept that the release is mandatory for itself, that it is the very being out of the expropriated space and motions in the exit are preliminaries for it and that the preliminary of the mandatory act is mandatory, we cannot accept this opinion; for preliminary of the mandatory act is mandatory only when there is no impediment, while such impediment exists here. For example, since to ride an expropriated vehicle in one's way to the pilgrimage to Mecca is prohibited *per se*, it is not qualified as mandatory even though one has performed a mandatory act by it. Here, motions in the exit are prohibited, since they are among instances of a prohibited act, i.e., occupying the expropriated space; hence, they are not qualified as mandatory because of their being preliminaries.

2. The answer to the question whether the prayers performed while exiting is acceptable or not is dependent upon what one chooses in the previous section:

2.1. One who holds that the exit is only mandatory, he should hold that performing the prayers in that case is of no problem, whether the time designated for it is enough or not – conditional upon performing of the prayers not necessitating any occupation additional to the motions in the exit, since that additional occupation is forbidden and prohibited. Should performing the prayers necessitate additional occupation: (2.1.1.) if the time is not enough for performing the prayers after the exit, the duty-bound should perform it in his exit contenting himself with the least mandatory acts of the prayers and gesticulate instead of bowing and bowing down, and (2.1.2.) if the time is enough for performing the prayers after the exit, he should wait and perform it out of the expropriated space.

2.2. One who holds that the exit is prohibited, he should hold that: (2.2.1.) if the time is enough for performing the prayers after the exit, the duty-bound should perform the prayers after the exit whether such performing necessitates additional occupation or not; and (2.2.2.) if the time is not enough for performing the prayers after the exit, there occurs interference and the duty-bound becomes uncertain whether to avoid the prohibited expropriation or to perform the mandatory prayers. Since the prayers should not be abandoned in any case, the duty-bound should perform the prayers while he abandons what necessitates additional occupation; he should gesticulate instead of bowing and bowing down and recite *sūra al-ĥamd* while walking and so on.

2.3. One who holds that the exit is neither mandatory nor prohibited, he should hold that performing the prayers while exiting is of no problem if it does not necessitate any additional occupation, even when the time is enough for performing the prayers after the exit.

CHAPTER 12

DENOTATION OF PROHIBITION AS TO ANNULMENT(*DALĀLA AL-NAHY ALA'L FASĀD*)

By denotation in this discussion is meant intellectual denotation. Hence, the dispute is over whether the nature of prohibition intellectually necessitates annulment of the prohibited or not. In fact, the dispute is over existence of intellectual implication between prohibiting something and its annulment.

The meaning of annulment is clear: the contrary to veraciousness in possession and privation fashion. Thus, what is capable of veraciousness can be qualified by annulment, and what is not so cannot. Of course, veraciousness of everything is due to itself. For instance, veraciousness of an act of worship means its conformity to the commanded act with respect to all parts and conditions, and its annulment means lack of conformity because of a shortage in the act done. The requisite of non-conformity to the commanded act is that the command will still remain and necessity of repetition within or out of the time will not be removed. On the other hand, veraciousness of a transaction is its conformity to all of its considered parts, conditions, and the like and its annulment is lack of such conformity. The requisite of non-conformity in a transaction is non-actualization of the desired effect of that transaction, such as transfer of ownership in the sale.

One important point to be borne in mind is that the object of prohibition should be capable of being qualified by veraciousness and annulment in order to be considered a matter of dispute; otherwise, it is nonsense to dispute whether prohibition of drinking wine necessitates annulment or not.

Since discussion varies a lot with regard to the act of worship and transaction, we deal with each of them separately.

Prohibition of Act of Worship (*al-'Ibāda*)

By act of worship in this discussion is meant its most particular sense, i.e., that whose acceptance is conditional upon the intention of proximity to God, or that which is the sheer burden made by God for proximity to Him. By that is certainly not meant what is actually an object of a command, for where something is assumed to be an object of actual prohibition, the assumption of directing a command to it will not be plausible. This case is not like that of conjunction of the command and the prohibition, since designations are not multiple here and the designation which is the object of command is itself the object of prohibition. Thus, by the prohibited act of worship is meant that whose nature is an object of command, even though it, as it is commanded, does not include the object of prohibition. In other words, by act of worship is meant a burden which would have been made as an act of worship had it been made by the lawgiver, even though no actual command is directed to it for some reason.

Prohibition of an act of worship can be of some kinds: (a) the prohibition is directed to the act of worship itself, such as prohibition of fasting in *'īd al-fiṭr* and *al-aḍḥā*, or performing the prayers by a woman in her menstruation; (b) it is directed to its part, such as prohibition of reciting some *sūras* in the prayers; (c) it is directed to its condition or condition of its part, such as prohibition of performing prayers in an expropriated or impure cloth; and (d) it is directed to its qualifier, such as prohibition of reciting *sūra al-ḥamd* in the prayers loudly when it must be recited quietly or vice versa.

The justifiable opinion is that the prohibition of act of worship necessitates annulment, whether it is of itself, of its part, of its condition, or of its qualifier; because of obvious contradiction between worship by which is meant proximity to God and His pleasure and prohibition of something whose committing causes wrath of God and distance from Him. It is impossible to become proximate by something causing distance and to attain pleasure by something causing wrath. It is also impossible to become proximate by something containing, something conditional upon, or something qualified by what is annoying, hated, and distance causing.

Prohibition of Transaction (*al-Mu'āmala*)

The divine lawgiver sometimes prohibits a transaction in order to depict that the prohibited thing is an impediment or something like that, and sometimes in order to dissuade from it because of displeasure of the object of prohibition and existence of something displeasing in it.

The first case is not a matter of dispute, for should the prohibition be made to depict that something is an impediment to the transaction it would clearly denote annulment of transaction where the impediment exists; as the prohibition denotes that non-existence of impediment is taken into consideration in the transaction, and where the impediment exists it contradicts what has been considered as a condition for veraciousness of the transaction.

As for the second case, the prohibition is either (1) of the essence of the cause, i.e., of creation of contractual tie, or of causing by the contractual tie creation of a transaction, such as prohibition of sale when *djumuʿa* prayers is being performed because of this verse: "O believers, when proclamation is made for prayer on the day of congregation (Friday), hasten to God's remembrance and leave the sale aside...," (62: 9) or (2) of the essence of the caused, i.e., of the very existence of transaction, such as prohibition of selling the Qur'ān .

1. The prevailing opinion in this connection is that the prohibition does not denote annulment of the transaction, for there is no contradiction, neither intellectually nor conventionally, between displeasure of the contract while causing a transaction and its approval by the divine lawgiver where the contract contains all considered conditions.
2. In this connection, there is disagreement among *Uṣūlīs*. Some hold that prohibition necessitates annulment, for veraciousness of every transaction is conditional upon the parties having religiously control over the contract not being under interdiction with regard to the object of transmission, while the very prohibition of the caused by the Lord makes the duty-bound incapable of that and removes his control over the contract. Thus, the condition taken into consideration in veraciousness of the transaction is not observed, and the transaction will necessarily be annulled.

However, one can say that attribution of annulment to the prohibition may only be assumed and disputed where the contract exists with all of its conditions, including those of contracting parties, and there exists nothing but the sheer displeasure understood from the prohibition. Here, it may be disputed whether or not such sheer displeasure contradicts veraciousness of the transaction. But it seems that there is no proof of such claim so that implication between the prohibition and annulment of the transaction may exist. This that the prohibition of the caused by the Lord makes the duty-bound incapable of acting and removes his control over the transaction means that prohibition of transaction denotes lack of a condition in the transaction by committing the prohibited act; and should such claim be correct, the case would doubtlessly be of the first state indicating that something is taken into consideration in the transaction.

Part III

Discussions of Authority

By this part is meant clarification of what is capable of being a proof of and is an authoritative proof of juristic precepts through which we may attain the actual divine precepts. Should we attain the actual precept through that proof, then, that would be the ultimate end; otherwise, we would be excused and would not be punished because of opposing the actuality. The reason why we are excused in case of error is that we have done our best in search for the ways capable of taking us to the Almighty's actual precepts in such a way that we become certain that a certain proof, such as single transmission, is approved by the divine lawgiver as a way to His precepts and is made an authoritative proof by Him in this connection. Thus, the error in which we are involved is because of the proof He has designated and not because of us. However, the reason why we are excused and how it is possible that something declared as an authoritative proof may be a failure while it is the divine lawgiver who has designated it, will be discussed in detail later.

Doubtless this part is the chief discussion and the ultimate end of discussions of *uṣūl al-fiqh*, for it is this part that provides the major premise of problems of both previous parts. For instance, the first part dealt with recognizing minor premises of literal appearances, such as "the imperative is apparent in the obligation," and this part discusses authority of literal appearances in an absolute manner and proves that "every appearance is an authoritative proof," which results that "the imperative is an authoritative proof in the obligation." Hence, wherever an imperative is found in a Qur'ānic verse or a *ḥadīth*, obligation of its object is inferred. Also, in the second part minor premises of intellectual judgments were discussed, and in this part authority of intellectual judgment will be proved, and those two make a syllogism.

Before dealing with the main topics, however, we should discuss some introductory issues.

INTRODUCTORY DISCUSSIONS OF THE THIRD PART

The subject matter of this part, in which objects and predicates of the former are discussed, is "whatever capable of being claimed to prove a juristic precept and to be an authoritative proof with regard to that precept." Therefore, if we can prove in this part by a certain, definite proof that a way is an authoritative proof (and we will prove later that such proof should be certain, definite and a conjectural proof will absolutely not be sufficient), we can take it and refer to it in order to prove juristic precepts; otherwise, we should reject and leave it. In short, the subject matter of this part is the essence of the proof *per se* and not the proof as it is proof – as some have claimed. As for its predicates and objects, they are authority of that certain thing which is either proved or negated.

According to what we said, discussions of this part include whatsoever which is said to be an authoritative proof. Thus, in addition to principal discussions of the Book, *Sunna*, consensus, and intellect, it includes discussing authority of report of single transmitter, appearances, celebrity, narrated consensus, analogy (*qiyās*), and the like. It also includes discussion of equilibrium and preferences (*al-ta'ādul wa'l tarādjīĥ*) in which determination of what is authoritative between two contradictory proofs is dealt with.

The Meaning of *al-Ĥudjdja*

Ĥudjdja literarily means whatsoever capable of being used as an argument against someone else through which one can overcome one's opponent in a dispute. Overcoming someone else is either by making him silent and nullifying his argument, or by making him accept one's argument – in this sense *ĥudjdja* being an excuser. In *uşūl al-fiqh*, however, *ĥudjdja* means that which proves its object but does not attain the level of certitude (*al-qaţ'*), i.e., it does not cause certitude with regard to its object – since in case of certitude it is the certitude which is *ĥudjdja*, though in its literal meaning. In other words, *ĥudjdja* is whatsoever revealing and indicating something else in such a way that the former proves the latter – its proving being made by the lawgiver, duty-maker as it is the actuality. This proving will be sound only by adding the proof which proves validity and authority of that revealing and indicates the thing in the divine lawgiver's view. Therefore, *ḥudjdja* in this sense does not include certitude (*al-qaṭʿ*), i.e., certitude is not called *ḥudjdja* in this sense, but in the literal sense; for, as will be explained, certitude is essentially a way and cannot be made an authoritative proof by anyone. *Ḥudjdja* in this sense is synonymous with *amāra*, proof (*al-dalīl*), and way (*al-ṭarīq*).

Amāra and *al-Żann al-Muʿtabar*

Uṣūlīs mostly use the term *amāra* (lit. sign) intending *al-żann al-muʿtabar* (the valid conjecture, i.e., the conjecture which is considered and made an authoritative proof by the divine lawgiver) and this may cause confusion that those two terms have the same meaning, while they do not. That usage is in fact a figurative one and not making another meaning for the word *amāra*. The literal object of denotation of *amāra* is whatever which is considered and made valid by the divine lawgiver because of its causing conjecture, such as the single transmission, and appearances. Here, either the name of cause, i.e., *amāra*, is used for its caused, i.e., conjecture, or that of the caused is used for its cause as it is *amāra* that causes conjecture. *Amāra* is figuratively called valid or particular conjecture because it always or mostly causes conjecture typically for most people – and that is why it is called typical conjecture (*al-żann al-nawʿī*). Since *amāra* is made valid and an authoritative proof by the divine lawgiver because of that, it will be an authoritative proof of all people even though it may not cause an actual conjecture for some of them. Hence, if an actual conjecture is not actualized by *amāra* for someone he should also follow it.

However, it should be noted that we would use all such terms as "the particular conjecture (*al-żann al-khāṣṣ*)," "the valid conjecture," "the authoritative conjecture (*al-żann al-ḥudjdja*)," and the like while we intend their cause, i.e., *amāra*. It should also be borne in mind that we would use the English expression "the authorized conjectural proof" precisely for *amāra* in this book.

Amāra and the Practical Principle

The term *amāra* does not include the practical principle (*al-aṣl al-ʿamalī*), but rather is contrary to it; for the jurist can refer to practical principles where there is no authorized conjectural proof, i.e., where he finds no authoritative proof of the actual juristic precept. As mentioned earlier in the definition of *ḥudjdja*, *amāra* proves its object, but the practical principle does not. Practical principles do not indicate the actuality; they are references to which the duty-bound refers when he is in the state of perplexity and doubt with regard to the actuality – they are at most excusers for the duty-bound.

To call practical principle *ḥudjdja* sometimes does not contradict that, for it is *ḥudjdja* in its literal sense, i.e., it would be an excuser for the duty-bound should he act in accordance with it and miss the actuality; as the Lord would punish the duty-bound should he not act in accordance with it and thereby miss the actuality.

The Criterion for Proving Authority of *Amāra*

Doubtless conjecture as it is conjecture cannot be the criterion for authority of *amāra* and one cannot rely on it for proving the actuality, for the Almighty has said, "Surely conjecture avails naught against truth" (10: 36), has blamed those who follow conjecture as it is conjecture in some verses including (6: 116): "They follow only conjecture, and they merely surmise," and has said, "Say: Has God given you leave or do you forge against God?" (10: 59) As can be seen in the last verse, God has declared what He has given leave as the opposite of forging against Him. Thus, what He has not given leave must be forging against him; and should one attribute a precept to God without His leave, it would definitely be forging against Him, blameful, and unlawful – as the verse declares. To act in accordance with conjecture, of course, and to believe that it is from God and proves His precepts is to attribute the precept to Him without His leave and hence falls into the category of forging against Him – which is unlawful. Thus, the primary principle necessitates that to act in accordance with conjecture as it is conjecture and to take it into consideration in order to prove divine precepts is not allowed – whatever its cause may be – for it avails naught against truth; hence, it is a null surmise and an unlawful forging.

However, should it be proved by a definite, authoritative proof that a particular conjecture caused by a specific cause is made by the divine lawgiver a way to His precepts, is considered an authoritative proof with regard to them, and is accepted as a sign for them, that conjecture would be out of scope of that primary principle; for it is not a surmise and forging against God. In fact, consideration of a valid conjecture which is definitely proved to be an authoritative proof is not consideration of conjecture as it is conjecture – though it is taken into consideration by the divine lawgiver because it is conjecture – but rather is consideration of certitude – that certitude which has made such cause of conjecture valid – and it will be explained later that certitude is essentially an authoritative proof in need of no authority maker. That is why valid conjectures are called *'ilmī,* i.e., attributed to knowledge, for their authority is proved by knowledge and certitude.

Now, we can sum up that the criterion for proving authority of *amāra* is the knowledge and certitude established for its validity and authority. Thus, should knowledge of its authority and certainty of permission of the divine lawgiver for its consideration not be actualized, we would not be allowed to take it into consideration, even though it may cause a prevailing conjecture, for its consideration in such case would be a surmise and forging against God. That is why *Uṣūlīs* have said that it would be sufficient for rejecting *amāra* to have doubt about its authority, or, to be more precise, not to have certitude for its validity; for the very lack of knowledge of that would be enough for knowledge of its non-authority, i.e., for unlawfulness of taking it into consideration and referring to it. In such cases, we are not in need of proof of its non-authority and invalidity; rather, as soon as certitude for authority of something is not actualized certitude for unlawfulness of taking it into consideration and referring to it in the position of action is actualized. Thus, certitude is taken into consideration in the object of authority of *amāra.*

In order to make that point clearer, let us take another way. First, conjecture as it is conjecture is not essentially an authoritative proof. This it self-evidently clear, for had conjecture been an essentially authoritative proof, prohibition of its following and consideration, even though in some cases, would not have been possible – as will be explained later – while following conjecture is doubtlessly prohibited in some Qur'ānic verses mentioned earlier. Secondly, since it is not an essentially authoritative proof, its authority should be accidental, i.e., it is taken from something else. Now, we ask of the nature of that else: if it is certitude, our claim is proved; otherwise, what is it? Nothing can be assumed but the very conjecture, for there is nothing else rather than those two whose authority can be considered. The second conjecture which proves authority of the first, however, is not an essentially authoritative proof, for there is no difference between one conjecture and another in this connection. Therefore, we ask of that second conjecture whose authority is taken from something else; what is that else? If it is certitude, our claim is proved; otherwise, it is a third conjecture. Then we ask of that third conjecture, which needs a fourth conjecture, and this leads to infinitive regression – which is impossible. The regression will not be stopped unless the chain ends in that which is an essentially authoritative proof, and that is nothing but certitude.

In other words, since conjecture is not an essentially authoritative proof, its authority must be accidental; and every accidental must refer to something essential – the essential authoritative proof being nothing but the certitude. Thus, it is proved that the criterion for authority of *amāra* is certitude, for authority of everything refers to it – whose authority is essential.

Essentiality of Authority of Certitude (Knowledge, *'Ilm*)

The meaning of authority of something being essential became clear from what we said. It means that its authority is raised from the very nature of its essence and is not taken from something else. Such thing is also not in need of any making by the divine lawgiver or any command by Him; rather, it is the intellect that commands the duty-bound to follow it. Such thing cannot be but certitude (or knowledge, i.e., that which is one hundred percent for certain) which is essentially a path to the factuality. The certitude must necessarily be followed, that necessity being an intellectual one originated by the fact that certitude is *per se* a path to the factuality and its reality is the very manifestation of the actuality. Thus, the essence of certitude is the very manifestation; it is not something which is endowed with manifestation. Since the certitude is essentially a path, as frequently repeated, it is neither plausible to be made a path by the divine lawgiver nor is it possible to be negated as a path; for both making and negating the essence and its requisites are impossible. Therefore, the certitude is an authoritative proof whatever its cause may be (contrary to *Akhbārīs*, who hold that certitude should not be followed when it is caused by intellectual preliminaries), for whomever it may be actualized (contrary to those who maintain that certitude is not valid if actualized for someone who becomes certain too much and too quickly (*al-qaṭṭā'*)), and whatever its object of denotation may be. In all such cases, the certitude is essentially a path to the actuality, and that is why no affirmative or negative change can be made in it. Yea, the only thing possible is to make the one who is wrongly certain realize that there is something wrong in the preliminaries of one's certitude. In that case, one's certitude will necessarily be changed into either possibility of or certitude in the contrary view – and there is nothing wrong with that.

The Position of Authority of *Amāra*

As said earlier, *amāra* is made an authoritative proof even in the case of possibility of acquiring knowledge, i.e., it is *per se* an authoritative proof whether or not the duty-bound can acquire knowledge of the actuality by referring, for instance, to the innocent-infallible Imām. Should *amāra* be an authoritative proof, one would be allowed to refer to it and act on its basis without referring to the innocent-infallible Imām in order to receive the actual precept. The reason why it is so will be explained in the coming discussions.

The Particular Conjecture and the Absolute Conjecture

By the particular conjecture (*al-żann al-khāṣṣ*) is meant every conjecture whose authority and validity is proved by a definitive, certain proof other than "the major closure proof (*dalīl al-insidād al-kabīr*)." It, therefore, means *amāra* which is an absolutely authoritative proof even when the door of knowledge is open. It is also called the knowledge-rooted (*'ilmī*) *path*, since, as said earlier, its authority is proved via knowledge and certainty.

By the absolute conjecture (*al-żann al-muṭlaq*) is meant every conjecture whose authority and validity is proved by "the major closure proof." It, therefore, means *amāra* which is an authoritative proof only when the door of knowledge and knowledge-rooted (*'ilmī*) is closed, i.e., closure of the door to both the very knowledge of precepts and knowledge-rooted paths leading to them.

In this book we will discuss only particular conjectures, for authority of some *amāras* is proved for us and there remains no room for the closure of door of knowledge and knowledge-rooted. However, we will discuss preliminaries of "the major closure proof" briefly for the sake of comprehensiveness of our discussion.

Preliminaries of the Closure Proof (*Dalīl al-Insidād*)

The proof known as "the Closure Proof" consists of four preliminaries. Should those preliminaries be accurate, intellect would judge that the duty-bound should act on the basis of any conjecture with regard to precepts – unless a conjecture whose non-authority is definitely proved, such as analogy (*qiyās*).

Those four preliminaries can be summarized as follows:

1. The door of knowledge and knowledge-rooted is closed in the most part of juristic precepts in our time when it is later than our holy Imāms'. This is the fundamental base of this proof upon which all other preliminaries are dependent.
2. It is not allowed to leave obedience of actual precepts which are known to us in summary fashion, nor is it permissible to reject them in the position of action. To leave and reject actual precepts can be actualized in two ways: either to treat ourselves as animals and children who have no burden, or to

refer to the principle of "clearance" and that of "non-existence of burden" wherever obligation or unlawfulness of something is unknown. Annulment of those two assumptions is self-evidently clear; therefore, we must take into consideration all actual precepts which are known in summary fashion.

3. To consider such precepts necessitates clarifying one's obligation, which, in turn, is restricted to one of the following four states: (3.1) to follow the one who believes in the openness of the door of knowledge, (3.2) to act on the basis of "precaution" in every problem, (3.3) to refer to the respective practical principle (the principle of clearance, that of precaution, etc.) in every problem as the circumstances necessitate, and (3.4) to refer to the conjecture where there is one, and to the practical principles where there is none.

Since referring to the first three states is not acceptable, we should take the fourth into consideration. The first is not acceptable, for how can one who believes in the closure of the door of knowledge refer to whom he considers wrong and ignorant in his believing in the openness of that door? The second is not plausible, for it necessitates intolerable hardship, or even disorder of the society if all duty-bounds are burdened with – which are both rejected in the Islamic law. And the third is not acceptable, for the existence of knowledge of mandatory and prohibited affairs in all doubtful problems in summary fashion prevents us from referring to the practical principles even though in some of them.

4. Thus, the only acceptable state is the fourth, i.e., referring to the conjecture. Although conjecture has two sides, i.e., the preferable (*al-rādjiḥ*) and the chimerical (*al-mardjūḥ=al-mawhūm*), one is merely allowed to refer to the preferable side; for preferring the chimerical side is intellectually reprehensible. Therefore, one is supposed to take the conjecture into consideration – unless a conjecture whose non-authority is definitely proved, such as analogy (*qiyās*). In case of definite knowledge of non-authority of a conjecture, one should refer to practical principles, precisely as one is supposed to refer to them in doubtful problems with regard to which no conjecture exists. There is no problem with referring to practical principles in such cases, for the knowledge in summary fashion is reduced to the detailed knowledge (*al-'ilm al-tafṣīlī*) of precepts proved by some authority and primary doubt (*al-shakk al-badwī*) with regard to other cases, in which one is supposed to refer to practical principles – as will be explained in the fourth part.

Commonness of Precepts between the Knowledgeable and the Ignorant

In addition to mass transmissions of holy Imāms, there is a consensus among Shiite scholars that the divinely precepts are common between those who are knowledgeable and who are ignorant of them, i.e., the divinely precept constantly follows its subject whether or not the duty-bound knows it; the duty-bound is charged with the duty anyhow. Thus, knowledge of precepts plays no role in their realization. The only role played by knowledge with regard to the burden is incontrovertible-making of burdensome precepts, in the sense that the duty-bound will not be punished because of opposing a precept except when he knows it – whether through a detailed or a summary fashioned knowledge, or an authoritative, valid proof which can replace the knowledge. Knowledge and what replaces it, therefore, is a condition for incontrovertible-making of the burden and not its complete cause – as some believe. That is why where, after the quest and despair, knowledge and what replaces it are not found, the duty-bound will not be punished because of opposing a precept; for punishing him in such case will be punishment without depiction, which is intellectually reprehensible – as will be explained in part 4.

The reason for commonness of precepts, apart from *ḥadīṯh*s and consensus, is clear:

1. Should the precept not be common between the knowledgeable and the ignorant, it would be peculiar to the knowledgeable; for to treat it as being peculiar to the ignorant is clearly unacceptable.
2. If it is peculiar to the knowledgeable, it means that the precept has been made dependent upon knowledge of it.
3. However, making the precept dependent upon knowledge of it is impossible, for it necessitates self-contradiction.
4. Therefore, the precept must be common between the knowledgeable and the ignorant.

The reason why it necessitates self-contradiction is that if the precept, obligation of the prayers for instance, be dependent upon knowledge of it, it necessities, or even it is the very meaning of dependent-making, non-obligation of the prayers *per se*. For it is assumed that obligation is directed to the prayers "whose obligation is known" as "something whose obligation is known," while assumption of knowledge of obligation of the prayers is impossible except when the obligation is directed to the prayers *per se*. Thus, that which was assumed to be directed to the prayers *per se* was not directed to the prayers *per se*, but rather to the known obligation peculiarly; and this is the self-contradiction which is obviously impossible.

In other words, to make the precept dependent upon its knowledge necessitates impossibility, which is impossibility of knowledge of the precept, and what necessitates impossibility is itself impossible; therefore, the very precept is impossible. For it is assumed that there is no precept before actualization of knowledge; then, when the duty-bound wishes to know what should he know? Actualization of knowledge without a subject whose actualization has already been assumed is not plausible. When actualization of knowledge is impossible, actualization of a precept which is made dependent upon knowledge will be impossible too, because of impossibility of precept without subject.

Thus, to make the precept dependent upon knowledge of it is impossible; and there remains no choice but commonness of the precept between the knowledgeable and the ignorant. This means that divinely precepts are directed to duty-bounds in cases of knowledge and ignorance both, i.e., they are directed to the ignorant as well– although the ignorant will be excused, i.e., he will not be punished because of opposing the precept he is ignorant of.

Why Is *Amāra* an Absolutely Authoritative Proof?

As was proved, *amāra* is an authoritative proof even in the case of openness of door of knowledge on the one hand and precepts are common between the knowledgeable and the ignorant on the other. Consideration of those two facts causes the following complicated problem: How is it possible that the divine lawgiver may allow duty-bounds to follow the conjectural *amāra* while it is a subject of possibility of such errors that cause missing the actuality while to allow missing the actuality is intellectually reprehensible? For instance, if *amāra* denotes lawfulness of an act while it is either mandatory or unlawful in the actuality, permission for following *amāra* will be permission for not performing the mandatory or committing the unlawful act while the act still maintains its actual obligation or unlawfulness on the one hand and it is assumed that the duty-bound can attain the knowledge of actuality on the other.

It is this problem that made some *Uṣūlīs* consider *amāra* as being a "cause" and not a "path" – the latter being the principle in this connection, as will be explained later. Should there be no way for consideration of *amāra* as a path, they would be right. For it is assumed that authority of *amāra* is definitely proved; hence, a good, which compensates for the good of the actuality in case of error of *amāra*, must lie in allowing duty-bounds to follow *amāra* so that the divine lawgiver's leave to cause missing the actually may not be considered reprehensible – since such causing is in favor of a higher, or an equivalent, good compared to that of the actuality. Thus, an apparent precept will be made as it is the actuality: it may be identical to the actuality where *amāra* is a success, or disagreeing with it where *amāra* is a failure.

However, since that problem can be solved in accordance with the principle that *amāra* is a path, there remains no room for treating *amāra* as a cause. The reason is that when it is assumed that there is a definite, certain proof which declares *amāra* an authoritative proof in such a way that one is allowed to follow it even when one can acquire the knowledge, that leave from the divine lawgiver, who knows the actuality and truths, must be due to something He knows and we do not know. That thing may be one of the two following points, and nothing else, both of which being intellectually acceptable without encountering any problem:

1. He knows that success of *amāra* in attaining the actuality is equivalent to, or exceeds, the knowledge attainable by duty-bounds, i.e., the divine lawgiver knows that error of the knowledge which is attainable by duty-bounds is equivalent to, or exceeds, that of an authoritative proof-made *amāra*.
2. He knows that not making specific *amāra*s an authoritative proof in acquiring precepts and limiting duty-bounds to the acquisition of knowledge will cause them hardship; especially when it is considered that they constantly follow such *amāra*s in their this-worldly affairs.

The second probability seems absolutely close to the factuality; for we have no doubt that burdening every individual with referring to the infallible-innocent Imāms or massive transmissions for acquisition of every precept will cause them intolerable hardship, especially when it is considered that this contradicts their practical conduct with regard to this-worldly affairs. Thus, it is very likely that the divine lawgiver has allowed duty-bounds to follow specific *amāra*s for the purpose of facilitation. It is clearly known that in Islam, which is based on the ease, the good of facilitation is among communal goods which are prior to individual goods of some duty-bounds which may sometimes be missed through following *amāra.*

No matter which probability is closer to the factuality, it is a matter of must that the divine lawgiver has not burdened duty-bounds strictly with regard to actual precepts in case of failure of *amāra*; that is, *amāra* is an excuser for duty-bounds and they will not be punished because of opposing some precept – it is not that another secondary precept is made through *amāra*. That is why wherever the divine lawgiver wishes attainment of the actuality in any case, such as cases engaging blood or pudenda, He has commanded duty-bounds to follow precaution and do not content themselves with conjectures.

Amāra Being a Path (*Ṭarīq*) or a Cause (*Sabab*)

By *amāra* being a path is meant that it is merely made to take duty-bounds to the actuality and to reveal the latter; if it is a success, the actuality will become incontrovertible, and if it is a failure, it will merely be an excuser for the duty-bound in opposing the actuality. By *amāra* being a cause is meant that it is a cause in generating a good in its outcome which is equivalent to causing elimination of the actuality in case of failure of *amāra*.

The justifiable opinion is the first. As mentioned earlier, to believe in the latter is dependent upon not believing in the former; for to believe in the latter is caused by inability to justify the former – which is the principle in this connection. However, since we are able to justify the former, there will remain no room for the belief in the latter. The former being the principle in this connection means that *amāra*, *per se*, must be a sheer path to its outcome; for it is to recount, express, and reveal the actuality. Furthermore, the wise take it into consideration because it reveals the actuality – and the conduct of the wise is the primary base in the authority of *amāra*. *Amāra* being treated by the wise as a cause is nonsensical.

CHAPTER 13

THE BOOK (*AL-KITĀB*)

The Holy Qur'ān, the Muslims' sacred book, is the everlasting miracle of the Holy Prophet Muĥammad, and is doubtlessly a divine mercy and guidance which "could not have been forged apart from God" (10: 37). Thus, it is the primary, definite authoritative source of the Islamic law, as its verses contain divine laws. As for other sources of the Islamic law, such as *Sunna* and consensus, they refer to the Qur'ān and are nourished by it.

However, it should be noted that the Qur'ān, whose authority with regard to the issuance is definitely established inasmuch it is transmitted massively from a generation to another, is not totally so with regard to its denotation; for it contains unambiguous (*muĥkam*) and ambiguous (*mutashābih*), the former being, in turn, divided into explicit-definite (*naṣṣ*) whose denotation is definite, and apparent (*żāhir*) whose denotation is dependent upon the belief in the authority of appearances. It also contains abolisher and abolished, general and particular, absolute and qualified, and ambiguous and clear which altogether make its denotation indefinite in a good number of its verses. It is necessary, therefore, to discuss the three following issues in order to establish its authority:

1. Whether its appearances can be considered authoritative proofs – a discussion to be left to the coming discussions of appearances,
2. Whether its restriction or qualification by another authority, such as single transmission and the like, is allowed – something discussed earlier in chapter 5, and
3. Whether its abolishment is allowed – a discussion not of that much use in the jurisprudence, but to be discussed for the sake of comprehensiveness.

Abolishment of the Book

Terminologically, *naskh* (abolishment) denotes removal of what is established in the religion, such as precepts and the like. By "establishment in the religion" is meant the real, actual establishment and not the apparent one because of literal appearance. That is why the removal of a precept which is established by the appearance of generality or absoluteness through a restrictor or a qualifier proof is not called *naskh*, but rather restriction, qualification, and the like. In the latter, the second proof which is given precedence over the appearance of the first is contextual evidence revealing the real intent of the divine lawgiver; it does not remove that precept but apparently, without any real removal of the precepts – contrary to the abolishment – and this is the real difference between abolishment on the one hand and restriction and qualification on the other.

The phrase "precepts and the like" is added so that the definition may cover both burdensome and conventional precepts as well as whatsoever whose establishment and removal is entrusted to the divine lawgiver as He is the Lawgiver. Thus, abrogation does not include existential things which are made by the divine lawgiver as He is the Creator.

Possibility of Abolishment of the Qur'ān

Some have doubted possibility of abolishment in general and that of the holy Qur'ān in particular. Here are the problems raised and their solutions:

1. What is removed in the abolishment is either an established precept or not. If it is established, it is impossible to be removed, and if it is not, there is no need for it to be removed. Therefore, abolishment must be interpreted either as the removal of an identical to the precept and not itself or as termination of time of validity of the precept.
The answer is that we choose the first, i.e., what is removed is an established precept. However, removal of an established precept does not mean its removal as it is established and while its establishment is assumed – which is impossible – rather, it is extinguishing an existent, which is not impossible. It should be noted that since precepts are made as verity propositions, in which the subject is assumed as being existent and not necessarily as being actual existent in the fact, they are established in the world of law-making by assuming the subject as existent and they will not be removed except by their legitimate removal; this is the meaning of removal of established precept and abolishment.
2. Precepts established by God must be of a good or an evil which exists in the object of the precept. That which is essentially of good cannot be turned to that which is essentially of evil, and vice versa, for it leads to

transformation of good to evil and vice versa. Therefore, abolishment is impossible, for it leads to either such impossible transformation or to the abolisher being unwise or ignorant of wisdom – which are both impossible with regard to the divine lawgiver.
The answer is that what is impossible is transformation of the essential good and evil to one another, while that is not the case with all precepts; for it is quite possible that a precept may have a temporary good – something, of course, not to be known except by God. Thus, when a precept is abolished it means that it has not been of essential good or evil, and there is nothing wrong with that kind of change.
3. If abolishment is because of termination of good of the precept, the time of validity of the precept should terminate when that good terminates, then. Now, the divine lawgiver who abolishes the precept is either aware of that from the very beginning or not. The latter is impossible with regard to the Almighty; so, the former is correct. This means that the precept has been temporal in the factuality, even though the abolisher had made it absolute in the appearance. Now, the proof of abolishment indicates and reveals the real intent of the abolisher, and this is the very meaning of restriction – with one difference: this is restriction with regard to time and not states. Thus, there will remain no difference between abolishment and restriction but in naming.
The answer is that although the abolished precept's time of validity terminates in the factuality and God is aware of that, it does not mean that the precept is temporal, i.e., it is qualified by time when it is made. Rather, like verity propositions, it is made in accordance with the good in an absolute manner. Hence, it remains established while the good exists, like other precepts which are made in accordance with their goods. Therefore, had the good been destined to last, the good would have been remaining constant. However, since the divine lawgiver knows that the time of validity of good terminates, He removes the precept and abolishes it.

This clarifies the difference between abolishment and restriction. The precept in the latter has been made qualified and restricted from the very beginning while the term has been apparently general. Then, the restricting proof comes and reveals the intent of the divine lawgiver – it does not remove what has been established in the factuality. In the former, however, since the precept has been made absolute, it is supposed to remain established should it not be removed by abolishment. Thus, abolishment is elimination of what is established (as said in the verse: "God eliminates and establishes whatsoever He wishes" 13: 39). Here, the very realization of the precept necessitates subsistence without there being any literal denotation of generality or absoluteness.

Principality of Non-Abolishment

It is a matter of consensus among all Muslim scholars of any sect that no Qur'ānic verse can be treated as abolished except where its abolishment is proved by a definite proof. It is also a matter of consensus that there are abolisher and abolished verses in the holy Qur'ān. The only matter of dispute is recognition of cases of abolishment. Thus, cases whose abolishment is proved definitely, which are very few, are treated so in *fiqh*. However, if the abolisher is conjectural and not definite, it is not an authoritative proof and must be ignored.

CHAPTER 14

SUNNA

Among Sunnī jurists, *Sunna* (lit. lifestyle) is "word, act, and acknowledgment (*taqrīr*) of the Prophet." That expression is originated by Muslim's being commanded by the holy prophet to follow his *Sunna*. Then, wherever the word *Sunna* is used in an absolute manner without being attributed to anyone, it is interpreted specifically as what contains a precept declared by the holy prophet, whether by his word, act, or acknowledgment.

As for Shiite jurists, since it is proved for them that words of infallible-innocent Imāms of the Household of the Prophet are, like those of the Prophet, authoritative proofs, they expanded the expression *Sunna* so that it may include "word, act, and acknowledgment of the infallible-innocent personality." The secret of that expansion is that holy Imāms are not like transmitters of words of the holy prophet so that their words should be authoritative proofs because they are trustworthy in transmission, but rather because they are appointed by God via the holy prophet in order to deliver factual precepts. That is why they do not make any judgment but in accordance with factual precepts as they are with God, and that happens either through inspiration, as happens for the holy prophet through revelation, or through receiving from the previous infallible-innocent personality, as Imām Ali said, "The holy prophet taught me a thousand windows of knowledge through each one opens for me a thousand windows." Therefore, their declaration of precepts is not of kind of transmission and narration of *Sunna*, nor of kind of *idjtihād* and inference from sources of law-making; but rather, they are themselves a source for law-making. Thus, their words are *Sunna* and not transmission of *Sunna*. However, they sometimes narrate traditions from the holy prophet, for the sake of transferring his precious epigrams, for arguing against others who do not believe in them, or for some other reasons.

As for proving their leadership and that their words are to be considered as those of the holy prophet, it is discussed in *'ilm al-kalām* (Islamic theology).

Now that *Sunna* in that broad sense is one of the sources of Islamic law-making:

1. If it happened that one could attain it in person by listening to the infallible-innocent personality, one has taken the factual precept from its main source in an absolutely certain manner with regard to transmission; such as taking from the holy Qur'ān and/or holy Imāms.
2. If it could not happen for one who is in search of factual precepts, as in times later than theirs, one has no choice, besides referring to the holy Qur'ān, but to refer to *ĥadīth*s narrating *Sunna*, whether through massive or single chain of transmission, while taking into consideration the extent of authority of the latter. Hence, *ĥadīth*s are not the very *Sunna*, but rather its narrator and revealer – though they are sometimes called *Sunna* figuratively inasmuch as they prove it. Thus, we have to discuss *ĥadīth*s in this chapter, since it deals with *Sunna*.

Denotation of Act of the Infallible-Innocent Personality

Doubtless act of the infallible-innocent personality (*al-Ma'ṣūm*), inasmuch as he is infallible-innocent, denotes that such an act is, at least, permissible; as his eschewal of an act denotes that it is, again at least, not mandatory. This cannot be a matter of doubt or dispute. However, his act may have a wider scope of denotation where some evidence exists; for instance, where it is certain that he is in the position of depiction of a precept or an act of worship, such as ablution or prayers. In such case, his act will denote the mode of act whether it is mandatory, recommended, etc. too according to what the evidence reveals. That appearance is doubtlessly an authoritative proof; as appearances of terms are authoritative proofs, without any difference. There are lots of cases in which jurists have argued for precepts of acts of ablution, prayers, pilgrimage to Mecca, and the like as well as their qualities by narrating act of the holy prophet or Imāms in such respects.

There are no doubts and disputes over those things. Matters of dispute in this connection are the two following:

1. Whether act of the infallible-innocent personality, without there being any further evidence, denotes more than permissibility. There are three opinions in this connection: it denotes that such thing is mandatory for us, it is recommended for us, and it denotes no more than permissibility. The justifiable opinion is the third, for there is nothing to prove either of such other two denotations.

It is argued for the first opinion that the verse: "You have had a good example in God's Prophet for whosoever hopes for God and the Last Day, and remembers God a lot," (33: 21) denotes that following the holy prophet in his acts is mandatory; and following his acts being mandatory necessitates that whatever he does should be mandatory for us even though it is not mandatory for himself – except what is proved by a certain proof that it is not mandatory for us. Some have said that should the verse not denote obligation of following the holy prophet, it would, at least, denote goodness and preference of following him.

To that argument, al-'Allāma al-Ĥilli replied that: "To follow someone is to do what he has done because it is his act and in the mode he has acted. Thus, if the act is mandatory, we will treat it as being done mandatorily; if it is recommended, we will treat it as being done as recommended; and if it is permissible, we will treat is as being permissible."

2. Whether the act of the infallible-innocent personality is an authoritative proof of us, i.e., whether the precept is common between him and us – in a case where the mode of what he has done is clear. The dispute is originated by the fact that some precepts are peculiar to the holy prophet in which Muslims are not common, such as obligation of night prayers and the like. Now, if it is known that what the infallible-innocent personality has done is peculiar to him it is doubtlessly peculiar to him and no Muslim shares him in that, and if it is known that it is not peculiar to him in any way it is doubtlessly common for all Muslims and his act is authoritative proof of us. The matter of dispute is a case where it is not known whether the act is peculiar to him or common for all Muslims without there being any evidence to determine any of them. There are three opinions in this connection: it is peculiar to him, it is common for all Muslims, and it has no appearance in either of them remaining thereby ambiguous.

The justifiable opinion is the second one, for the holy prophet is primarily a human being burdened by all duties. Thus, he is principally common with all people in all divine duties, except what he is treated by the Almighty as different.

Denotation of Acknowledgment (*Taqrīr*) of the Infallible-Innocent Personality

By acknowledgment is meant a case where someone performs an act in the presence of the infallible-innocent personality and the latter remains silent while he is aware of what the former is doing and is in the state of capability of informing the former if he is wrong in what he is doing. The state of capability occurs when the time is enough for depiction and when there is no obstacle for that, such as fear, dissimulation, despairing of influence of advising, and the like. Such silence of the infallible-innocent personality and taking no action with regard to what someone has done is called *taqrīr*.

Doubtless such an acknowledgment, accompanied by those conditions, is apparent in that such an act is permissible where its prohibition is probable and is lawful and acceptable where it is an act of worship or transaction. For should it be unlawful in the actuality or suffer from deficiency it was upon the infallible-innocent personality to prohibit the doer if he is knowledgeable of what he is doing, because of obligation of commanding to good and prohibiting from bad, and to expound the precept as well as mode of the act if the doer is ignorant of the precept, because of obligation of teaching the ignorant.

The case is the same where someone explains a precept or quality of an act of worship or transaction in the presence of the infallible-innocent personality while he is capable of depiction but he remains silent, since this is acknowledgement of what he has said.

The Massive Report (*al-Khabar al-Mutawātir*)

The report is of two principal kinds: massive (*mutawātir*), and single (*wāḥid*). Massive is a report which causes confidence in one's soul in such a way that all doubts are removed and definite certainty occurs because of report of massive transmitters whose collusion in lying is impossible. On the contrary, single report, in its *uṣūlī* sense, means that which is not massive even though reporters may be more than one.

What should be emphasized with regard to the massive report is that in a report which has several mediators, like reports of old events, all conditions of massive report must be actualized in each generation; otherwise the report is not to be treated as massive, for the conclusion is pursuant to the inferior preliminary. The reason is clear: a report with several mediators is in fact made of several reports, for each generation reports the report of its previous one. Therefore, report of the last generation must be a massive report of a massive report of a massive report, and so forth, up to a massive report of the very incident or words; and it is clear that should conditions of massive report not be actualized in any generation the report would not be massive, but rather single.

The Single Report (*Khabar al-Wāhid*)

The single report, which, as said earlier, is the one not attaining the level of massive report, may sometimes provoke knowledge even though the reporter may be one – and that is where the report is overwhelmed by evidence provoking knowledge of truthfulness of the report. Such a report is doubtlessly an authoritative proof, for acquisition of knowledge is the utmost end, as there is no authority beyond knowledge and authority of every authoritative proof affair rests upon it.

However, where the single report is not overwhelmed by such evidence, even though it may be overwhelmed by some evidence provoking confidence but not knowledge, there is a major disagreement among *Uṣūlīs* as to its authority as well as conditions of its authority. The disagreement, especially among Shiite scholars, refers, in fact, to the existence or otherwise of definite proof supporting authority of the single report; for it is a matter of consensus among them that the single report as it provokes personal or typical conjecture is not considerable – as conjecture *per se* is definitely not authoritative proof in their opinion. Thus, those who deny authority of single report merely deny existence of such a definite proof, while others believe that it does exist.

As for opinions in this connection, some have denied authority of single report in an absolute way, such as al-Sayyid al-Murtaḍā, Ibn Barrādj, Ibn Zuhra, and Ibn Idrīs who claimed that there is a consensus among Shī'a scholars that the single report is absolutely not an authoritative proof. However, that opinion has found no support from others who came after Ibn Idrīs. Some *Akhbārīs* have said that all *hadīths* collected in Shiite well-known books, especially *al-Kutub al-Arba'a* (the Four-fold Books, i. e., *al-Kāfī* by al-Kulainī, *Man Lā-Yahḍuruh al-Faqīh* by al-Shaikh al-Ṣadūq, and *Tahdhīb al-Ahkām* and *al-Istibṣār fī-mā Ikhtalaf min al-Akhbār* both by al-Shaikh al-Ṭūsī) are definitely truthful. Others, who believe in the authority of single report but not in an absolute way hold different views as to the criterion for its authority maintaining that it is its being considered by Shī'a jurists, righteousness of the transmitter or only his being trustworthy, the sheer conjecture of being uttered by authorities without taking into consideration qualities of the transmitter, and so forth.

What we have to do is to find out whether it is basically an authoritative proof or not, and then the extent of denotation of proofs in this connection.

Proofs of Authority of Single Report from the Book

It should be noted that one who argues Qur'ānic verses for authority of single report does not claim that they are explicit–definite in their denotation – they are at most apparent. If so, how can one argue something conjectural for proving authority of something else whereas the proof of authority, as proved earlier, must be definite-certain? The answer is simple: as will be seen, authority of appearances of the holy Qur'ān is proved by definite proofs; therefore, arguing them ends finally in knowledge and would not be argumentation for conjecture by conjecture. Thus, we merely mention some verses for the authority of single report making ourselves content with proving their appearance in the desired.

> ***1. Verse 6, sūra 49:*** "O believers, if an evil-doer comes to you with a report, make clear, lest you afflict a people unwittingly and then repent of what you have done."

Implicatures of "condition" and "qualifier" of this verse are argued for proving authority of single report. However, it seems that arguing the former is enough. Apart from detailed discussions on this verse, we can argue that the verse declares that the report as it is report is supposed to be confirmed by people and be taken into consideration as that is their practical conduct, otherwise the Almighty would have not prohibited from consideration of report of an evil-doer as he is evil-doer. Hence, God whishes to draw attention of the believers not to rely on every report by everyone. Rather, they must deal with a report by an evil-doer with caution and investigate to find out whether it is true, lest they afflict a people in an unwise way which may harm them. The secret is that the evil-doer is not supposed to be confirmed in his reporting, that is why his report must not be accepted. Thus, implicature of condition of the verse denotes that report of a pious person is supposed to be true, that is why one is not supposed to avoid afflicting a people in an unwise way through investigation his report – its implication being authority of such a report. In short, the verse reveals authority of report of a pious person since his report is supposed to be true, contrary to report of an evil-doer.

> ***2. Verse 122, sūra 9:*** "It is not for the believers to go forth totally; therefore, why should not a party of every section of them go forth to become learned in religion and to warn their people when they return to them, that haply they may beware?"

Arguing this verse for the authority of single report is dependent upon two preliminaries:

2.1. The first part of the verse, i.e., "It is not for the believers to go forth totally," as something preparing the ground for the reasoning; for it is apparent in the negation of obligation of going forth of all believers to the holy prophet for learning the religion. This part is either predicative by which being meant configuration of obligation and thereby is really configurative, or predicative by which being meant emphatic announcement of non-actualization of such a thing from all believers since it is almost impossible – its necessity being non-obligation of going forth of all. No matter which one is considered, the verse denotes non-obligation of going forth of all, whether predicatively or configurationally.

However, the divine lawgiver as He is divine lawgiver is not supposed to negate obligation of something, whether predicatively or configurationally, unless when He is in the position of removal of supposition of or belief in the obligation of that thing. On the one hand, the wise are supposed to believe in the obligation of going forth; for learning the religion is intellectually obligatory for everyone, and acquisition of certainty of that, which is usually restricted to hearing from the holy prophet, is also an intellectual obligation. Hence, believers are truly right in believing in the obligation of going forth to the holy prophet in order to acquire knowledge of precepts. On the other hand, going forth of all believers from all parts of Islamic land to the holy prophet for the acquisition of knowledge of precepts whenever they encounter a problem is no doubt practically impossible – in addition to causing severe difficulties.

Thus, this part of the verse indicates that God, the All-Merciful, wished to remove that duty and difficulty from believers by removing obligation of going forth of all of them. However, that removal does not necessitate removal of obligation of going forth for learning the religion in principle; for necessities should be dealt with within the limits of necessity, and difficulty will clearly be removed by removal of obligation of going forth of every one. That is why God has made another legitimate way for learning the religion other than that of learning it in a definite way by hearing from the holy prophet himself, and that way is explained in the second part of the verse: "therefore, why should not a party of every section of them go forth to…." The letter فـ (to be translated as "therefore") clearly indicates that this way is dependent upon negation of obligation of going forth of all believers.

2.2. The second part of the verse, which is mainly argued by *Uṣūlīs* for proving authority of single report: "Therefore, why should not a party of every section of them go forth to become learned in religion and to warn their people when they return to them, that haply they may beware?" It is argued that when God, the Al-Merciful, announced non-obligation of going forth for everyone, He stimulated believers to follow another way, i.e., to send a party of every section of them so that they convey to others the precepts they have learned when they return. In fact, that way is the best, and indeed the only, one for acquisition of knowledge.
Thus, the verse as a whole expounds an intellectual affair, which is obligation of knowledge and learning. Now that the definite knowledge, through going forth of everyone to the holy prophet in order to learn the religion, is not possible, God has allowed believers to send a party of every section of them in order to learn – and it is this party which is entrusted with teaching others. Furthermore, not only God has allowed them to do so, but He has made that thing obligatory for them. That obligation is inferred from لولا (to be translated as "why should not"), which is for stimulation; and from end of going forth, which is learning for the sake of teaching others so that they may beware – in addition to the intellectual obligation of learning, as said above. All those are clear evidence for obligation of learning the religion for a party of every section in order to teach others religious precepts. That obligation is, naturally, collective and not individual.
Now that obligation, or at least lawfulness, of learning of a party of every section for the sake of teaching others when they return to them is inferred from the verse, it must be inferred that the Almighty has made their reporting precepts an authoritative proof for others; otherwise, making such a going forth lawful in the way of obligation or permission would be absurd and in vain when the obligation of going forth of all is negated. Furthermore, should reporting precepts not be an authoritative proof, there would remain no way for learning them – a way which can be an excuser for the duty-bound or can be used as an argument for and against him.
In short, removal of obligation of going forth from all and deeming that of a party of believers to learn the religion and to teach others is a clear proof for authority of reporting precepts, even though that reporting may not provoke definite knowledge. Since the verse is absolute with regard to making the warning conditional upon provoking knowledge, it should be absolute with regard to

accepting the warning and teaching; otherwise, that solution legitimized by God would be absurd and in vain not being capable of actualizing the purpose for which going forth was legitimized.

It should be noted that arguing that verse for the authority of single report is not dependent upon going forth of a party of every section being mandatory. Rather, that way being legitimized by the Almighty even though in the way of permissibility would be enough, for its very legitimizing necessitates legitimizing authority of reporting precepts on the part of the one who has learned. Therefore, there is no need of prolixity for inferring obligation from the verse.

One problem remains: What is mandatory is going forth of a party of every section, and a party consists of at least three persons; hence, the verse does not cover the report of one or two persons. What can solve the problem is that there is no denotation in the verse that the party should collectively warn their people when they return to them. Therefore, the verse is absolute in this connection, and its absoluteness necessitates that report of a single person should also be an authoritative proof when he reports singly.

We do not discuss other verses presented to prove authority of single report, as they have no such denotation.

Proofs of Authority of Single Report from *Sunna*

It is obviously clear that one cannot argue the very single report for the authority of single report, since it is obviously a vicious circle. Rather, reports argued must be definite; either by being massive, or by being overwhelmed by definite evidence. As for *ĥadīths* available in this connection, they are doubtlessly not massive in their terms, i.e., there are no massive reports containing such words as "authority of single report;" they are at most massive in their concepts, i.e., one can say that the concept of authority of a single report where the reporter is reliable in his reporting is confirmed in some massive reports – as asserted by al-Shaikh al-Ĥurr al-'Āmilī in his *Tafṣīl Wasā'il al-Shī'a.*

Al-Shaikh al-Anṣārī has narrated some groups of *ĥadīths* by consideration of which altogether one becomes certain that report of a single reporter who is reliable and trustworthy in his reporting is definitely treated as an authoritative proof on the part of holy Imāms. Here, we mention those groups briefly:

1. What is said by holy Imāms with regard to referring people to such preferences as the reporter being more righteous-trustworthy, truthful, and the like in case of contradiction of *ĥadīths*. (Some of those *ĥadīths* will be

mentioned later in the discussion of "equilibrium and preferences.") Had report of a single reporter who is reliable and trustworthy in his reporting not been an authoritative proof, assumption of contradiction of *ḥadīth*s and preference giving would have been absurd – as it is clear.

2. What is said by holy Imāms with regard to referring single reporters to their single companions, as Imām's referring to Zurāra by saying, "If you wish to hear a *ḥadīth*s, you should refer to the man sitting here," and Imām's positive answer when someone said, "Sometimes I need to ask you, but I cannot see you whenever I wish. Is Yūnus b. 'Abd al-Raḥmān reliable so that I may learn my religious teaching from him?" The second *ḥadīth* indicates that it has been taken for granted that one should accept words of a reliable reporter; that is why he asks Imām whether Yūnus is reliable in order to conclude that he can refer to him for learning religious teachings.

3. *Ḥadīths* encouraging narration, writing, and conveying traditions, such as the famous prophetic *ḥadīth*: "Whosoever saves forty *ḥadīth*s for my followers will be raised as a knowledgeable scholar in the hereafter," and the like.

4. *Ḥadīths* blaming those who forge falsehood against the holy prophet and Imāms and warning people against them. Had acceptance of single reports not been prevailing among Muslims, there would have remained no room for forging falsehood against them, fear of that, or warning against those who forge; for such forging would be fruitless if Muslims were not to accept single reports.

As such words as truthful, trustworthy, and the like used in those *ḥadīth*s indicate, the single report in question is the one reported by such a person whose lying is nearly improbable in such a way that the wise do not take probability of his lying into consideration.

Proofs of Authority of Single Report from Consensus

A good number of scholars have claimed that there is a consensus among Shī'a on the authority of report of a single transmitter if he is truthful and trustworthy in his reporting, even though his report does not provoke knowledge. The chief figure among those is al-Shaikh al-Ṭūsī; but he conditioned that upon the single report being narrated by Shī'a transmitters from the holy prophet or Imāms, the transmitter being precise and not being accused of lying in his reporting. On the other hand, another group of Shī'a scholars, pioneered by al-Sayyid al-Murtaḍā, have claimed such a consensus among Shī'a on non-authority of single report and treated it as analogy (*qiyās*) whose non-authority is quite well-known among Shīʿa. He asserts every now and then that "the single report neither provokes knowledge nor causes an act."

Occurrence of such a contradiction between claims of two contemporary scholars, the first of whom being studied at the second, who were both expert on Shīʿa teachings and were not that heedless to claim something without an exhaustive research is astonishing. That is why later scholars have attempted to find some compromise solution, one being that the single report claimed by al-Sayyid al-Murtaḍā as being a matter of consensus of non-authority is the one which is narrated by Sunnīs, and al-Shaikh al-Ṭūsī agrees with him on that. A second one is that by single report al-Sayyid al-Murtaḍā has meant the one opposite to that which is taken from trustworthy transmitters, recorded in authentic books, and accepted by all Shīʿa scholars – something al-Shaikh al-Ṭūsī agrees with. A third one is that the single report claimed by al-Shaikh al-Ṭūsī as being a matter of consensus of authority is the one which is overwhelmed by some evidence provoking knowledge of its truthfulness – something al-Sayyid al-Murtaḍā agrees with. A fourth one is that by knowledge al-Sayyid al-Murtaḍā has meant the sheer confidence and not a certainty into which no probability can penetrate, and this interpretation brings those two claims close to one another. The more reliable compromise solution is the fourth, the first, and the second respectively.

However, no matter one can find a compromise solution, it is al-Shaikh al-Ṭūsī's claim that is acceptable, for all Shīʿa scholars, including the very al-Sayyid al-Murtaḍā and Ibn Idrīs, have always referred to trustworthy single reports narrated in Shiite reliable books. In short, one who doubts existence of consensus in this connection can find no consensus in Shīʿa jurisprudence.

Proofs of Authority of Single Report from the Conduct of the Wise

It is doubtlessly and definitely clear that the wise (i.e., human beings as they are intellectual creatures), though having various tastes and approaches to affairs, have only one practical conduct with regard to the single report: On the one hand they take report of one whom they trust and are confident that he is truthful and not a liar into consideration, and on the other hand they rely on trustworthy single persons in order to convey their words. The secret of that conduct is that the wise do not take the weak counter-probabilities into consideration; they ignore the probability of falsehood of report of the trustworthy person as well as that of his mistake, heedlessness, or error.

People's lives are based upon that practical conduct. Should that conduct not exist, their social order would become chaotic and anxiety would dominate their lives, because of scantiness of reports provoking knowledge in terms of transmission and context.

Muslims, in particular, are like other people in this connection and have had the same practical conduct from early Islam with regard to receiving religious precepts. Have Muslims ever hesitated to learn their religious duties from the holy prophet's and holy Imāms' companions?

When, on the one hand, the practical conduct of the wise is to take the report of a trustworthy single into consideration, and, on the other hand, the divine lawgiver has not prohibited from following that way, we can infer, as will be explained in detail in chapter 19, that the divine lawgiver has confirmed that way; for He is among the wise, and even their chief. Otherwise, if He had adapted another way in conveying religious precepts, He would have announced and depicted that way having ordered believers to follow it.

As confirmed by a good number of celebrated scholars, this proof is the main proof in this connection. If one can supposedly find some way to refute other proofs, he will not be able to do so with regard to this one.

The only doubt cast upon this argument is that the second premise of the proof is not actualized here, since the divine lawgiver has prohibited from following that way in such Qur'ānic verses that forbid believers from following conjecture, as explained earlier, among which being the single report which does not provoke knowledge. However, that doubt can be removed by realizing that such verses do not include single report of the trustworthy person, for consideration of that report in the conduct of the wise is not an instance of observing conjecture. Rather, it is an instance of knowledge, since the wise, due to their nature and practical conduct, ignore the probability of that report being in opposition to the factuality. Thus, single report of the trustworthy person is basically not included in the conjecture, and that is why those verses cannot prohibit from consideration of single report of the trustworthy person. If one wishes to prove that one is in need of a particular proof, and such proof is missing.

Anyhow, could those verses be capable of prohibiting from consideration of single report of the trustworthy person, appearances, and the like for which a conduct of the wise exists, it would be revealed and known among Muslims and they would have no practical consensus on taking them into consideration. This is a definite proof of such verses not being capable of prohibiting from consideration of single report of the trustworthy person; hence, we are in need of no more proof in this connection.

CHAPTER 15

CONSENSUS *(IDJMĀʿ)*

Being defined as consensus of Muslim jurists, that of Muslim community, and so on, *idjmāʿ* is considered one of the three-fold or four-fold free-standing sources of religious precepts by Sunnī *Uṣūlīs* and jurists. Shīʿa *Uṣūlīs* and jurists, however, do not treat consensus as a free-standing source, but rather as a way through which *Sunna* can be revealed. Thus, authority and innocence are for words of the infallible-innocent personality, which may sometimes be revealed by the consensus, and not for the consensus *per se*. That is why Shīʿa jurists sometimes treat unanimity of opinion of a few individuals whose unanimity is technically not called *idjmāʿ* as consensus, because of its definite revelation of opinions of the infallible-innocent personality on the one hand, and do not consider a consensus which does not reveal opinions of the infallible-innocent personality as *idjmāʿ* even though it is technically called so on the other.

Considering the difference between Sunnī and Shīʿa in this connection, we have to deal with the issue separately. Before that, however, one point should be noted: it is obviously clear that consensus of all people, or a specific people, as it is consensus has no implication to revealing divine precepts; for it is not of unanimity of opinion of the wise as they are the wise which is an authoritative proof like the Book and *Sunna*. Unanimity of opinion of the wise as they are the wise is in fact the very intellectual proof, as will be discussed later, and not the technical consensus. The reason why a consensus of people which is not included in the unanimity of opinion of the wise as they are the wise cannot be considered a source for religious precepts is that such a consensus may be caused by people's habits, beliefs, emotions, or sentiments which are of human characteristic and the divine lawgiver transcends them. Should consensus of people as it is consensus be an authoritative proof, consensus of other people who follow other religions should be an authoritative proof as well – something no Muslim believes in. Thus, some other proof must be presented by Sunnī jurists with regard to the authority of consensus.

Sunnī Approach to the Consensus

As mentioned earlier, Sunnī *Uṣūlīs* and jurists treat the consensus as a free-standing source for religious precepts arguing some Qur'ānic, traditional, and intellectual proofs. They cannot argue the consensus itself, for it is obviously a vicious circle.

As for the Qur'ānic proof, they have argued some verses the clearest of which being the verse 115 of *sūra* 4: "But whoso makes a breach with the Prophet after the guidance has become clear to him, and follows a way other than the believers, him We shall turn over to what he has turned to and We shall roast him in Hell – an evil homecoming," since it makes following the way of believers obligatory; and when believers have a consensus it becomes their way whose following is obligatory.

To refute that argument, suffice it to narrate what al-Ghazzālī has said in this connection: "The appearance of the verse is that whoso troubles the Prophet and follows a way other than that of believers in following and assisting him as well as repelling his enemies We shall turnover him to what he has turned to; as if to eschew troubling the Prophet is not deemed sufficient and to follow the way of believers in defending him and submission to his commands and prohibitions is added." (*al-Mustaṣfā*, 1, 111) As al-Ghazzālī admits, no verse of all other verses argued in this connection is apparent in the authority of consensus.

With regard to *Sunna*, some *ĥadīth*s, claimed to be massive in their concepts, conveying the meaning of "My *umma* (community; i.e., followers) will not be unanimous in the error" are argued in order to prove innocence of Muslim community, so that their consensus may be treated as an authoritative proof and a free-standing source for inferring religious precepts.

Apart from being authentic and massive or otherwise, those *ĥadīth*s do not prove such a claim, for unanimity of the community means that of all community and not a part of it, while by consensus Sunnīs mean unanimity of people of Medina, that of people of Mecca, Medina, Kūfa, and Baṣra, that of those who are qualified to unbind and bind, that of companions, that of *Uṣūlī* jurists, and so forth – according to various opinions presented by Sunnī sects and scholars. How can one find consensus of all Muslim *umma*, which consists of a variety of peoples and individuals, in all times on anything but necessities of religion, such as obligation of prayers, fasting, and the like, which are not of the type of consensus in question? Obligation of such things is not in need of authority of consensus.

The intellectual proof presented is that when Companions give a verdict considering themselves as being certain, there must be a definite proof; for they do not become certain but because of existence of a definite evidence. And when their number increases to the level of massive report, both lie and mistake on their part normally becomes impossible. If disciples of Companions and disciples of disciples become certain of what Companions have been certain of, their missing the truth will normally become impossible.

That argument, however, cannot be treated as a sound reasoning. For consideration of consensus as a free-standing source for religious precepts means that it is not a way through which opinion of the infallible-innocent personality is revealed. If so, since those who have reached a consensus, whoever they are, are not innocent, their being wrong, mistaken, or neglectful is quite possible – though their lying is not considerable – as it is quite possible that their consensus might be caused by their beliefs, habits, and the like. Thus, how can such a consensus implicate a divine law? Furthermore, should that intellectual proof be sound, consensus of all people and followers of all religions would be an authoritative proof and not that of Muslim community, Muslim jurists, or companions of the holy Prophet alone – unless innocence of Muslims should be proved by a specific proof, and in that case it is that proof which establishes authority of consensus and not this intellectual reasoning.

Shiite Approach to the Consensus

As said earlier, consensus as it is consensus would have no value in Shī'a jurisprudence should it not reveal opinion of the infallible-innocent personality, and that is why it is not considered a free-standing source for religious precepts. In fact, authority is for the revealed, i.e., *Sunna*, and not for the revealer, i.e., consensus; and consensus precisely plays the role of massive report – with one difference: the latter reveals the very words of the infallible-innocent personality (and that is why it is called lexical proof *(al-dalīl al-lafẓī)*) while the former reveals the opinion of the infallible-innocent personality and not his words (and that is why it is called thematic proof *(al-dalīl al-lubbī)* which conveys the theme and not the terms). Now that consensus is an authoritative proof because of revealing opinion of the infallible-innocent personality and not *per se*, there is no need for unanimity of all; rather, that of those whose unanimity reveals words of the infallible-innocent personality would be sufficient, no matter how many they are – as explicitly asserted by some great Shī'a jurists and *Uṣūlīs*.

As for the ways through which the consensus reveals opinion of the infallible-innocent personality, they are claimed to be up to twelve four of which being more considerable. However, since most of later Shī'a jurists and *Uṣūlīs* have raised doubts about them and followed some specific way called "the way of surmise (*ṭarīqa al-ḥads*)," we will discuss this way only. According to the way of surmise, when one observes that all Shī'a jurists have a consensus on a precept while they disagree too much on most of precepts, one will definitely become certain that their consensus is rooted in the holy Imām's opinion and, being handed down from generation to generation, they have received it from their Imām – as is the case with consensus of followers of all other creeds and sects with regard to which no one doubts that the matter of consensus is taken from their leader. It should be emphasized that in the way of surmise, consensus of all jurists of all times, beginning from the era of holy Imāms, must be actualized; for disagreement of one earlier generation, and even one single known outstanding jurist, prevents actualization of certitude in this connection.

Since this book is an introductory work, we do not discuss doubts raised as to whether this argument for justification of way of surmise is sound.

All detailed discussions and arguments in Shiite *uṣūl al-fiqh* on the authority of consensus as well as the ways through which the consensus reveals opinion of the infallible-innocent personality deal with *al-idjmā' al-muḥaṣṣal* (the acquired consensus), i.e., a consensus which is acquired by a jurist who has searched all opinions of all jurists in person. It is this kind of consensus whose authority is a matter of dispute.

However, a case where a jurist has acquired a consensus and then has reported it to others (which is called *al-idjmā' al-manqūl*, i.e., the reported consensus), is also a matter of dispute and different opinions are presented in this connection. Some have considered the reported consensus an authoritative proof since it is a single report, some have treated it as not being an authoritative proof since it cannot be considered an instance of single report, some have considered it an authoritative proof where it reveals religious precepts in the view of the one who is reported to and not the reporter alone, and others have held some other different views in this regard. However, as mentioned earlier, since this book is an introductory work on the one hand and discussions concerning consensus, both acquired and reported, are complicated on the other, we content ourselves with this brief presentation referring our readers to Shiite detailed *uṣūlī* books.

CHAPTER 16

THE INTELLECTUAL PROOF (*AL-DALĪL AL-'AQLĪ*)

By the intellectual proof as a free-standing source other than the Book and *Sunna* is meant any judgment of the intellect which provokes certainty of divinely precepts; in other words, any intellectual proposition through which definite knowledge of divinely precepts is acquired. It is obviously clear that if the intellectual proof is treated as something free-standing, it naturally cannot be an authoritative proof except where it provokes certitude – which is an authoritative proof by essence. That is why it cannot include conjectures and those intellectual preliminaries which do not provoke certitude as to divinely precepts, such as analogy (*qiyās*) and the like. To be exact, the intellectual proof is the judgment of intellect that an established religious or intellectual precept implicates another religious precept, such as intellect's judgment in the questions of replacement, the preliminary of the mandatory act, and other dependent intellectual proofs discussed earlier. Some other examples of intellectual proof are judgment of the intellect that burdening without depiction is impossible, which implicates religious precept of clearance from obligation (*al-barā'a*); its judgment that the more important precept must be given priority in case of interference of precepts, which implicates actuality of the more important precept on the part of God; and its judgment that divine precepts necessarily conform judgment of the wise as to "the praised opinions (*al-ārā' al-maḥmuda*)." Such implications are real, actual affairs which are perceived by the intellect either naturally, because of being among primary premises and natural premises whose syllogisms are with them, or via acquisition, because of leading to primary premises and natural premises through which the intellect should know those implications in certitude. Should the intellect know an implication in certitude while it is assumed that it knows the implicated in certitude, it must necessarily know the implicating, i.e., the divine lawgiver's precept, in certitude – and it was proved earlier that certitude is an essentially authoritative proof to which leads authority of every authoritative affair. Thus, such intellectual implications are major premises of intellectual propositions by being added to their minor premises religious precepts may be achieved.

The intellectual proof is exclusive to such implications because the intellect can initially not achieve religious precepts independently, i.e., it has no way to know that such a thing has such a religious precept without benefiting from implications. The reason is that religious precepts are dependent upon instruction; for they are neither among primary premises nor among observable things, they can neither be observed by eyes nor can be experienced or guessed. Therefore, there remains no way to know them but to hear from the one who is appointed by the divine lawgiver to deliver them, i.e., the prophet. Criteria for precepts can also not be known but through hearing from the one who delivers precepts, for we have no rules through which we may know secrets of divine precepts as well as criteria upon which they are dependent – and remember that "surmise avails naught against truth (Qur., 10: 36)."

Justification of Authority of the Intellect

As said earlier, by the intellectual proof is meant what provokes knowledge of religious precepts and makes one know them in certitude – certitude being essential authoritative proof to which referring authority of every authoritative affair. The intellect is the distinguishing feature of human beings which proves God and His unity, prophethood, resurrection, and all other fundamental teachings of every divine religion. Should the intellect not be an authoritative proof, there would remain no reliable way to the acquisition of sound beliefs. That is why the seventh S̲h̲īʿa Imām, Imām al-Kāżim, has said, "God has two authorities: an outward authority and an inward one. As for the outward, it is prophets and Imāms; as for the inward, it is intellects." (al-Kulainī, 1: 15)

Although one is naturally allowed to doubt minor premises of intellectual arguments, i.e., whether intellectual implications exist in independent as well as dependent intellectual proofs, one has no way to doubt authority of the intellect where the implication exists. Some *Ak̲h̲bārīs*, however, have claimed that religious precepts cannot be acquired unless when they are proved via *Sunna* of holy Imāms. That opinion can be justified in some ways the best of which being that religious precepts are confined to being known through *Sunna* of holy Imāms. However, it was proved in the discussion of commonness of precepts between the knowledgeable and the ignorant that conditioning precepts to knowledge of them is absolutely impossible, let alone conditioning them to a knowledge provoked by a certain cause.

CHAPTER 17

AUTHORITY OF APPEARANCES
(ĤUDJDJIYYA AL-ŻAWĀHIR)

Preliminary Notes

1. In the first part, whose end was explanation of minor premises of principality of appearance, appearances of some disputed terms were taken into consideration from a general aspect. In this chapter, we discuss the major premise of principality of appearance, i.e., authority of appearance.
2. The discussion of authority of appearance is pursuant to the discussion of the Book and *Sunna*. It means that appearances are not independent, separate, free-standing proofs; rather, their authority is needed to be proved for the sake of consideration of the Book and *Sunna*. Thus, principality of appearance is a complementary to the authority of the Book and *Sunna*; for it is obviously clear that one cannot treat the Book and *Sunna* as authorities except when their appearances are authoritative proofs – since explicit-definite phrases, whose denotation is definitive, in those two sources are very rare.
3. It was proved earlier that conjecture is principally forbidden to be followed except where a definite proof proves its authority. Appearances are among conjectures; therefore, we should look for a definite proof for their authority so that we may take appearances of Quranic verses and *ĥadīth*s into consideration. That proof will be presented in this chapter.
4. The discussion of appearances needs the two following steps:

   4.1. Whether a specific term is apparent in a specific meaning. The whole first part dealt with discussing appearances of some terms whose appearances were a matter of dispute, such as terms of commands and prohibitions, those of general and particular, and so on. In fact, they are some minor premises of the principality of appearance.

   4.2. Whether a term whose appearance is recognized is an authoritative proof in its specific meaning from the divine lawgiver's view so that both the divine lawgiver and duty-bounds can argue it. That is the major premise by adding its minor premises one will be allowed to take appearances of Qur'ānic verses and *ḥadīths* into consideration and act on their basis.

5. The first step, i.e., recognition of minor premises of principality of appearances, is generally concerning two issues:

5.1. The issue of convention of the term. Should the convention be recognized, the term would necessarily be apparent in the meaning specified; such as appearance of the imperative in the obligation, that of conditional sentence in some implicatures, and so forth.

5.2. Whether a general or particular evidence exists as to whether the meaning is meant by the term. The need to evidence appears either in case of intending other than what the term is specified for, or in case of commonness of a term in more than one meaning. Should the evidence exist, the term will be apparent in what the evidence denotes, no matter the evidence is joint or separate.

In case of doubt over those two cases, there are some ways for knowing convention of terms as well as general evidence some of which being as follows:

a) One searches various usages of the term and exercises his own opinion if one is among experts on the language and rhetoric.

b) One refers to signs of literalness, such as preceding other meaning, and the like.

c) One refers to opinions of lexicographers, although validity of this way is a matter of dispute. In this connection, it should be noted that, initially, one will not be justified in referring to opinions of lexicographers for the issue of convention, since lexicographers are chiefly concerned with reporting those meanings in which the terms are commonly used without caring much about distinguishing literal from figurative meanings – except al-Zamakhsharī in *Asās al-Balāgha*, and some works on philology. Nevertheless, in case lexicographers explicitly declare that a meaning is literal, one may accept it only if such declaration provokes knowledge of convention. Otherwise, there must be a proof of authority of the conjecture caused by lexicographers' opinions so that referring to their opinions may be justifiable. Here are some proofs presented in this connection:

c.1) Consensus. It is said that there is a comprehensive consensus, without even a single objector, on accepting the opinion of lexicographers even though the opinion may be declared by a single lexicographer. That claim, however, is absurd; since neither does such a consensus exist among all jurists nor is it an authoritative proof, for the infallible-innocent personality does not refer to the opinion of lexicographers so that his agreement about this issue may be revealed.

c.2) The conduct of the wise. To refer to trustworthy experts in all such affairs that are in need of skill and independent persuasion such as medicine, engineering, and the like – among which being lexicography and complicated science of terms – is definitely a practical conduct of the wise; and it is absolutely clear that the lexicographer is considered an expert by the wise. On the other hand, no prohibition from that practical conduct is proved on the part of the divine lawgiver. It is concluded from those two premises that the divine lawgiver agrees with them and is satisfied with that conduct.

However, agreement of the divine lawgiver cannot be discovered merely through His prohibition not being proved, as will be explained in detail in chapter 19; there must exist three conditions none of which being existent here. For neither is the divine lawgiver in need of referring to experts so that He may have a practical conduct in this connection, nor is the conduct of the wise in referring to opinions of lexicographers even in religious affairs proved, nor does a definite proof announcing agreement and confirmation of the divine lawgiver exist – on the contrary, Qur'ānic verses which prohibit from following conjecture sufficiently prove prohibition from that practical conduct.

c.3) The intellectual proof. It is a definite judgment of the intellect that the ignorant must refer to the knowledgeable; and since that intellectual judgment is among the praised opinions on which the wise are unanimous, the divine lawgiver, who is among the wise and even their chief, should have judged the same. This proof is very close to the factuality, and not only justifies but necessitates the reference to the opinions of lexicographers.

Justification of the Authority of Appearance

The only proof of authority of appearance is the conduct of the wise, which consists, as said earlier, of two premises:

1. The practical conduct of the wise and their unanimity of opinion is doubtlessly established on that the speaker can content himself with the

appearance of his words in communicating his ideas to others; the wise do not oblige the speaker to use only such words that are definite with regard to which no other meaning is probable. On the other hand, based on that practical conduct, they take appearances of words of every speaker into consideration for understanding his ideas whether or not his words are explicit-definite. That is why the appearance is an authoritative proof for both the speaker against the hearer if the latter predicates the former's words upon something contrary to the appearance and the hearer against the speaker if the former claims that he has meant something contrary to the appearance. It is the legal procedure that the appearance of a judicial confession or acknowledgment should be taken into consideration even though the term may not be explicit-definite.

b) It is also indubitably clear that the holy lawgiver has not taken a way other than that of the wise in His communications; for the lawgiver is considered among the wise, and even their chief; therefore, He should have confirmed that conduct. This argument is sound, since there is no problem with the divine lawgiver having the same conduct and way on the one hand and no prohibition from Him is proved in this connection on the other.

It is necessarily and definitely concluded from those two premises that the appearance is treated as an authoritative proof by the divine lawgiver: for Him against the duty-bound, and as an excuser for the duty-bound.

However, some doubts have been cast upon generality of either of those premises; of each we will discuss only one:

Authority of the Appearance with regard to Those Whose Communication Is Not Meant

In his book *al-Qawānīn al-Muĥkama*, al-Qummī (d. 1810) has held that the appearance is not an authoritative proof with regard to those whose communication is not meant – by them being meant people of our time and the like who were not orally addressed by the Book and *Sunna*. He argues that the holy Qur'ān did not address those who were not present; the Qur'ān is not like usual books which are written to communicate with whoever reads them. As for *Sunna*, *ĥadīths* of innocent-infallible personalities in the position of answering questions have merely meant communication of ideas to questioners and no one else.

However, that idea is not sound and is criticized by all later scholars. The reason is that such statement is ambiguous; it is not clear what is meant by negation of authority of appearance with regard to those whose communication is not meant. If by that is meant that:

1. The speech has no essential appearance with regard to such persons; then, it is clearly untrue.
2. The wise have no practical conduct to ignore the probability of existence of evidence in the appearances with regard to those whose communication is not meant; then, it is a claim without any proof. In fact, what is known from the conduct of the wise is something contrary to that, for the wise do not differentiate in acting on the basis of literal appearance between those whose communication is meant and those whose communication is not meant.
3. The intellect allows the wise speaker to count on some evidence which is unprecedented and unknown to other than the one whose communication is meant; then, it does not harm the authority of appearance proved by the conduct of the wise – although it is sound *per se*. What makes the appearance an authoritative proof is negation of probability of existence of evidence by the conduct of the wise and not negation of that probability by judgment of the intellect, and none of them implicates the other, i.e., lack of negation of probability of existence of evidence by the intellect does not implicate lack of that negation by the conduct of the wise – the latter being influential in the authority of appearance. The fact is that this statement is not precise, or correct; for the appearance will not be appearance unless where a probability of existence of evidence which is not negated by the intellect exists; otherwise, the speech will be explicit-definite (*naṣṣ*) and not appearance.

Generally speaking, the speech is apparent, and not explicit-definite which conveys the objective definitely, only when it is associated with such possible intellectual probability or probabilities as error, negligence, deliberateness of the speaker (for some reason), or that of designation of evidence no matter hidden or unhidden from others. Furthermore, the appearance is not an authoritative proof unless where the practical conduct of the wise ignores such probabilities, i.e., it does not consider them in the position of consideration of the appearance.

Thus, this justification of that opinion is not acceptable, for it proves, at most, that existence of hidden evidence from the one whose communication is not meant is probable since it is not reprehensible if a wise man does so; therefore, existence of evidence is intellectually possible. However, this does not contradict the practical conduct of the wise to ignore such probability.

Should it be accepted that authority of the appearance differs from the one whose communication is meant to others, the point would be examining its efficacy with regard to the holy Qur'ān and *Sunna.* Since duties mentioned in the Qur'ān are obviously common for all duty-bounds with no peculiarity to those whose communication is meant, there must exist no evidence which is hidden for those who are not orally addressed. In fact, the holy Qur'ān has doubtlessly not addressed only those whose communication is meant.

As for *Sunna*, *ĥadīth*s indicating it contain duties for all duty-bounds and mean communication with everybody including those who are not orally addressed; they rarely deal with questions peculiar merely to the addressee – cases in which the duty should be generalized in order to include others as well, because of the rule of commonness of all duty-bounds in all duties. On the other hand, should such evidence exist, trustfulness of transmitter of *ĥadīth* necessitates mentioning that. Otherwise, the principle of lack of evidence negates existence of such evidence.

Authority of Appearances of the Book

Some *Akhbārīs* have allegedly held that appearances of the holy Qur'ān are not authoritative proofs and one is not allowed to take them into consideration in his religious duties without referring to their interpretation by holy Imāms.

Before examining soundness of that idea, we have to mention that those who believe in the authority of appearances of the Book do not mean:

1. Authority of all parts of the Book in which some ambiguous verses, whose arbitrary interpretation is not allowed, exist. However, existence of ambiguous verses cannot prevent from taking appearances of the Book into consideration, for it is not that difficult for an expert to distinguish ambiguous from unambiguous;
2. Permissibility of hastening to act in accordance with ambiguous verses without thorough investigation, in the Book and *Sunna*, of whatsoever capable of changing the appearance, such as abolisher, restrictor, evidence of figurative meaning, and so forth; and
3. Validity of acting in accordance with the appearances of the Book on the part of everybody, even though he has no knowledge of whatsoever plays a role in understanding themes of its verses. That is why the lay cannot claim understanding appearances of the Book and act on their basis. That is not something peculiar to the holy Qur'ān; it applies to every scholarly/scientific

text which needs precision. For although such texts have appearances to be understood on the basis of terminology and grammatical rules capable of being used as arguments for and against both their authors and addressees, a layman cannot refer to them to become an expert on that science using such appearances as arguments for and against without studying them at a learned expert – and should he do that, he would definitely be blamed by the wise.

Now, what do those *Akhbārīs* mean by their denial of authority of appearances of the holy Qur'ān? If they mean what we have just mentioned, i.e., impermissibility of hastening to consideration of them without thorough investigation of whatsoever capable of changing its appearances, that is absolutely correct and natural. However, we mentioned that it does not mean that appearances of the Book are absolutely out of reach of everybody and that no one has authority to refer to them. And if they mean that one should only deal with what is received from holy Imāms and is absolutely not allowed to consider Qur'ānic appearances in cases where no depiction from holy Imāms exists, even though one is among experts on the language and other sciences necessary for understanding them while one has quested for whatsoever capable of being evidence of change of appearances, this is something improvable by the proofs they have presented. On the contrary, there are a good number of *ḥadīth*s referring people to the holy Qur'ān, such as what commands them to compare contradictory *ḥadīth*s with the Qur'ān and to accept the one which is in agreement with it, to compare not only contradictory but all *ḥadīth*s with the Qur'ān, to annul such conditions of contracts which contradict it, and some specific *ḥadīth*s allowing consideration of its appearances.

Furthermore, to refer to *ḥadīth*s of holy Imāms means consideration of appearances of their words and not those of the Book. Now, one may ask whether everybody is allowed to refer to appearances of *ḥadīth*s without being among people of knowledge and deliberation, without questing for probable evidence, and without being an expert on whatsoever plays a role in understanding their themes. Add to this that, contrary to the Book, *ḥadīth*s are in need of investigation of their chain of transmission on the one hand and are often narrated through conveying the meaning and not recounting the very words of holy Imāms on the other.

In short, although it is correct that understanding the Qur'ān is complicated and only experts can deal with it, it does not mean that its words have no appearances and its appearances are not authoritative proofs – as is the case with any other technical, scholarly text.

CHAPTER 18

THE CELEBRITY *(AL-SHUHRA)*

Literally, *al-shuhra* means obviousness and clarity of something. Terminologically, however, it is of two applications: one is in the science of *ḥadīth* where any *ḥadīth* whose transmitters are less than the level of massive report (*mutawātir*) is called *mashhūr* (i.e., celebrated) or sometimes *mustafīd*, and the other is in the jurisprudence where any opinion of jurists on a juristic problem which is abundant but not at the level of consensus is called *mashhūr* (and sometimes the very jurists are called the same, as in "*mashhūr* says so," or "*mashhūr* holds that....").

Thus, *shuhra* is of two varieties:

1. *Shuhra* in the *ḥadīth*. In this kind, it is not necessary that jurists should have taken that *ḥadīth* into consideration in a celebrated way as well; they may or may not do so. However, we will mention in chapter 21 that such celebrity provokes preference of the celebrated *ḥadīth* over others, and that is why the celebrated *ḥadīth* is an authoritative proof from this aspect.
2. *Shuhra* in the verdict, meaning celebrity of a verdict of jurists which provokes the belief in its conformity to the factuality – though not at the level of certitude. This is, in turn, of two varieties:
2.1. It is known that such *shuhra* is dependent upon a specific *ḥadīth* available to us. This kind is called "practical celebrity (*al-shuhra al-'amaliyya*)" and we will discuss in chapter 21 whether it compensates for the weakness in the chain of transmission and/or for the weakness in the denotation.
2.2. It is not known on what that celebrity is dependent, whether there exists a *ḥadīth* in conformity with the celebrity but the celebrity did not consider it or it is not known whether the celebrity has considered it, or there is no *ḥadīth* at all. This kind is called "celebrity of verdict (*al-shuhra al-fatwā'iyya*)."

It is this celebrity of verdict that is the matter of dispute here, for some jurists have allegedly held that this kind of celebrity, as it is celebrity, is an authoritative proof over juristic precepts and, like single report, should be included in particular conjectures, while others hold that there is nothing that can confirm its authority. The latter is the justifiable opinion, and all proofs claimed for its authority, as listed below, are null and void:

1. Proofs arguing authority of single report denote that of celebrity as well through accordant implicature; for the conjecture actualized by celebrity is stronger than the one actualized by single report. Thus, celebrity takes priority over single report with regard to authority.
This argument is not sound, for it depends upon the criterion of authority of single report being its causing conjecture so that what provokes stronger conjecture should be given priority in authority, while that is a mere probability and has no supporting proof – if what is proved not being non-consideration of actual conjecture.
2. Generality of argumentation in the verse 6 of *sūra* 49, "lest you afflict a people unwittingly" (see chapter 14, proofs of authority of single report from the Book) proves authority of celebrity; for the argumentation reveals that what prohibits from accepting report of an evil-doer without investigation is unwittingly afflicting denoting thereby that whatsoever does not lead to unwittingly afflicting is an authoritative proof. Since this is the case with celebrity, one should take it into consideration.

Should it be accepted that this part of the verse is argumentation, however, it should be noted that this reasoning is consideration of "generality of opposite of argumentation" and not "generality of argumentation," and there is no indication of opposite of argumentation in the verse in a necessary manner. Let us take an example. Should doctor prohibit patient from some food because it is sour, it would not mean that the patient is allowed to, or must, eat whatsoever is not sour. The case is the same here, for unlawfulness of consideration of report of an evil-doer without investigation because one is not safe from unwittingly afflicting does not denote obligation of consideration of whatsoever is safeguarded from that. In other words, such argumentation in the verse denotes that unwittingly afflicting is an obstacle to effectiveness of origin of authority of a report, but does not denote that origin of authority exists in whatsoever in which no obstacle lies. Lack of obstacle in celebrity does not necessitate existence of origin of authority in it.

As for authority of single report of a righteous-trustworthy person, it was not inferred from generality of argumentation, but rather from implicature of condition whose authority is a matter of certainty.

*****

It is quite well-known that great scholars do not dear oppose celebrity unless with a strong, clear proof which makes them confident in their diverging from celebrity. They usually insist on following the celebrity and finding a proof in favor of it, even though the contrary proof may be stronger. This is not because of imitation or belief in the authority of celebrity, but rather due to honoring opinions of great scholars.

This is a common point in all kinds of science and art, for to oppose majority of men of research in any branch of knowledge is not that easy, except when there exists a strong proof and motivation. A fair-minded scholar always treats himself as being wrong in comparison with the celebrity and is afraid of being in double ignorance, especially when the opinion of celebrity is in accordance with the precaution in religious affairs.

CHAPTER 19

THE CUSTOM *(AL-SĪRA)*

By the custom is meant continuity of practical conduct of people to do or to leave something. By people, in turn, is meant either all people of every folk and creed, whether Muslim or non-Muslim – this custom being called "the custom of the wise (*sīra al-'uqalā'*)" and by recent *Uṣūlīs* "the conduct of the wise (*binā' al-'uqalā'*)" – or only Muslims as they are Muslims or a specific sect of Muslims such as Shī'a – this custom being called "the custom of the people of the religion (*sīra al-mutasharri'a*)," or "the religious custom (*al-sīra al-shar'iyya*)," or "the Islamic custom (*al-sīra al-Islāmiyya*)." Since the discussion differs in kind as to those two customs, we deal with them separately.

Authority of the Conduct of the Wise

The proof called "the conduct of the wise (*binā' al-'uqalā'*)" consists of two premises:

1. The wise as they are the wise (i.e., human beings as they are intellectual beings and not as they are animate creatures with some emotions, desires, customs, and the like) have such a practical conduct. This reveals that such a conduct is originated by the intellect and not other human faculties.
2. The divine lawgiver has not prohibited from following that conduct. This reveals that He has recognized that conduct; for He is among the wise, even chief of the wise and creator of the intellect, and therefore has no other judgment.

The conclusion is that the divine lawgiver has confirmed that conduct and has had no other way in this connection; otherwise, He would have announced and depicted His specific way ordering believers to follow it.

It should be noted, however, that the divine lawgiver's agreement with the conduct of the wise could not be discovered merely through His prohibition not being proved, but rather there must exist some conditions so that one may deduce the divine lawgiver's agreement with a conduct of the wise:

2.1. There should not be a problem with the divine lawgiver having the same conduct and way. Should the divine lawgiver having the same conduct and way be impossible, agreement of the divine lawgiver cannot be discovered from His prohibition not being proved – as is the case with referring to experts such as lexicographers, for need of the divine lawgiver to experts is nonsensical and makes no sense so that He may have a practical conduct in this connection.
2.2. Should the divine lawgiver having the same conduct and way be impossible, it must be proved that the practical conduct has been prevalent even as to religious affairs in the time of infallible-innocent personalities so that one can infer their acknowledgment from their silence and deduce that the divine lawgiver has been in agreement with the wise. This is the case with, for example, the principle of continuity of the previous state (*aṣāla al-istiṣĥāb*) which is an authoritative proof in the case of doubt about the previous state; for, on the one hand, it is nonsensical that the divine lawgiver should doubt about persistence of His precept, and, on the other hand, the conduct of the wise as to consideration of the previous state has been prevalent in religious affairs. Now, since the conduct of the wise has been prevalent even in religious affairs and the divine lawgiver has not prohibited from that, we can deduce that He has confirmed the conduct in question.
2.3. Should the divine lawgiver having the same conduct and way be impossible while neither of the two previously mentioned conditions exists, there must be a specific, definite proof announcing agreement and confirmation of the divine lawgiver. Otherwise, agreement of the divine lawgiver with the conduct is merely a conjecture, and "Surely conjecture avails naught against truth." (Qur., 10:36)

In other words, in any custom of the wise, the divine lawgiver (2.3.1.) is either expected to be in agreement with the wise since there is no problem with that, as in the case of single report,(2.3.2.) or is not expected to be in such agreement because of existing a problem, as in the case of the principle of continuity of the previous state (*aṣāla al-istiṣĥāb*).

If the former, if it is proved that the divine lawgiver has prohibited from the conduct, that conduct is definitely not of authority, and if not, it is definitely discovered that He is in agreement with the wise. For He is among the wise, even chief of the wise and creator of the intellect; had He not confirmed that conduct having a specific way in this connection other than that of the wise, He would have announced and depicted that way prohibiting believers from following their own conduct.

If the latter, (2.3.2.1.) it is either known that the conduct of the wise as to its consideration has been prevalent in religious affairs, as is the case with *istiṣḥāb*, or (2.3.2.2.) that is not known, as is the case with referring to experts for meanings of words.

In (2.3.2.1.), the very lack of establishment of divine lawgiver's prohibition from that custom is sufficient for discovering His agreement with the wise, for that is something He cares about. Had He not confirmed that while that custom is observed by His vicegerent, He would have prohibited duty-bounds from following that custom and conveyed that prohibition to them in any way possible. Thus, the very lack of establishment of prohibition reveals His agreement, for it is obviously clear that an actual prohibition which is not conveyed to and has not reached duty-bounds cannot be regarded an actual, authoritative prohibition.

As for (2.3.2.2.), the very lack of establishment of divine lawgiver's prohibition from that custom is not sufficient to reveal His agreement, for it is probable that He has prohibited the wise from that custom in religious affairs and they did not do so, or they may have arbitrarily not followed that custom in religious affairs and it is not upon the divine lawgiver to prohibit them from following that custom in irreligious affairs – had He not confirmed that in such affairs. That is why we are in need of a specific, definite proof in order to take such custom into consideration in religious affairs.

Authority of the Custom of the People of the Religion

The custom of the people of the religion, i.e., Muslims, to do or to eschew something is in fact a kind of consensus. It is even the highest level consensus, for it is an actual consensus of all Muslims while consensus on verdicts is a literal one and made only by scholars.

Such conduct is of two kinds, for it is sometimes known that it has been prevalent in the time of infallible personalities in such a way that the infallible personality has exercised, or, at least, confirmed it, and sometimes that is not known or it is known that such custom has appeared after infallible personalities' time.

If the former, that custom is undoubtedly a definite, authoritative proof of agreement of the divine lawgiver and is, *per se*, an indicator of religious precepts. It is this point that differentiates between custom of the people of the religion and custom of the wise; for the latter is in need of another proof proving its confirmation by the divine lawgiver, even though through lack of establishment of His prohibition.

As for the latter, there is no way to rely on that for discovering agreement of infallible personalities in a certain manner, as was the case with consensus. The case is even worse and lower with this one, as will be explained. Consideration of the way customs take shape in human communities, including Muslims', clarifies the influence of irreligious habits on human emotions: some influential person does something in order to satisfy his own desires or for some other reason such as imitating other cultures, then comes someone else who follows the first, and thereby the act continues and gradually becomes prevalent among people without there being someone who prohibits them from that wrong act because of neglectfulness, heedlessness, fear, and the like. That act is conveyed by the first generation to the second and other coming generations and becomes a custom of Muslims. In this case, should someone cast doubts upon that custom, which has become sacred with the passage of time, and blame Muslims because of their heedlessness, he would definitely be treated as someone against the Islamic laws and customs.

That is why we cannot treat present Muslim customs as being present in early Islam; and when we doubt authority of something we have to treat it as unauthorized, for there is no authority but through knowledge and certainty.

As for the extent of an authorized custom of the people of the religion, it proves lawfulness of something if it is a custom of doing, and lawfulness of eschewing and lack of obligation if it is a custom of eschewal. There is no denotation of obligation or unlawfulness, even preference or disapproval, in any custom of doing or eschewing; for the act is, *per se*, ambiguous having no denotation more than lawfulness of doing or eschewing.

CHAPTER 20

THE (JURISTIC) ANALOGY *(AL- QIYĀS)*

Qiyās, to be defined precisely later, is a matter of major dispute among Muslim scholars of different sects. Following their infallible-innocent Imāms, Shī'a scholars have denied its authority; and among Sunnī sects, followers of Dāwūd b. Khalaf, called al-Żāhiriyya, and Ĥanbalīs hold the same. The first one who took the analogy into consideration and used it widely was Abū Ĥanīfa (in the second Hijri century). That method, however, was later on adopted by Shāfi'īs and Mālikīs and used by some in such an extremist way that they preferred it to the consensus and rejected some *ĥadīths* by it.

Definition of *Qiyās*

Qiyās is defined variously the best of which being "establishment of a precept for something by a motive (*al-'illa*) because of its establishment for something else by that motive." The first thing is called "subordinate (*al-far'*)," the second "principle (*al-aṣl*)," and the common motive "encompassing (*al-djāmi'*)." In fact, *qiyās* is a function performed by the arguer in order to infer a juristic precept for something whose precept is not depicted by the divine lawgiver inasmuch as such a function provokes certainty or conjecture as to the precept of that thing. This function is the very predication of the subordinate upon the principle with regard to the proved precept of the principle through which the arguer grants the same precept to the subordinate – if obligation, obligation; if unlawfulness, unlawfulness; and so forth – in the sense that he argues that the subordinate should have the same precept with the principle because of commonness of the motive. Thus, that arguer's function becomes a proof of religious precepts, since it provokes certainty or conjecture that the divine lawgiver has the same judgment.

Pillars of *Qiyās*

From what said earlier, we can conclude that *Qiyās* has four pillars:

1. The principle (*al-aṣl*), something whose precept is known,
2. The subordinate (*al-far'*), something whose precept is to be discovered,
3. The motive (*al-'illa*), also called the encompassing (*al-djāmi'*), the common facet between the principle and subordinate which necessitates establishment of the precept, and
4. The precept (*al-ḥukm*), the kind of precept which is proved for the principle and is to be proved for the subordinate.

Authority of *Qiyās*

It was frequently said that authority of any conjectural proof is due to knowledge. Thus, *qiyās*, like all other conjectural proofs, would not be an authoritative proof except in the two following states:

1. It *per se* provokes knowledge of the precept, or
2. There is a definite proof which proves its authority.

Provoking Knowledge

Juristic *qiyās* is an analogy, and it is proved in the science of logic that analogy provokes nothing but probability; for similarity of two things in something, even in many things, does not necessitate their similarity in all aspects and properties. Yea, when aspects of similarity between the principle and the subordinate become more and stronger, probability becomes stronger and may reach the level of conjecture – but never that of certainty and knowledge – and, as frequently emphasized, conjecture avails naught against truth.

Of course, should we know, no matter through which way, that the similarity aspect is the complete cause for the precept in the principle with the divine lawgiver on the one hand and that the same complete cause with all of its properties exists in the subordinate on the other, we would definitely know that the subordinate has the same precept; for this is not juristic analogy, but rather logical syllogism which definitely provokes certainty and knowledge. However, the problem is that we have no way to discover that the encompassing is the complete cause of the precept. It was thoroughly discussed in chapter 16 that canons of precepts cannot be captured by intellects and the only way to know them is to hear from the person appointed by the Almighty to deliver precepts to people. The only intellectual way to canons of precepts is intellectual implication, and juristic analogy makes no intellectual implication as to the principle and the subordinate.

Definite Proofs Proving Authority of *Qiyās*

Followers of *qiyās* have argued the Book, *Sunna*, consensus, and the intellect for proving authority of *qiyās*. However, all such proofs are nullified even by some Sunnī scholars, such as Ibn Ĥazm in his book *Ibṭāl al-Qiyās*. Since dealing with such proofs and their nullification is beyond the level of an introductory work on the one hand and Shiite position on *qiyās* will be clarified in the coming discussion on the other, we will not deal with them.

Shiite Position on *Qiyās*

Following Ahl al-Bayt, Shī'a scholars have absolutely denied authority of *qiyās*, for it provokes nothing but conjecture (which, according to the Qur'ān (10: 36), avails naught against truth) on the one hand and no acceptable, definite proof is argued to support it on the other. One *ĥadīth* will suffice to present Shiite position on *qiyās*:

Abān b. Taghlib narrates that he asked Imām Dja'far al-Sādiq (the sixth Imām), "What do you say on compensation of a woman's finger cut by a man?"

Imām replied, "Ten camels."
I asked, "Two fingers?"
Imām replied, "Twenty."
I asked, "Three?"
Imām replied, "Thirty."
I asked, "Four?"
Imām replied, "Twenty."

Being astonished, I asked, "A man cuts three fingers of a woman and gives thirty camels but cuts four fingers and gives twenty?! We heard this when we were in Irāq and we used to say one who said this was Satan!"

Imām replied, "Calm down Abān! This is the holy Prophet's judgment that woman equals man up to the third of compensation, but when it comes to the third hers becomes half. O Abān, you are arguing *qiyās*, while arguing *qiyās* against *Sunna* obliterates the latter."(al-Kulainī, 7:300)

CHAPTER 21

EQUILIBRIUM AND PREFRENCES
(*AL-TA'ĀDUL WA'L TARĀḎJĪĤ*)

This chapter deals with the question of contradiction of proofs. By equilibrium in the title is meant that two proofs are equal in whatsoever necessitating preference of one to another, and by preferences is meant whatsoever necessitating preference of one to another where they are not equal – by infinitive being meant subject in the latter, i.e., preferrer.

Since incompatibility of proofs is of various kinds, we have to discuss them separately.

Contradiction (*al-Ta'āruḍ*)

Contradiction between two proofs occurs where either of them nullifies and repudiates the other. Such repudiation is either in all denotations or some of them, in such a way that assumption of subsistence of authority of either of them along with that of the other is impossible and one cannot act in accordance with both of them.

Conditions of Contradiction

Contradiction of proofs occurs only where the following conditions exist:

1. Neither of two proofs being definite; for should one of them be definite untruth of the other would be revealed, and it is obviously clear that untrue cannot contradict true. As for both of them being definite, it is absolutely impossible.
2. Actual conjecture not being considered in the authority of both, since actualization of actual conjecture as to two contradictory proofs is also impossible. Of course, actual conjecture may be taken into consideration

particularly in one of them.

3. Denotations of two proofs contradicting one another, even though in parallel and in some aspects, so that mutual repudiation may occur. The criterion is that they would result in what cannot religiously be made and is impossible in the actuality, even though such impossibility being caused by something outside of their very denotations; as is the case with contradiction of proofs of obligation of Friday prayers and that of obligation of żuhr prayers on Friday, since there is no contradiction between those two proofs *per se* inasmuch as conjunction of obligation of two prayers in a specific time is not impossible, but as it is known through another proof that only one prayers is obligatory at a given time they repudiate one another.

4. Either of two proofs possessing conditions of authority, in the sense that either of them is an authoritative proof whose following is mandatory if there appears no contradictory proof – though one unspecified proof would become unauthorized as soon as contradiction occurs.

5. Relation of two proofs not being that of interference, as will be explained later.

6. Relation of two proofs not being that of sovereignty, as will be explained later.

7. Relation of two proofs not being that of entry, as will be explained later.

Primary Principle as to Contradictory Proofs

The primary principle as to contradictory proofs is mutual falling (*al-tasāquṭ*), i.e., neither of two proofs may be treated as an authoritative proof – though the secondary principle is option, as will be explained later. For contradiction causes mutual repudiation and leads to non-actuality of one unspecified proof, i.e., either of them becoming obstacle to actuality of the other; hence, neither of them will possess constituents of actual authority so that it may make the actuality incontrovertible and mandatory. That is why they both become unauthorized. However, should one of them be endowed with a preferrer, as will be explained later, it is that one which must be taken.

Secondary Principle as to Contradictory Proofs

Although the primary principle as to the contradictory proofs is mutual falling, there are so many *ḥadīth*s revealing another principle in this connection. Shiite scholars, however, disagree on what is inferred from such *ḥadīth*s and hold three opinions:

1. Option as to taking either of them. This is the celebrated opinion, and even allegedly a matter of consensus.
2. To cease and follow the way of precaution.
3. Obligation of taking the one which accords with the precaution, and if neither of them is so one will have the option to take either of them.

As for the option, it should be noted that it is a primary and not a continuous one, in the sense that one is merely allowed to choose one of the two contradictory *ḥadīth*s at the beginning, but one should follow it afterwards and has no option any more.

Customary Gathering (*al-Djam' al-'Urfī*)

By gathering is meant taking two proofs altogether. It is an intellectual judgment that taking two seemingly contradictory proofs altogether is more plausible than leaving either of them. This judgment is due to the fact that contradiction does not occur unless all constituents of authority exist in either of them as to both chain of transmission and denotation, as was mentioned earlier. In case of existence of all constituents of authority, i.e., existence of the origin, nothing may cause leaving the proof but existence of an impediment to the efficacy of the origin; and that impediment can be nothing but their mutual repudiation. On the other hand, possibility of gathering both proofs as to their denotations leaves no room for certainty of their mutual repudiation, which leads to lack of certainty as to the existence of impediment to the efficacy of authority with regard to the proof. Thus, how can one judge that one or both of those proofs is no longer authoritative proof?

However, it should be noted that such judgment of the intellect is not absolute, but rather is conditional upon the gathering being "customary" or "acceptable," in the sense that it should not be in a way that custom of people of the language does not confirm it on the one hand and no third proof supports it on the other.

Preferrers

According to *ḥadīth*s, if one of the two contradictory proofs is endowed with a preferrer, it should definitely be taken; but what the preferrers are is a matter of dispute. That dispute is beyond the level of an introductory work; hence, we merely mention that preferrers include such affairs as being in accordance with celebrity, conforming to the holy Qur'ān, not being uttered due to dissimulation, positive qualities of transmitters, and the like.

Interference (*al-Tazāḥum*)

What differentiates between contradiction and interference is that in the former the two proofs repudiate one another in the position of lawgiving while in the latter they are not so and it is the duty-bound who cannot take both of them in the position of obedience, such as the case where someone is going to be drowned and the only way to save him is an expropriated land. Here, there is no contradiction between "Do not expropriate" and "Save one who is going to be drowned" in the position of lawgiving at all. However, the duty-bound cannot take both of them in the position of obedience; he should eschew either the command or the prohibition.

The intellectual judgment in such cases is option: since taking both proofs is not possible, eschewing both of them is unlawful, there is no preferrer in this connection, and preferring without any preference is impossible, there remains no way but to leave the way of obedience in hands of the duty-bound inasmuch as subsistence of actual burden in either of them is impossible on the one hand and nothing exists to cause removal of burden in both of them on the other. Since this judgment is among independent intellectual judgments, it reveals agreement of the divine lawgiver in this connection.

The important point, however, is to find out what the preferrers as to the interference are. It is obviously clear that preferrers should refer to the importance of one of the two proofs in the view of divine lawgiver: what is more important in His view is the one which should be given priority. But how can one find which of the two proofs is more important? Here, we mention some criteria for that:

1. Where one of the proofs has no substitutes while the other has some. In case of interference, what has no substitute is doubtlessly more important than the one having some; for the divine lawgiver has permitted to eschew the one with substitute and observe its substitute in case of compulsion while He has not permitted that as to the one without substitute. Hence, to give the one with substitute priority over the one without substitute causes elimination of the latter while to give the latter priority over the former

leads to taking both burdens altogether in the position of obedience.

2. Where one of the proofs is constricted or urgent while the other is not so, such as purification of the polluted mosque (which is urgent) and performing prayers while there is still time. It is obviously clear, as was the case with the previous state, that giving the constricted or urgent duty priority over the other leads to taking both burdens altogether in the position of obedience while giving the latter, which has a vertical substitute, priority over the former causes elimination of the former.

3. Where one of the proofs has a specific time while the other is not so while both of them are constricted, such as performing daily prayers in the last part of their time and performing prayers of eclipse also in the last part of its time. Since daily prayers are of specified time in their very law-making, they are to be given priority over prayers of eclipse – which is not of specified time in its very law-making and has accidentally encountered shortage of time.

4. Where one of the proofs should be given priority due to its importance being obviously known in Islam, such as what concerns people's rights especially their blood, and what is a pillar (*rukn*) in an act of worship.

Sovereignty (*al-Ĥukūma*) and Entry (*al-Wurūd*)

By *sovereignty* is meant a case where one of the two proofs is supposed to be given priority over the other because of its sovereignty while both of them are still authoritative proofs, i.e., neither of them repudiates the other. (Examples will be given where differences are expounded.)

"Entry" is used for a case where something is not included in something else – in a real manner, but through depiction of the divine lawgiver and not existentially – like the relation between authoritative conjectural proof (*amāra*) and such intellectual practical principles as clearance and option. As you remember, the object of intellectual principle of clearance is "lack of depiction," while the proof which makes the conjectural proof authoritative treats it as depiction – through declaration of the divine lawgiver – and thereby the object of intellectual principle of clearance is removed by such divine declaration. Also, the object of practical principle of option is perplexity, while the authoritative conjectural proof, because of the proof which has made it authoritative, makes one part preferable and thereby removes perplexity.

Thus, the difference between sovereignty and entry is that in the latter one proof really removes the object of the other, though through divine declaration, while in the former no proof removes the other's denotation in a real manner; the removal is figurative and because of treating what is denoted by the divine declaration as an existent affair.

In order to make differences of four apparently similar expressions of *al-ĥukūma, al-wurūd, al-takhṣīṣ*, and *al-takhaṣṣuṣ*, let us take one sample of the command "Revere Muslim scholars" and the prohibition "Do not revere impious Muslim scholars" in some different ways:

Should a certain Zayd not be a Muslim scholar, Zayd would obviously not be supposed to be revered. This is *takhaṣṣuṣ* (non-inclusion), since Zayd is *really* and *existentially* not included in the object.

Should that Zayd be a Muslim scholar but an impious one, he would be supposed to be revered if there were no prohibitions, since he is included in Muslim scholars. However, taking both the command and the prohibition necessitates that he should not be revered, for he is impious. This is *takhṣīṣ* (restriction), which restricts revering to the pious Muslim scholars.

Thus, *takhaṣṣuṣ* is *non-inclusion* in the *object* while *takhṣīṣ* is *expelling* from the *judgment.*

Now, suppose that a certain Bakr is a lay but pious man. If a predicative sentence such as "Lay but pious people are scholars" is declared, Bakr is included in the command of revering scholars and should be revered while he is not a scholar. This is ĥukūma. If a predicative sentence such as "An impious person is not a scholar" is declared, that Zayd who was an impious scholar is removed from the command of revering scholars and should not be revered while he is a scholar. This is another kind of *ĥukūma.* Thus, ĥukūma is inclusion or exclusion of something in or from an object by a *predicative sentence* through expanding or limiting realm of the object or subject.

Part IV

The Practical Principles

Introduction

Doubtless every follower of the religion knows, in summary fashion, that there are some divine obligatory precepts, whether compulsory or unlawful, that all duty-bounds, whether knowledgeable or ignorant, must observe. Such knowledge in summary fashion makes actual, obligatory duties incontrovertible; and since the intellect necessitates clarification of one's obligation it becomes obligatory for duty-bounds to struggle for seeking knowledge of such duties through a reliable way whose following should make them certain of clearance from liability. That is why we believe in the obligation of knowledge-seeking in the one hand and of the quest for proofs of such duties on the other.

However, knowledge-seeking does not lead to precept finding in all probable cases; that is why the duty-bound may sometimes doubt what his duty is and wonder what to do. The divine lawgiver has taken such cases into consideration and made some practical duties for him in order to refer to them when necessary and act in accordance with them to become certain that he will not be punished in the hereafter because of negligence in performing his duties.

Uṣūlīs have realized that such duties, which are general and not peculiar to certain parts of jurisprudence, are of four kinds: the principle of clearance from liability (*aṣāla al-barā'a*), the principle of precaution or liability (*aṣāla al-iḥtiyāṭ* or *ishtighāl*), the principle of option (*aṣāla al-takhyīr*), and the principle of continuity of the previous state (*aṣāla al-istiṣḥāb*). That is realized because doubt is generally of two kinds:

1. The doubtful has a previous state while that state is taken into consideration by the divine lawgiver; this is the position of principle of continuity of the previous state,
2. The doubtful does not have a previous state or that state is not taken into consideration by the divine lawgiver, and this is, in turn, of three kinds:
   2.1. The duty is absolutely unknown, i.e., it is not known even generically; this is the position of the principle of clearance from liability,
   2.2. The duty is known in summary fashion while precaution is possible; this is the position of principle of precaution or liability, and
   2.3. The duty is known in summary fashion while precaution is not

possible; and this is the position of principle of option.

Before dealing with any of those principles in detail, we have to mention some general points as to the practical principles:

1. By doubt is meant both real doubt, i.e., a case wherein both sides are equal, and the invalid conjecture; for the latter is treated as the former. In fact, the latter is really a kind of the former, for perplexity of the duty-bound will not be removed by following it and he remains doubtful whether or not he has cleared his obligation.

2. To doubt something with regard to its precepts is of two kinds:

2.1. The doubt is an object of the actual precept, such as doubting *rak'as* of the prayers, for it sometimes causes change of the real precept into separate *rak'as*.

2.2. The doubt is an object of apparent precept. It is this kind that is the matter of discussion here.

3. It should be emphasized that referring to practical principles is allowed only when the jurist has quested for the authorized conjectural proof of the precept which is the matter of dubiety and despaired of finding it. Thus, there would be no room for exercising practical proofs where the quest is possible and existence of an authorized conjectural proof is probable. The quest and despair in this connection is a matter of must for jurists, for knowing and learning precepts are obligatory. That is why the jurist would not be excused should he oppose an actual duty by exercising a practical principle, especially that of clearance.

4. It has been customary to open this part by discussing the principle of clearance – because, perhaps, it has been the major dispute between *Uṣūlīs* and *Akhbārīs*. Here, we follow the same pattern.

CHAPTER 22

THE PRINCIPLE OF CLEARANCE *(AṢĀLA AL-BARĀ'A)*

It should preliminarily be noted that the doubt as to its object, i.e., the doubtful, is of two kinds: the doubtful is a universal precept, such as doubting whether smoking is unlawful or it nullifies fasting, which is called "the dubiety concerning the precept *(al-shubha al-ḥukmiyya)*," and the doubtful is an objective affair, such as purity of certain water or whether a certain liquid is wine or vinegar, which is called "the dubiety concerning the object *(al-shubha al-mawḍū'iyya)*." Since on the one hand the former may be caused by "lack of proof," "ambiguity of proof," or "contradiction of proofs" and on the other hand the dubiety in both of them is either concerning obligation or unlawfulness, we will have eight separate topics in this connection. However, since the discussion on the dubiety as to obligation is secondary to that as to unlawfulness without any differences, we will deal with the problem in question in the five following discourses: (1) the dubiety concerning the precept as to unlawfulness because of lack of proof, (2) the dubiety concerning the precept as to unlawfulness because of ambiguity of proof, (3) the dubiety concerning the precept as to unlawfulness because of contradiction of proofs, (4) the dubiety concerning the object as to unlawfulness, and (5) the dubiety concerning the precept as to obligation because of lack of proof, because of ambiguity of proof, because of contradiction of proofs, and concerning the object.

1. The Dubiety concerning the Precept as to Unlawfulness Because of Lack of the Proof

Generally speaking, there are two opinions in this connection: non-obligation of precaution by eschewing the act, and obligation of precaution by eschewing the act; the former being declared by *Uṣūlīs* and the latter by *Akhbārīs*. In order to prove their opinions, *Uṣūlīs* have argued the four-fold proofs, i.e., the Book,

Sunna, consensus, and intellect first and nullified *Akhbārīs'* proofs secondly.

1.1. *Uṣūlīs'* Proofs of Clearance

1.1.1. The Book

1.1.1.1. The verse 7 of *sūra* 65: "God charges no soul (with a burden) save with what He has given him." To argue this, it is asserted that by "what" is meant the burden, and to give something is due to the thing given. To give a burden is to depict it; hence, as clearly emphasized in the verse, God will charge no soul with a burden which He has not depicted.

To that argumentation, it is replied that by "what" two other meanings, i.e., "possession" and "the sheer doing or abandoning something," may be meant as well, and this prevents from predicating "what" upon the burden and arguing the verse for the clearance. Should the first be meant – and it is supported by contextual evidence, which is the previous phrase of the verse: "Let the man of plenty expend out of his plenty; as for him whose provision is stinted to him, let him expend of what God has given him" – the phrase would mean that God charges no soul with the burden of expending money save the possession He has given him. Should the second be meant, the phrase would mean that God charges no soul save to its capacity (as mentioned in some other verses such as 2: 286). Any attempt for gathering those three meanings in one word would be in vain, for there is no encompassing word to cover all of them. Furthermore, consideration of burden as the meaning of "what" will not solve the problem; as depiction is attributed to God, it is apparent in depicting through usual means, i.e., revelation and sending prophets – something happened. This that some precepts are not delivered to us because of evil-doing of some unrighteous people in the past does not mean lack of depiction by the Almighty.

1.1.1.2. The verse 15 of *sūra* 17: "We have never been to chastise, until We send forth a Messenger." To argue this, it is asserted that to send a messenger is an allusion to depicting precepts to duty-bounds. Thus, God will not punish duty-bounds because of opposing unknown burdens before they are depicted to them – and this is obviously "clearance."

To that argumentation, it is replied that the phrase explicitly conveys negation of this-worldly chastisements of previous peoples and not chastisement in the hereafter which is the matter of dispute here. Thus, there is no such denotation in the verse in question.

CONCLUSION. Although some other verses are argued in this connection, none of them can prove clearance – as admitted by men of research among *Uṣūlīs* and shown in the two examples mentioned above.

1.1.2. *Sunna*

There are some ten *ḥadīths* argued in this connection. However, we discuss only one of them known as the prophetic *ḥadīth* of Removal (*al-Raf'*):

"Nine things are removed from my people: error, forgetfulness, what they have done under duress, *what they do not know*, what they cannot endure, what they have done under compulsion, to take as a bad omen, jealousy, to think of createdness [of the Almighty] so long as one has not uttered it."

The preliminary discussion. To argue this *ḥadīth* for the clearance, it is usually asserted that (a) removal is not used in its literal sense in the *ḥadīth*, for those affairs *do* exist among Muslims, (b) in order for the speech not to be a lie we should consider something as omitted – as necessitated by the denotation of necessitation, and (c) that thing could be (c.1.) all effects in all nine phrases, (c.2.) the apparent effect in each phrase, or (c.3.) reproach in all nine phrases. Then, it is usually discussed at length which of the three probabilities mentioned above should be adopted.

On the other hand, some *Uṣūlīs* have argued that removal in the *ḥadīth* should mean repelling, either figuratively, or literally – since removal, at the plane of its occurrence, is also literally repelling, for it repels efficacy of origin of something as to subsistence of that thing in the moment subsequent to its origination.

However, neither of those two argumentations is sound. The first is not so because one is allowed to refer to the denotation of necessitation only when such thing is necessary, while it will be clarified that the removal is used in its literal sense in the *ḥadīth* without occurrence of any lie. As for the second, its annulment will be known through consideration of the difference between removal and repelling.

In order to approach the *ḥadīth* in an appropriate way, we should consider the difference between removal and repelling first. Doubtless, removal occurs as to something which exists, that is why assumption of existence of the removed thing in an earlier time or plane is necessary – the removed thing exits even though the removal has not occurred yet – while in the literal usage of repelling nothing is considered but its being subsequent to the existence of origin of something, for repelling is preventing from efficacy of origin of something as to its actualization. Thus, both removal and repelling are supposed to be considered only when existence of origin of something is already assumed, but they differ from one another as to need for assumption of prior existence of the effect. In the former, it is assumed that the origin has affected that thing in an earlier time or plane, while what is considered in the latter is preventing from efficacy of the origin in the same time or plane. Of course, the actual existence of the removed thing is not necessary in veraciousness of literal usage of removal; rather, its allegedly existence, even though by consideration of existence of its origin, is sufficient, for the wise consider existence of origin of something as existence of that thing and treat it as if it exists.

It becomes clear, then, that there is no problem with predicating the removal in the *ḥadīth* upon its literal meaning in all nine affairs, since the sheer consideration of existence of something prior to the removal – when its origin does exist – is sufficient for veraciousness of usage of removal. Thus, removal in the *ḥadīth* means that canons (*milākāt al-aḥkām*), in spite of existence of their origins, are repelled as to efficacy in making such precepts for such affairs, because of *grace-bestowing* upon Muslims. However, repelling as to efficacy in making precepts differs with regard to the nine-fold affairs, since (a) in "taking as a bad omen, jealousy, and thinking of createdness [of the Almighty]" it is as to precept making, (b) in "error, forgetfulness, what they have done under duress, what they cannot endure, and what they have done under compulsion" it is as to inclusion of them in generality and absoluteness of precepts (whose result would be peculiarity of precepts to other than such things), and (c) in "what they do not know" is as to making the precaution obligatory despite the fact that canons necessitate such obligation, i.e., canons necessitate making precaution with regard to probable duties obligatory, but *ḥadīth* of removal declares that origins of precepts are repelled as to efficacy in making the precaution obligatory – because of grace-bestowing upon Muslims.

It should be noted in this connection that:

1. Effects removed by *ḥadīth* of removal should be qualified by neither "existence" nor "non-existence" of those affairs; for should they be qualified by existence of such affairs (as in the obligation of penance in "homicide in error") the effect cannot be removed in case of occurrence of that affair, for it causes self-contradiction (what is considered the object of precept is not the object, and this is absurd) – the object of an effect requires existence of that effect and cannot cause its non-existence – and should they be qualified by non-existence of such affairs their removal would be due to removal of the

object and not because of the *ḥadīth* (as in retaliation in case of "intentional homicide" which is qualified by non-existence of error; if homicide is caused by error the object of retaliation, i.e., intention and non-existence of error, is automatically removed).

2. As *ḥadīth* of removal declares God's grace-bestowing upon Muslims, any affair whose removal contradicts grace-bestowing is not removed. For instance, although a "compelling contract" is done under compulsion, it is valid, for one who sells his property under compulsion is in an urgent need, and if his contract is treated as null and void his situation becomes worse – something contrary to grace-bestowing.

3. What is removed in "jealousy" and "thinking of createdness [of the Almighty] so long as one has not uttered it" is their unlawfulness, which would have been made should grace-bestowing not be declared; and what is removed in "taking as a bad omen" is unlawfulness of quitting something because of a bad omen: although people should not quit anything because of a bad omen, *ḥadīth* of removal declares that they have not committed a sin if they do so. By removal in "error, forgetfulness, what they have done under duress, and what they have done under compulsion" is meant that whatsoever done in such cases has no religious effect and is considered null.

The primary discussion: how ḥadīth of removal denotes clearance. There is no dispute that the *ḥadīth* denotes clearance with regard to the dubiety concerning the object. Therefore, should one doubt whether certain water is pure, one would treat that water as pure, and should one doubt whether certain liquid is wine or vinegar, one would be allowed to drink it.

The matter of dispute is whether the *ḥadīth* includes the dubiety concerning the precept as well so that when one lacks knowledge of unlawfulness of certain thing, because it has no precedent in early Islam and there is no proof in favor of it in the sources, one is allowed to do it according to the principle of clearance.

Those who oppose such inclusion argue that on the one hand contextual coherence necessitates that by "what they do not know" should be meant the doubtful *object* and not precept, since by the relative pronoun in "what they have done under duress," "what they cannot endure," and "what they have done under compulsion," is meant the act that they have done under duress, they cannot endure, or they have done under compulsion; hence, by the relative pronoun in "what they do not know" should also be meant an act which is doubtful, such as a specific drinking which is not known whether it is wine or vinegar drinking. On the other hand, there is no inclusive affair capable of encompassing both the dubiety concerning the precept and the dubiety concerning the object – so that we may consider that by the relative pronoun is meant that inclusive affair – for what is removed in the dubiety concerning the precept is the very object of ignorance, i.e., the unknown actual precept, and attribution of removal to it is of attribution of something to what it is for, while the object of ignorance in the dubiety concerning the object is primarily the external thing and only secondarily the religious precept, and since the external thing is not removable by itself attribution of removal to it would be of attribution of something to other than what it is for – and these two cannot be both used in one usage and one attribution. Now, which of them should be preferred? The answer is "the doubtful object," for, although the attribution is apparent in being directed to what it is for and this gives priority to dubieties concerning precepts, contextual coherence, which is a stronger appearance than that appearance, necessitates peculiarity of the relative pronoun to dubieties concerning objects.

To the first argumentation, *Uṣūlīs* have replied that there is no such contextual coherence in the *ḥadīth*, for "to take as a bad omen, jealousy, and to think of createdness [of the Almighty]" are included in it while it is obviously clear that by them the act is not meant. As for the second argumentation, it can be said that by the relative pronoun in "what they do not know" is meant "the religious unknown precept in an absolute sense" which includes both dubieties concerning precepts and objects, since there is no difference between those two dubieties but that the origin of doubt in dubieties concerning precepts is lack or ambiguity of proof while in dubieties concerning objects it is external things, and difference in the origin of doubt makes no difference in attribution of removal to the relative pronoun.

Thus, one can argue the *ḥadīth* of removal in order to prove clearance in cases of probability of unlawfulness against those who believe that in such cases the duty-bound is supposed to follow the way of precaution. However, it should be noted that the principle of clearance can be exercised only after the quest for all probable proofs and despair of finding any; no one is allowed to act in accordance with that principle before the quest and despair.

1.1.3. Consensus

Although some *Uṣūlīs* have attempted to present some ways to prove that there is a consensus among Shī'a scholars on the clearance, all such attempts are in vain, for *Akhbārīs* are obviously against that claim and emphatically insist that duty-bounds must follow the way of precaution and avoid doing anything whose unlawfulness is probable.

1.1.4. The Intellect

The intellect undoubtedly judges that punishment without depiction is reprehensible. In other words, it judges independently, without any need to religious judgments, that it is reprehensible to reproach and punish someone without there being a depiction available to him – of course when he has made a thorough quest for probable existing proofs but has found nothing. This intellectual rule, which cannot be a matter of dispute and is accepted by *Akhbārīs* as well, is the major premise of a syllogism which proves clearance: there is no depiction with regard to the dubiety concerning the precept as to unlawfulness where there is no proof (the minor premise), punishment without depiction is reprehensible (the major premise), then, there would be no punishment should one not avoid such dubiety. As mentioned above, the major premise cannot be a matter of dispute; it is the minor premise which is disputed: *Akhbārīs* claim that proofs proving obligation of precaution are to be considered as depiction. That is why *Uṣūlīs* should nullify proofs argued by *Akhbārīs* as to obligation of precaution so that they can argue this intellectual proof.

On the other hand, there is another intellectual proof in this connection argued by *Akhbārīs* for proving obligation of precaution: obligation of repelling the probable harm. According to this rule, there is a probable harm in doing the dubiety concerning the precept as to unlawfulness where there exits no proof (the minor premise), repelling the probable harm is obligatory (the major premise), then, to avoid the dubiety concerning the precept as to unlawfulness in case of lack of proof is obligatory.

Since these two intellectual proofs seem to contradict each other, we have to find out which of them should be given priority over the other. It should be noted that the subject matter of the former is "lack of depiction" and that of the latter is "the probable harm."

In order to prove intellectual obligation of precaution, it is said that the relation between those two rules is entry on the part of latter, since it is a depiction for the necessity of precaution. This argumentation, however, is not sound; for by the harm is meant either:

a. Other-worldly harm, i.e., the rule declares that probability of unlawfulness implicates harm and punishment in the hereafter; then, there is no room for the minor premise of the syllogism – though its major premise is all right. The major premise is all right because repelling otherworldly probable harm is intellectually obligatory, since it is a probability of eternal misery and unblessedness. The minor premise has no room because the rule has no subject matter. As mentioned earlier, the subject matter of this rule is probable – here, the otherworldly – harm, and that harm is negated by the intellectual rule of reprehensibility of punishment without depiction. It is concluded, then, that the relation between those two rules is entry on the part of the former and not the latter.

Should one attempt to nullify this argumentation and assert that the rule of obligation of repelling the probable harm brings about a probability of harm and makes a minor premise for it, we would reply that this is not acceptable, for a rule cannot make a subject matter for itself. This argumentation is like the following reasoning: "This is wine." "Why?" "Because wine is unlawful!"

Or :

b. This-worldly harm, i.e., the rule declares that probability of unlawfulness implicates this-worldly harm; then, there is no room for neither the minor nor the major premise of the syllogism: minor premise, because the criteria for precepts are not always harm, but rather actual good and evil which are not of kind of harm; and major premise, because the intellect has no judgment that any this-worldly harm should be repelled, but rather there are some definitive, let alone probable, harms which are always undertaken by the wise for some this-worldly motives.

1.2. *Akhbārīs'* Proofs of Precaution

1.2.1. The Book

1.2.1.1. The verse 102 of sūra 3:

"… Fear God as He should be feared."

It is inferred from this verse that to fear God as He should be feared is obligatory, for God has commanded that and the command is apparent in the obligation. To fear God as He should be feared with regard to the case in question means to avoid whatsoever whose unlawfulness is probable, and this is the way of precaution.

Uṣūlīs have said that to fear God means to avoid committing whatsoever God has forbidden and eschewing whatsoever He has commanded. But doing whatsoever whose unlawfulness is probable without there being a single proof of its unlawfulness on the one hand and permission of both the intellect and the divine lawgiver to do it on the other does not contradict God-fearing.

It should be noted, however, that *Akhbārīs'* argument is focused on fearing God as He should be feared and not fearing Him in an absolute sense.

1.2.1.2. The verse 36 of sūra 17:

"And do not pursue that you have no knowledge of."

To argue this verse, it is said that to pursue what one has no knowledge of is unlawful, for Gad has prohibited from that and prohibition is apparent in unlawfulness. To do what whose unlawfulness is probable and not to avoid dubieties is to pursue what one has no knowledge of, and this is forbidden and unlawful.

Uṣūlīs have replied that to do what one has both intellectual and religious proofs for its permissibility is not to pursue what one has no knowledge of – which is forbidden.

There are some other verses argued as to obligation of precaution, but all such argumentations are nullified by *Uṣūlīs.*

1.2.2. *Sunna*

There are a huge number of *ḥadīth*s argued by *Akhbārīs* as to obligation of precaution. However, they can all be classified into four categories only two of which being discussed here:

1.2.2.1. What denotes unlawfulness of issuing juristic decisions with no knowledge, such as, "it is upon duty-bounds to say what they know and to stop where they have no knowledge of," (al-Kulainī, 1:43) and the like.

To that, *Uṣūlīs* have replied that to do what one has both intellectual and religious proofs for its permissibility is not to issue juristic decision without knowledge.

1.2.2.2. What denotes that to stop where there is dubiety is better than to sink into perishment, such as, "stop where there is dubiety, for stopping where there is dubiety is better than sinking into perishment,"(al-Kulainī, 1: 50) and the like, in which the divine lawgiver has commanded duty-bounds to stop in such cases and follow the way of precaution.

Uṣūlīs have said that such *ḥadīth*s should be predicated upon dubieties accompanied by summary-fashioned knowledge, for their appearances convey that perishment, which is punishment, has already existed in a plane prior to the command to stop. The reason is that they have treated sinking into the perishment as the cause for commanding to stop; hence, the doubted duty must have been incontrovertible in the plane prior to the command to stop so that the argumentation can be plausible and sinking into dubiety can be considered sinking into perishment and punishment. Thus, dubieties in such *ḥadīth*s must be those accompanied by summary-fashioned knowledge, or primary dubieties before the quest for probable proofs.

1.2.3. The Intellect

Two intellectual proofs are attributed to *Akhbārīs* for obligation of precaution:

1.2.3.1. Intellectual rule of obligation of repelling the probable harm. *Uṣūlīs*' reply to this argument was discussed at length earlier.
1.2.3.2. Since we have knowledge in summary fashion that there are so many unlawful affairs among dubieties on the one hand and summary-fashioned knowledge makes duties incontrovertible on the other, to follow the way of precaution through avoiding all dubieties becomes obligatory; for it is the intellect's judgment that definite liability necessitates definite clearance.

To that argument, it is replied that such summary-fashioned knowledge is reduced to *the detailed knowledge of* unlawfulness as to what is proved by sources and *primary doubt* with regard to other cases – the latter being an instance of principality of clearance, as proved earlier.

2. The Dubiety concerning the Precept as to Unlawfulness Because of Ambiguity of the Proof

Since an ambiguous proof has no denotation and should be treated as non-existent on the one hand and proofs presented earlier have no peculiarity to the case of lack of proof on the other, clearance is proved for this case as well.

3. The Dubiety concerning the Precept as to Unlawfulness Because of Contradiction of Proofs

The discussion here is pursuant to what was discussed in chapter 21 where criteria for preferring one proof to another were explained in detail. In short, should one proof be preferable, it would be taken into consideration and the other would be left aside the dubiety being thereby dissolved. Otherwise, one would have the right to choose any of proofs, as was explained there.

4. The Dubiety concerning the Object as to Unlawfulness

All proofs presented as to the dubiety concerning the precept serve here as well and prove clearance with regard to objects. Furthermore, there is a consensus among both *A<u>kh</u>bārīs* and *Uṣūlīs* on the clearance here.

5. The Dubiety as to Obligation concerning the Precept Because of Lack of the Proof, Because of Ambiguity of the Proof, Because of Contradiction of Proofs, and concerning the Object

Since proofs and criteria are the same in dubieties as to both unlawfulness and obligation, clearance with regard to all these four cases is definitely proved. Furthermore, there is again a consensus among both *A<u>kh</u>bārīs* and *Uṣūlīs* on the clearance in such cases.

CHAPTER 23

THE PRINCIPLE OF OPTION (*AṢĀLA AL-TAKHYĪR*)

The position of principality of option is where the generic compulsion is known while it is not known whether that compulsion is obligation or unlawfulness. In such case, either both sides are instrumental or one side is religiously, the former having, in turn, happened in one occurrence or multiple occurrences. Thus, we should deal with the problem in the following separate state:

1. The case where both sides are instrumental, in one occurrence; like the case where one definitely knows that he has sworn but one is doubtful whether one has sworn *to do* a certain permissible affair in a specific time (to do that affair in that time becoming obligatory in such case) or *not to do* it in the same specific time (to do that affair in that time becoming unlawful, then). As the summary-fashioned knowledge cannot make the known affair incontrovertible, because of impossibility of precaution in such case due to impotence of the duty-bound against actualizing both probabilities, its existence becomes as non-existence as to making "the definite obedience" obligatory or "the definite opposition" unlawful (as will be explained in detail in chapter 24). On the other hand, "the probable obedience" is inevitable. Hence, the intellect judges that the duty-bound has the option to do or to eschew, in the sense that he has actually no choice other than that. Thus, this is an existential, involuntary option and not an actual or apparent precept made by the divine lawgiver; for the latter would be acquiring what is already acquired – something impossible. However, there is a dispute whether (1.1.) such thing can have an apparent permissibility, (1.2.) proofs of clearance embrace that, (1.3.) the unlawfulness should be given priority, for repelling evil is prior to acquiring interest, or (1.4.) none of those is possible. As for the apparent permissibility, it cannot be made, for the duty-bound is certain of its non-existence, since he definitely knows that there is a compulsion on the part of the Lord either to do or to eschew in such a way

that permissibility, which is permission to both doing and abandoning, is impossible.

Inclusion in the clearance is also impossible, for the option judged by the intellect is prior to exercising clearance, since that intellectual option is due to the ineffectiveness of summary-fashioned knowledge and effectiveness of clearance is doubtlessly subsequent to the ineffectiveness of summary-fashioned knowledge.

The third probability is also nonsensical, for should such probability of evil cause unlawfulness, it would be more plausible to do that as to the primary dubiety inasmuch as there exists no probability of good, while in such cases clearance is doubtlessly effective.

Thus, it became clear that none of such probabilities is considerable and there is an intellectual option in such cases.

2. The case where both sides are instrumental but in multiple occurrences, like the case where one definitely knows that one has sworn, but he is doubtful whether one has sworn *to do* a certain permissible affair every Friday, for instance, or *to avoid doing* it every Friday. Here, since the summary-fashioned knowledge is effective as to making the definite opposition unlawful, one is not allowed to do that certain affair on one Friday and to eschew it on another. On the other hand, observing "the definite obedience" is impossible, as explained in the first case. The result, therefore, would be an intellectual *primary* option, meaning that one is allowed to choose *at the beginning* either of those two probabilities, but one must observe that choice constantly without any change in mind.

3. The case where both sides are religiously, or one certain side is so. Here, since the definite opposition is possible, by doing or eschewing with the intention of proximity to God, it is definitely unlawful. Therefore, one is not allowed to do without the intention of proximity to God where the mandatory act is religiously or eschew without the intention of proximity to God where the unlawful act is so. Rather, one must do or eschew in accordance with the probable obedience. The result is that the intellectual option in this case is conditional upon not necessitating the definite opposition.

*****

1. Should one side be more important where canons are definitely known, like when one wonders whether the animate thing one wishes to shoot is a human being whose killing is unlawful or an animal whose killing is permissible, one has no option anymore and should take the more important side into consideration. However, in cases where canons are not known in a definite way and the probability is not that strong to make the precaution necessary, one still has the option no matter how important one side seems.

2. In cases where following the way of precaution is not possible in one act but is possible by repeating the act, such as performing the prayers both completely and shortened, the summary-fashioned knowledge would become incontrovertible and the precaution and observing the definite obedience would be mandatory.

CHAPTER 24

THE PRINCIPLE OF LIABILITY (PRECAUTION) (*AṢĀLA AL-IḤTIYĀṬ or ISHTIGHĀL*)

Contrary to the principle of clearance which was concerned with the case where one was doubtful whether or not one was charged with a burden, the principle of liability deals with the case where one definitely knows that there exists some burden but wonders what one is charged with, i.e., the doubt is concerning *al-mukallaf bih*. The criterion for the doubt concerning what one is charged with is that the doubt is (a) over the very object of the duty, i.e., performing or eschewing which is wished either itself or its opposite, or (b) the object of object, i.e., an external affair as it is doubted – when, of course, one has already known that it is externally actualized.

Another preliminary point is this discussion is that knowledge of something is either detailed or summary-fashioned. There is no difference between those two kinds of knowledge as to the nature of knowledge. The difference lies in the *object of knowledge* being known in the former in detail and in the latter in summary fashion. The summary-fashioned knowledge is a mixture of knowledge and ignorance, and is accompanied by two or more detailed doubts as to every object of knowledge. Now, the question is that (1) whether summary-fashioned knowledge makes a duty incontrovertible in such a way that its overlooking should cause punishment or is like preliminary doubts necessitating no incontrovertible-making, and, if the former, (2) whether such incontrovertible-making is like a prerequisite so that its effectiveness may be prevented even as to the definite opposition and duty-negating principles may be exercised as to all parts of summary-fashioned knowledge, or is like a cause so that giving permission to oppose it, neither absolutely nor as to the definite opposition, may be possible.

The justifiable opinion as to (1) is that the summary-fashioned knowledge makes its object incontrovertible, precisely as the detailed knowledge does. For there is no difference between those two kinds of knowledge but being in detail and in summary fashion, and that makes no variety as to their function. The criterion for the intellect's judgment as to the liability and obligation of obedience is merely recognizing nature of the Lord's command, without considering any other property. As for (2), the justifiable opinion is that incontrovertible-making is like causality as to both the definite opposition and the definite obedience; it does not allow occurrence of even a single opposition to "the known in summary fashion." For such allowing necessitates contradiction: on the one hand the intellect judges that it is mandatory to avoid all parts as a preliminary to avoiding the unlawful existing among doubtful affairs, and on the other hand it allows committing some parts – an obvious contradiction. Furthermore, it is treated by the intellect as the Lord's permission to disobey Him, and this is obviously impossible.

It should be noted, however, that the summary-fashioned knowledge would become controvertible and would allow the duty-negating principles to be exercised in other parts in the two following cases:

1. Should there exist a practical principle or an authorized conjectural proof that proves existence of "the duty in accordance with the known in the summary-fashioned" in some parts, in such a way that it makes avoiding one part as a substitute for avoiding the known in summary fashion.
2. Should there exist a practical principle or an authorized conjectural proof that causes actual reduction or quasi-reduction of the summary-fashioned knowledge. The "actual reduction" *(al-inĥilāl al-ĥaqīqī)* is that the knowledge changes from summary fashion into detailed, such as the case where the duty-bound knows in summary fashion that one of the two bowls is religiously impure and then realizes that one certain bowl is so. Here, the other bowl would be treated as pure, since the dubiety concerning it has changed into a primary one. The "quasi-reduction" *(al-inĥilāl al-ĥukmī)* is that the summary-fashioned knowledge is subsistent, but it is no longer effective; such as the case where one of the two bowls which are parts of a summary-fashioned knowledge of religious impurity becomes part of another summary-fashioned knowledge of religious impurity with another bowl. The second summary-fashioned knowledge cannot affect the part in question whose obligation of avoiding had become incontrovertible by the first summary-fashioned knowledge, since it would be a kind of acquiring what is already acquired.

The third preliminary point is that parts of summary-fashioned knowledge are either two divergent things (*mutabāyinain*) or the least and the most of one thing (*al-aqall wa'l-akthar*), the dubiety in each being either concerning unlawfulness or obligation and as to the precept (which in turn is caused by lack of proof, ambiguity of proof, or contradiction of proofs) or the object. All these topics will be discussed in this chapter in an arrangement appropriate to any discussion.

And the final preliminary point is that observing precaution in all kinds of compulsory duty is preferable, both intellectually and religiously; for the intellect undoubtedly judges that to do whatsoever is probably desired by the Lord and to eschew whatsoever is displeasing to Him is absolutely good, and there are several *ĥadīths* confirming that. That is why observing precaution is conditional upon nothing but actualization of its object, i.e., the probability of duty, and precaution is constantly good even though it necessitates repetition of the act on the one hand and the duty-bound is capable of removing the dubiety through the quest for the duty on the other.

1. The Dubiety Being over Two Divergent Things

1.1. The Dubiety concerning Unlawfulness

1.1.1. The Dubiety concerning the Object

1.1.1.1. The Small-Scale Dubiety (*al-Shubha al-Maĥşūra*)

When the doubtful exists between two or more specified and limited things, the dubiety is called *the small-scale dubiety*. For instance, one knows that the liquid existing in one of these two or more specified bowls is religiously impure and its drinking, therefore, is unlawful.

The definite opposition. Is ignoring the summary-fashioned knowledge and committing all doubtful things, i.e., the definite opposition, in the small-scale dubiety allowed? The answer is negative. For it was proved earlier that the summary-fashioned knowledge is like a cause as to making the duty incontrovertible; hence, it is impossible to prevent its effectiveness as to making its object, which is definitely known, incontrovertible; either by the intellect (through the rule of reprehensibility of punishment without depiction, since the summary-fashioned knowledge is *depiction*) or by the religion (since no apparent precept can be made in this case inasmuch as following an apparent precept in a plane where the actual precept is preserved leads to contradiction). In other words, on the one hand one knows in summary fashion that the unlawful *does* exist among doubtful affairs and this makes the duty incontrovertible, and on the other hand nothing exists to allow one to eschew that knowledge. On the one side generality of the command to avoid religiously impure liquid includes this case, for peculiarity of the command to something which is known in detail has no support, on the second the intellect allows charging duty-bounds with avoiding an unlawful affair which exists among two or more things as well as punishing those who oppose such a duty, and on the third side no permission giving exits in the religion – on the contrary, all religious proofs of clearance which denote lawfulness of any of doubtful things *do* denote unlawfulness of what is known in summary fashion.

The definite obedience. Is committing one of the doubtful things in the small-scale dubiety allowed or is it mandatory to avoid all parts and to observe the definite obedience? The latter is justifiable, for it was proved earlier that the summary-fashioned knowledge is, like the detailed knowledge, a depiction and makes its object incontrovertible. In fact, the summary-fashion knowledge is a detailed knowledge as to its object; it is considered summary merely because its object is doubtful as to being included in the precept.

*****

Concerning the small-scale dubiety, the two following points should be borne in mind:

1. To avoid every doubtful thing becomes mandatory only when the duty as to the actual unlawful is incontrovertible in all assumptions, i.e., every one of doubtful things is such that should one assumedly be certain that it is the unlawful thing the duty as to avoiding would be incontrovertible. Otherwise, avoiding the other part would not be mandatory, such as the case where (a) there is no duty as to it at all, like when one knows that a drop of wine is dropped into one of the two bowls one of which is wine or religiously impure because of being mixed with some wine, (b) the duty is known in one of them but instead of being incontrovertible it is suspended until the duty-bound becomes capable of committing it, like when the duty-bound knows that the religiously impure thing has touched one of the two things he is not capable of committing one of them specifically, and (c) to commit one particular part is intellectually possible but the duty-bound is considered strange to that due to circumstances, like when one doubts whether the religiously impure bowl is this or the one which is not applicable to one. The reason is that in (a) there is no knowledge of occurrence of duty as to avoiding that which is touched by

the drop, for had the religiously impure bowl touched the drop no duty as to avoiding would have been generated (inasmuch as it has already been impure having the command to be avoided); hence, the doubt as to obligation of avoiding the other part is a doubt concerning the duty and not concerning what one is charged with, and in such cases the principle of clearance is exercised; in (b) the dubiety is over existence of an incontrovertible duty and not over something with which one is charged in an incontrovertible manner, and in (c) although the duty as to avoiding the other bowl is intellectually possible, it is not customarily incontrovertible, and to direct an incontrovertible duty as to avoiding something with which the duty-bound is not supposed to deal is not plausible. That is why should some parts of the summary-fashioned knowledge not be supposed to be dealt with on the part of the duty-bound, the summary-fashioned knowledge would no longer be effective as to them. Such case may occur where (c.1) the duty-bound has customarily no power over it as it is in a country very far from his place, (c.2) he has no religious power over it as it is owned by another person, or (c.3) it is customarily very unlikely that he will be obliged to use it, as in the case of a soil one is not customarily going to use it for bowing down in one's prayers.

2. It is not differentiated in the obligation of avoiding doubtful affairs between the case where they are of one kind, such as where the duty-bound knows that the liquid in one of these bowls is religiously impure, and where they are of different kinds, such as where he knows that either the liquid in this bowl is religiously impure or the liquid in that bowl is expropriated; for the proofs mentioned earlier include the latter as well.

1.1.1.2. The Large-Scale Dubiety (*al-Shubha Ghair al-Maḥṣūra*)

There are several definitions presented for the large-scale dubiety most of which suffering from incorrectness. However, we mention some of them without dealing with their problems:

1. It is treated by people as being large-scale dubiety, such as one in one thousand,
2. The parts are abundant in such a way that counting them in a short time, or absolutely, is difficult,
3. The parts are abundant in such a way that the wise do not take the summary-fashioned knowledge existing among them into consideration and treat it as no knowledge,

4. Abundance of parts causes hardship and difficulty with the definite obedience, and it is clearly known in the Islamic jurisprudence that the hardship removes duties,
5. Abundance of parts is that much that weakens the probability in each of them.

The definite opposition. According to what was proved earlier that the summary-fashioned knowledge is like cause and makes its object incontrovertible, there will be no difference between the small-scale and the large-scale dubieties and the definite opposition is unlawful in this kind as well.

The definite obedience. Although there is no difference between the small-scale and the large-scale dubieties, as said above, there is a very considerable celebrity, very close to the level of consensus, among Shī'a scholars that the definite obedience in the large-scale dubiety is not mandatory. Furthermore, there are many *ḥadīth*s which confirm that, such as words of the fifth Imām, al-Bāqir, in response to Abu l-Djārūd's remarks that he saw some people using organs of dead animals in making cheese: "Should all that exists on earth be unlawful because of a certain place in which people use organs of dead animals in making cheese?! If you know that it is made by organs of dead animals do not eat, but if you do not know, buy, sell, and eat." That is why we hold that in the large-scale dubiety, the definite obedience is not mandatory.

*****

Concerning the large-scale dubiety, the three following points should be borne in mind:

1. Should parts of that which is doubted among the large-scale dubiety be abundant in such a way that the ratio between all of them to the doubtful things and one thing to the small-scale dubiety be the same (sometimes called the dubiety of abundant in the abundant), such as the case where one knows that flesh of five hundred of fifteen hundred sheep of a flock are unlawful, the case would be treated as the small-scale dubiety.
2. Proofs proving non-obligation of precaution in the large-scale dubiety do not denote that all parts can be committed in the dubiety concerning unlawfulness and all parts can be eschewed in the dubiety concerning obligation. Rather, the amount one knows in summary-fashioned knowledge must be eschewed in the dubiety concerning unlawfulness and done in the

dubiety concerning obligation.

3. The summary-fashioned knowledge not being incontrovertible in the large-scale dubiety does not mean overlooking the doubt and treating it as non-existence. It means that the other unspecified part is treated as a substitute for what is known in summary fashion: to be done in the dubiety concerning obligation, and be eschewed in the dubiety concerning unlawfulness.

1.1.2. The Dubiety concerning the Precept

An example of this kind is unlawfulness of the third *adhān* on Fridays whose determination is a matter of dispute. Precisely as in the dubiety concerning the object, the definite opposition is unlawful and the definite obedience is mandatory here.

1.2. The Dubiety concerning Obligation

1.2.1. The Dubiety concerning the Precept

Such dubiety (which is caused by lack of proof, ambiguity of proof, or contradiction of proofs) occurs where it is doubted whether something is mandatory or is characterized by other precepts save unlawfulness, such as the doubt whether in the Occultation time one must perform *żuhr* or *djumuʿa* prayers on Fridays.

1.2.1.1. Because of Lack of Proof

The definite opposition and the definite obedience. The definite opposition, i.e., performing neither *żuhr* nor *djumuʿa* prayers on Fridays in the Occultation time, is absolutely unlawful, precisely because of what was explained on the dubiety concerning unlawfulness. For the same reason, the definite obedience is also mandatory, and in such case the duty-bound must perform both prayers on Fridays.

1.2.1.2. Because of Ambiguity of Proof

The definite opposition and the definite obedience. The same reason proves that the definite opposition is unlawful and the definite obedience is mandatory. Such duty is even clearer here, for although the proving proof is ambiguous, the very precept is addressed to duty-bounds in a detailed fashion and there is no ambiguity in the addressing *per se.*

1.2.1.3. Because of Contradiction of Proofs

According to *ĥadīths*, which encounter no opposition in this connection, the duty-bound has the option to act according to any of the proofs in such cases.

1.2.2. The Dubiety concerning the Object

An example of this kind is the case where one knows that one has forgotten to perform one of daily prayers but wonders whether it was noon or afternoon prayers.

The Definite Opposition and the Definite Obedience. The definite opposition is unlawful and the definite obedience is mandatory, and the reasoning is the same. Thus, in the example mentioned above, one must perform both noon and afternoon prayers.

2. The Dubiety Being over the Least and the Most of One Thing

This dubiety is, in turn, of two kinds: "independing" *(istiqlālī)* and "relational"*(irtibāṭī)*. An example of the former is where one knows that one has not performed a number of one's daily prayers but doubts the number of them and wonders whether they were six, for instance, or four (in the dubiety concerning obligation), or one knows that one ejaculated and knows that recitation of Qur'ānic *sūras* containing specific verses upon the recitation of which one must bow down is unlawful in such cases but wonders whether recitation of the whole *sūra* is unlawful or only that of the verse (in the dubiety concerning unlawfulness). An example of the latter is that one knows that performing prayers is mandatory but wonders whether *sūra*, i.e., recitation of one *sūra* after *sūra al-ĥamd*, is part of prayers (in the dubiety concerning obligation), or one knows that sculpturing an animating objects is unlawful but wonders whether sculpturing the whole body of such objects is so or making some parts is also unlawful (in the dubiety concerning unlawfulness).

The difference between the two is that the duty in the latter is one in case of obligation of the most but obedience of the least must be realized within the most, while in the former the duty is multiple causing multiplicity of reward and punishment in case of obedience and disobedience, obedience of the least being realized even though not being done within the most.

2.1. The Independing Least and Most

In all cases of this kind (i.e., the dubiety concerning the precept as to both unlawfulness and obligation caused by either lack of proof, ambiguity of proof, or contradiction of proofs as well as the dubiety concerning the object whether concerning unlawfulness or obligation) the clearance from liability to the most will undoubtedly be exercised, for addressing in such cases is reduced to some independent addresses which causes actual reduction of the summary-fashioned knowledge to a detailed duty as to the least and a primary doubt as to the most.

2.2. The Relational Least and Most

2.2.1. The dubiety concerning the precept whether as to unlawfulness or obligation, caused by either lack of proof, ambiguity of proof, or contradiction of proofs

2.2.1.1. The dubiety over object of the duty

2.2.1.1.1. *The dubiety over parts of a composite commanded act.* An example of this kind is to doubt whether *sūra* is part of prayers (in which case the prayers without *sūra* being the least and with sūra being the most). In such cases, the clearance from liability to the most will undoubtedly be exercised, for the summary-fashioned knowledge, which is the cause of obligation of precaution, is reduced to a detailed duty as to the least and a primary doubt as to the most. However, the least is undoubtedly mandatory, for there is a detailed knowledge as to its obligation, no matter such obligation being independent or within the most – should the most be mandatory.

2.2.1.1.2. *The dubiety over conditions of and impediments to the commanded act.* Precisely because of the same reasons, what is exercised here is the principle of clearance.

2.2.1.1.3. *The dubiety in analytical composite affairs.* This means that the affair in question is composed of genus and differentia. An example of this kind is "animal" in "feed an animal," where one doubts whether the absolute "animal" is commanded to be fed or the qualified "rational animal," i.e., human being which is composed of animal (genus) and rational (differentia).

It should be noted that the doubtful additional property is sometimes (a) intellectually among constituents of what it is a property of, such as differentia as to the genus, since genus cannot be found externally without differentia and therefore it must be actualized within a species should it become object of a duty, (b) customarily among constituents of what it is a property of, as in "Buy a horse for me" and then "Buy an Arabian horse for me," in which being Arabian is not an intellectual constituent of the horse but Arabian is customarily considered species other than Turkmen, for instance, horse, and (c) not among constituents of what it is a property of, neither intellectually nor customarily.

In (a), since the external existence is considered in the duty and genus alone has no external existence and therefore cannot be actualized, genus together with one of the differentiae must be the object of duty. The result is that when feeding an animal becomes mandatory, it becomes an optional mandatory as to the differentiae; hence, the dubiety would be over determination and option and not over the least and the most. In other words, since genus alone is not, and cannot be, object of the duty so that it may be considered the definite amount, but rather in the *absolute command*, such as "feed an animal," the object of obligation is animal with one of the differentiae in an optional manner, and in the *qualified command*, such as "feed a rational animal," it is animal with a definite differentia – the dubiety becomes over determination and option in which determination should principally be adopted, and not over the least and the most in which clearance as to the property is exercised.

In (b), the intellect considers "the definite amount" and "the known in a detailed way" existent; hence, the summary-fashioned knowledge is reduced and clearance as to the doubtful additional is exercised; for the property is not an intellectual constituent on the one hand and common consent cannot be taken into consideration in this connection on the other.

In (c), there is no problem with exercising the clearance as to the doubtful additional property.

2.2.1.2. The dubiety over causes

It is quite well known in the Islamic law that some specific kinds of washing are mandatory for the sake of religious purity. Now, the question is that whether the commanded in such cases is the purification caused by such washings and washings themselves are only commanded because they cause purification, or they are the very actual commanded. On the basis of the former, the commanded affair is a simple designation and specific kinds of washing are merely causes of actualization of that designation. This is an example of this topic.

The prominent opinion among Shī'a scholars is that where it is doubted whether something is taken as part or condition in a cause the clearance would absolutely not be exercised, no matter such causes are religious, intellectual, or customary; for charging with the simple designation is known in detail and to doubt whether something is considered as a condition or part in its actualization refers to the doubt whether or not obedience will be actualized without that thing, and it is absolutely clear that in such cases it is the principle of liability that must be exercised and not that of clearance.

2.2.2. The dubiety concerning the object whether as to unlawfulness or obligation

This kind of dubiety concerning the object of duty is possible and occurs where the object of duty is related to the external things, such as the command to respect religious scholars. Since number of religious scholars differs from time to time and place to place, the object of duty may become more or less; for the proposition is reduced to multiple propositions according to the number of religious scholars. Now, in case of doubting whether certain individual is a religious scholar, should he be so the object of duty would become more – and this is the most – and should he not be so the object of duty would become less – and this is the least. Hence, to doubt whether certain individual is a religious scholar leads to the dubiety concerning the object of duty being between the least and the most. A juristic example of this kind is to doubt whether cloth of one who is performing the prayers is made of parts of an animal whose flesh is prohibited to be eaten – a case where the prayers is annulled.

It is obviously clear that the clearance would be exercised here; for the doubt is over existence of another proposition, i.e., whether the doubtful individual is an instant of religious scholars, and it was proved earlier that in all cases where reduction as to the doubtful instance occurs the clearance is undoubtedly exercised. Thus, in the example mentioned above, one is allowed to perform one's prayers in such a cloth.

CHAPTER 25

THE PRINCIPLE OF CONTINUITY OF THE PREVIOUS STATE
(AṢĀLA AL-ISTIṢḤĀB)

When the duty-bound becomes certain of a precept or an object, then his precious certainty changes into uncertainty and he doubts subsistence of what he was certain of previously, he wonders what to do: should he act in accordance with what he was certain of, or should he not act so? The problem is that in both cases the duty-bound fears opposition of the actuality. However, there is a juristic principle in this connection which removes such perplexity: the principle of continuity of the previous state (*aṣāla al- istiṣḥāb*). The Arabic term *istiṣḥāb* is derived from ṣuḥba meaning accompanying somebody or taking something with oneself. The expression, therefore, means to take what one has been previously certain of with one to the present time. That is why the best definition of *istiṣḥāb* is "to judge that what has previously been is subsistent." Before dealing with opinions on the authority of *istiṣḥāb*, we should expound what it really is.

Constituents of *Istiṣḥāb*

In order for *istiṣḥāb* to be called *istiṣḥāb* or to be covered by the coming proofs of its authority, the following pillars should exist:

1. Certainty. By this is meant certainty of the previous state, whether it is a precept or an object having a precept.
2. Doubt. By this is meant doubt over subsistence of the definite affair. It should be noted that the doubt includes both real doubt and invalid conjecture.
3. Conjunction of certainty and doubt, in the sense of simultaneous occurrence of certainty and doubt. This does not mean that origins of

those two are simultaneous; for sometimes the origin of certainty is before that of doubt, such as where one is certain on Thursday that one's cloth is religiously pure and on Friday doubts whether it is still pure or has become impure; sometimes the origin of certainty is after that of doubt, such as where one doubts on Friday whether one's cloth is religiously pure and this doubt continues until Saturday when one becomes certain that one's cloth has been pure on Thursday; and sometimes origins of those two occur simultaneously, such as where one becomes certain on Friday that one's cloth has been religiously pure on Thursday and at the same time on Friday doubts whether that purity has been subsistent until Friday – all of these being subject to *istiṣḥāb*. This component differentiates *istiṣḥāb* from "the rule of certainty" which is absolutely different and will be discussed later. An example of the latter is where one is certain that one's cloth is religiously pure on Friday and then on Saturday one doubts whether one's cloth was pure on Friday. Here, the question is not subsistence of purity; it is casting doubt upon the very previous certainty and changing the very certainty into doubt.

4. Unity of objects of certainty and doubt. Ignoring the time, this means that the doubt is over the very thing that has been the matter of certainty. This component differentiates *istiṣḥāb* from "the rule of origin and impediment."

5. The time of the definite affair preceding that of the doubtful one. This means that the doubt must be over subsistence of what has already been existent in certain fashion. Should the time of the definite affair be subsequent to that of the doubtful one, which is called reverse *istiṣḥāb* (*al-istiṣḥāb al-qahqarā*), it would not be an authoritative practical principle.

Proofs of Authority of *Istiṣḥāb*

As for the opinions on the authority of *istiṣḥāb*, at least twelve ones are known most of which differentiating between some cases and others. However, since this is an introductory work on the one hand and we will prove absolute authority of *istiṣḥāb* on the other, there is no need to deal with those opinions. Hence, we will discuss proofs of absolute authority of *istiṣḥāb* straight away.

1. The conduct of the wise

Doubtless the wise (i.e., human beings as they are intellectual creatures), though having various tastes and approaches to affairs, treat something they have been certain of as subsistent in case of doubt over that until they make sure that the previous state is changed. On the other hand, the divine lawgiver has not prohibited from following that conduct. This reveals that He has recognized and confirmed that conduct; for He is among the wise, even chief of the wise, and therefore has no other way in this connection – otherwise He would have announced and depicted His specific way ordering believers to follow it (as was explained in detail in chapter 19).

2. *Ĥadīths*

Several *ĥadīth*s, which are the chief proofs of authority of *istiṣĥāb*, are argued by *Uṣūlīs* of which we discuss only two:

2.1. Zurāra's first authentic ĥadīth.

Zurāra, who was a great companion of the fifth and sixth Imāms, narrates that:

I asked Imām, "A man who has performed minor ablution sleeps. Do one or two winks of sleep make another minor ablution mandatory?"

Imām replied, "O Zurāra, sometimes eyes sleep while the heart and ears have not slept. When eyes and ears sleep, performing minor ablution [for prayers and the like] becomes mandatory."

I asked, "If something moves near him but he does not realize [should he perform minor ablution again]?"

Imām replied, "No, until he becomes certain that he has slept. Until a clear sign [of sleeping] comes. Otherwise, he is certain of his minor ablution, and he should never break the certainty by doubt. Rather, he breaks certainty by another certainty."

To argue this *ĥadīth*, it is said that the predicative sentence "he is certain of his minor ablution" is in fact the consequent in the conditional sentence "if he is not certain that he has slept, then his certainty of his minor ablution subsists," in the sense that what can remove the certainty of minor ablution, i.e., certainty of sleeping, has not occurred. This is a preliminary to depict that the doubt does not remove the certainty of minor ablution and it is the certainty of sleeping that can remove it. In other words, doubt as it is doubt cannot remove and break the certainty and it is only the certainty that can break the certainty. Thus, "he is certain of his minor ablution" is as the minor premise and "he should never break the certainty by doubt" is as the major premise. This major premise denotes the rule of *istiṣĥāb*, i.e., continuity of the previous certainty and not breaking it by the coming doubt, and conveys that no previous certainty is broken by a coming doubt.

2.2. Zurāra's second authentic ĥadīth.

Again Zurāra narrates that:

I asked Imām, "Some drops of blood or semen touched my cloth. I marked my cloth to wash it when I found water. Then, the time of prayers came and, forgetting that there was something wrong with my cloth, I performed my prayers. Then, I remembered that. [What should I do?]"

Imām replied, "Wash it and repeat your prayers."

I asked, "If I did not know where it was dropped while I was certain of its dropping on my cloth, but when I looked for it I could not find it and it was only after the prayers that I found it [what should I do]?"

Imām replied, "Wash it and repeat your prayers."

I asked, "If I thought that it was dropped but I was not certain of that and when I looked I found nothing, then I performed my prayers and I saw it [What should I do]?"

Imām replied, "Wash it but do not repeat your prayers."

I asked, "Why is it so?"

Imām replied, "Because you were certain of your purity and then doubted that, and you are never supposed to break the certainty by the doubt."

I asked, "If I were certain that it was dropped on my cloth but I was not certain where it was dropped so that I wash it?"

Imām replied, "Wash the area where you think it is dropped so that you become certain of your purity."

I asked, "Would it be mandatory to quest for the impurity if I doubted whether or not some impure object has touched it?"

Imām replied, "No. By doing that you merely wish to remove your psychic doubt."

I asked, "If I saw it while I was in prayers?"

Imām replied, "Break the prayers and repeat it if you were doubtful of some part of your cloth and you saw it….."

Two phrases of *ĥadīth* are argued for the authority of *istiṣĥāb*:

a. "Because you were certain of your purity and then doubted that….," since by certainty of purity is meant certainty of purity before doubting whether or not an impure object touched the cloth.

b. "…And you are never supposed to break the certainty by the doubt," since by the certainty is meant the certainty as it is certainty and not a specific one, i.e., certainty of purity alone; for treating the doubt as countering the certainty and attributing "not to break" to the doubt clearly reveals that the criterion for unlawfulness of breaking is the aspect of certainty as it is certainty and not that of certainty qualified by purity as it is qualified by purity.

CONCLUSION. Considering denotations of all proofs, we come to this conclusion that *istiṣḥ̂āb* is an authorized practical principle with regard to all kinds of doubts which are of previous states, whether as to objects or precepts.

Secondary Discussions of *Istiṣḥ̂āb*

The Rule of Certainty (*Qā'ida al-Yaqīn*)

This rule, in which the doubt is called the penetrative doubt (*al-shakk al-sārī*), deals with the case where one doubts the very thing one was certain of. For instance, one is certain on Friday that one's cloth is religiously pure, then on Saturday one doubts whether one's cloth *was* religiously pure on Friday. In such case, the doubt penetrates into Friday and the certainty of Friday changes into doubt. Such case is not included in the proofs of authority of *istiṣḥ̂āb*, for it is not "to judge that what has previously been is subsistent," as nothing has previously been certain. On the other hand, there is no other proof in favor of this rule; that is why it cannot be treated as an authoritative proof of religious precepts.

Continuity of the Previous State of the Universal (*Istiṣḥ̂āb al-Kullī*)

By *istiṣḥ̂āb al-kullī* is meant *istiṣḥ̂āb* of the universal where one is certain of its existence within one of its instants but later on doubts subsistence of the very universal. This doubt over subsistent of the universal within its instances can be considered in three ways – called varieties of *istiṣḥ̂āb al-kullī*:

1. The doubt is over subsistence of the universal because of doubting subsistence of the very instance one was certain of.
2. The doubt is over subsistence of the universal because of the doubt over determination of the instance one was certain of, in the sense that the instance is either definitely subsistent or is definitely removed. In this case, one is summarily certain of existence of an instant of the universal instants and thereby is certain of existence of the universal within that, but one is doubtful whether that actual instant has a long lifespan and therefore is

definitely subsistent in the second time or has a short lifespan and therefore is definitely removed in that time – that is why one is doubtful about subsistence of the universal.

An example of this variety is where one observes something in one's cloth and becomes certain in summary fashion that it is an impure object, but one does not know whether it is urine or semen and then performs minor ablution. Here, one is certain of the universal defilement within that instance: if it is urine, the defilement is minor and is definitely removed by minor ablution, but if it is semen, the defilement is major and is definitely not removed by minor ablution. Could the universal *istiṣḥāb* be exercised, the universal defilement would be treated as being subsistent and thereby effects of universal defilement, such as unlawfulness of touching letters of the holy Qur'ān, would be actualized. However, effects of minor or major defilement in particular, such as unlawfulness of entering mosques, could not be realized.

3. The doubt is over subsistence of the universal because of the doubt over existence of another instant instead of the one whose generation or removing is definitely known, i.e., the doubt is caused by the probability of existence of another instant. In this case, should the second instant actually be existent, the universal would be subsistent through it; otherwise, the universal would become non-existent due to the annihilation of the first instant.

This variety is of two kinds:

3.1. It is probable that the second instant is originated in the vessel of existence of the first one, and

3.2. Probable origination of the second instant is simultaneous with the removal of the first, which, in turn, may be actualized through changing the first into the second or mere accidental simultaneity of removal of the first and origination of the second.

As for the authority of *istiṣḥāb al-kullī*:

In (1) there is no dispute among *Uṣūlīs* that *istiṣḥāb* is exercised as to both the universal and instant, in the sense that religious effects of both the universal and the instant with its individual characteristics should be actualized.

In (2) *istiṣḥāb* is exercised as to the universal, but not as to the instant. Therefore, in the example mentioned earlier touching letters of the holy Qur'ān is unlawful because of *istiṣḥāb* of the universal, but entering mosques is permissible because of principle of non-existence of contribution of individual characteristics.

In (3), *istiṣḥāb* is absolutely not exercised. For it is obviously clear that, first, unity in kind is not sufficient in *istiṣḥāb* inasmuch as it means subsistence of something externally. By *istiṣḥāb al-kullī* is not meant *istiṣḥāb* of the very quiddity as it is quiddity, since it is nonsensical; rather, *istiṣḥāb* of the quiddity as it has an external existence, in order to actualize its actual precepts. Secondly, it is also clear that the relation between universal and its instants is the same with the relation of fathers and children, for the universal has no existence but accidentally and through its instants. In (3), a portion of the universal is actualized but it is certainly removed, and origination of the other portion of the universal in the second instant has been doubtful from the very beginning. Thus, the definite affair and the doubtful affair are not the same, and a major constitute of *istiṣḥāb* is missing.

This is the difference between c and b, for in b subsistence of the very portion of the universal, which is really actualized and certainly originated, is doubted, as it is not known whether it is the one attributed to the long instant or the short one.

Selected Bibliography

Al-'Āmilī, al-Ĥurr, *Tafṣīl Wasā'il al-Shī'a ilā Taĥṣīl Masā'il al-Sharī'a*, al-Maktaba al-Islāmiyya, Tehran, 1376 A.H.

Al-Anṣārī, al-Shaikh Murtaḍa, *Farā'id al-Uṣūl*, Mu'assasa al-Nashr al-Islāmī, Qum.

Al-Budjnūrdī, Mīrzā Ĥasan, *Muntahā al-Uṣūl*, Mu'assasa al-'Urūdj, Tehran,1421 A.H.

Al-'Irāqī, Aghā Ḍiya' al-Dīn, *Nihāyat al-Afkār*, Mu'assasa al-Nashr al-Islāmī, Qum, 1405 A.H.

Al-Iṣfahānī, Muĥammad Ĥusain, *Nihāyat al-Dirāyat fi Sharĥ al-Kifāyat*, Mu'assasa Āl al-Bayt li Iĥya' al-Turāth, Beirut, 1418 A.H.

Al-Iṣfahānī, Muĥammad Ĥusain b.'Abd al-Raĥīm, *al-Fuṣūl fi 'Ilm al-Uṣūl*, Lithograph.

Al-Iṣfahānī, Muĥammad Taqī b.'Abd al-Raĥīm, *Hidāyat al-Mustarshidīn*, Lithograph.

Al-Khū'ī, al-Sayyid Abulqāsim, *Muĥāḍarāt fi Uṣūl al-Fiqh*, Mu'assasa al-Nashr al-Islāmī, Qum, 1419 A.H.

Al-Khurāsānī, Muĥammad Kāẓim, *Kifāyat al-Uṣūl*, Mu'assasa al-Nashr al-Islāmī, Qum,1424 A.H.

Al-Kulainī, Muĥammad b.Ya'qūb, *al-Kāfī*, Islāmiyya Publications, Tehran, 1407 A.H.

Al-Muẓaffar, Muĥammad Riḍā, *Uṣūl al-Fiqh*, Mu'assasa Maṭbū'ātī Esmā'īliyān, Qum, 1421 A.H.

Al-Nā'īnī, Mīrzā Muĥammad Ĥusain, *Fawā'id al-Uṣūl*, Mu'assasa al-Nashr al-Islāmī, Qum,1424 A.H.

Al-Qumī, Mīrzā Abulqāsim, *al-Qawānīn al-Muĥkama*, Lithograph.

Al-Ṭabāṭabā'ī, al-Sayyid Muĥammad Ĥussain, *Ĥāshiyat al-Kifāyat*, Bonyād-e Elmī va Fekrī-ye Allāmeh Ṭabāṭabā'ī.

Al-Ṭabrisī, Abu 'Alī Faḍl b. al-Ĥasan, *Madjma' al-Bayān fi Tafsīr al-Qur'ān*, Dar Iĥyā' Turāth al-'Arabī, Beirut, 1339 A.H.

INDEX *

A

al- a'amm, 9
al-a'ammī, 9
Abān b. Taghlib, 157
abolishment, 117, 118, 119, 120
absolute, 16, 61, 63, 64, 110
absolute conjecture, 110
absoluteness of the position, 24, 61
absoluteness, 6, 9, 10, 12, 21, 22, 23, 24, 25, 26, 34, 35, 36, 40, 48, 61, 62, 63, 64, 71, 118, 120, 129, 172
Abū Baṣīr, 35
Abū Ĥanīfa, 155
accordant, 32, 57, 58, 148
acknowledgment, 121, 123, 124, 142, 152
acquired consensus, 136
actual, 17
actual precept, 1, 71, 72, 74, 75, 76, 104, 110, 168, 174, 187
actual reduction, 186, 193
al-adā', 20
al-'adad, 43
'adam ṣiĥĥat al-salb, 5, 10
adumbration, 41, 46
Akhbārīs, 109, 125, 138, 144, 145, 168, 169, 170, 174, 175, 176, 177, 178, 179
akhdh bi'l dalīlayn, 21
al-akthar, 53
al-alfāż, 2
al-'Allāma al-Ĥillī, 123
amāra, 71, 106, 107, 108, 109, 110, 113, 114, 115, 163
ambiguous, 65
'āmm, 4
analogy, 105, 110, 111, 130, 137, 155, 156, 157
antecedent, 5, 33, 34, 35, 36, 38
apparent, 1, 2, 6, 7, 15, 16, 26, 27, 29, 34, 35, 38, 40, 41, 42, 49, 51, 52, 56, 57, 58, 62, 63, 65, 69, 70, 71, 74, 104, 114, 117, 118, 124, 126, 127, 134, 139, 140, 143, 168, 170, 171, 174, 176, 177, 181, 187
apparent precept, 2, 71, 74, 114, 168, 181, 187
appearances of terms, 2, 122
al-aqall wa'l-akthar, 53, 187
al-ārā' al-maĥmuda, 137
aṣāla al-'umūm, 6
aṣāla al-ĥaqīqa, 6
aṣāla al-istiṣĥāb, 152, 167
aṣāla al-iṭlāq, 6
aṣāla al-takhyīr, 167
aṣāla al-żuhūr, 6
Asās al-Balāgha, 140
al-aṣl, 2, 106, 155, 156
al-aṣl al-'amalī, 2, 106
authoritative conjecture, 106
authoritative proof, 32, 41, 46, 51, 52, 54, 55, 56, 58, 62, 63, 72, 75, 76, 104, 105, 106, 107, 108, 109, 110, 113, 114, 120, 122, 123, 125, 128, 129, 130, 133, 134, 135, 136, 137, 138, 139, 141, 142, 143, 147, 148, 152, 153, 156, 160, 161, 201
authority of appearances, 46, 126, 145
al-awāmir, 15
al-'aynī, 18

* *al* – in Arabic terms is not considered in the index.

B

al-barā'a al-'aqliyya, 74
al-barā'a al-shar'iyya, 74
belated, 19, 20
belatedness, 24
binā' al-'uqalā', 7, 151
bi-shart lā, 23
bi-shart shay', 23
burdensome precepts, 2, 16, 31, 88, 112

C

canons, 156, 157, 172, 183
causes, 37, 38, 45, 54, 63, 87, 90, 91, 100, 106, 113, 115, 124, 131, 160, 162, 163, 168, 172, 186, 190, 193, 194, 195
celebrity, 147
celebrity of verdict, 147, 148
certitude, 65, 76, 105, 106, 107, 108, 109, 136, 137, 138, 147
clear, 65
clearance from obligation, 2, 71
closure proof, 110
collective, 18
command, 85
compelling, 69, 70, 173
condition, 33, 34
conditional, 16
conditioned-by-something, 23
conjunction, 3, 38, 82, 83, 84, 85, 86, 87, 88, 91, 92, 93, 100, 160
consensus, 3, 58, 68, 72, 75, 76, 105, 112, 117, 120, 125, 130, 131, 132, 133, 134, 135, 136, 140, 141, 147, 153, 154, 155, 157, 161, 170, 174, 179, 190
consequent, 33, 34, 35, 36, 37, 38, 199
constricted, 19
constrictive, 41
contextual denotation, 44
contextual evidence, 5, 6, 7, 8, 9, 16, 21, 22, 24, 28, 32, 35, 39, 40, 41, 42, 118, 170
continence, 29, 30
continuity of the previous state of the universal, 201
contradiction, 63, 159, 179, 192
convention, 3, 4, 5, 6, 8, 12, 30, 48, 61, 140
convention by determination, 3, 8
convention by specification, 3, 8
custom, 151
custom of the people of the religion, 151, 153, 154
custom of the wise, 151, 152, 154
customary gathering, 161

D

al-dalāla al-iltizāmiyya, 31
al-dalāla al-siyāqiyya, 44
al-dalīl al-'aqlī, 137
al-dalīl al-faqāhatī, 2
al-dalīl al-idjtihādī, 1
dalīl al-insidād, 110
dalīl al-insidād al-kabīr, 110
al-dalīl al-lafẓī, 135
al-dalīl al-lubbī, 135
dalāla al-nahy ala'l fasād, 99
al-dawām, 30
Dāwūd b. Khalaf, 155
definite, 17, 21, 41, 49, 54, 58, 63, 65, 105, 107, 111, 114, 117, 120, 124, 125, 126, 127, 128, 129, 132, 133, 134, 135, 137, 139, 141, 142, 143, 152, 153, 156, 157, 159, 178, 181, 182, 183, 185, 186, 187, 190, 191, 192, 194, 197, 198, 203

definite obedience, 182, 186, 188, 190, 191, 192
dependent intellectual proofs, 68
depiction, 21, 22, 24, 25, 35, 42, 62, 63, 71, 73, 112, 122, 124, 137, 145, 163, 170, 175, 176, 187, 188
derived, 13
designated, 5, 61, 62, 87, 88, 89, 90, 91, 92, 94, 96, 104
designation, 9, 10, 38, 39, 40, 41, 43, 47, 53, 85, 86, 87, 88, 89, 90, 91, 94, 95, 96, 100, 143, 194, 195
detailed knowledge, 111, 178, 185, 188, 193
determinate, 18
al-đidd al-ʿāmm, 79
al-đidd al-khāṣṣ, 80
disaccording, 32, 57, 58
divine lawgiver, 7, 55, 64, 68, 71, 74, 77, 80, 83, 100, 101, 104, 106, 107, 108, 109, 113, 114, 115, 118, 119, 127, 132, 133, 137, 138, 139, 140, 141, 142, 151, 152, 153, 154, 155, 156, 162, 163, 167, 177, 181, 199
al-djāhil al-qāṣir, 3, 72
djamʿ bayn al-dalīlayn, 21
al-djāmiʿ, 155, 156
al-djamʿ al-ʿurfī, 161
dubiety concerning the concept, 52, 55
dubiety concerning the instance, 52, 54, 55
dubiety concerning the object, 169, 173, 174, 191, 193, 195

E

emphasis, 26, 27
encompassing, 47, 51, 54, 61, 155, 156, 170, 174
encompassing generality, 47
entry, 163
equilibrium and prefrences, 159
exclusiveness, 35, 36, 37, 43
exclusivity, 42
excuser, 105, 107, 114, 115, 128, 142
explicit, 6, 41, 49, 58, 65, 117, 126, 139, 142, 143
extended, 19

F

al-farʿ, 155, 156
fasting, 8
al-fawr, 24
fawrī, 19
figurative, 6, 8, 14, 44, 50, 52, 65, 106, 140, 144, 164

G

general, 4
general opposite, 79
al-ghāya, 42
ghayr al-muwaqqat, 19
ghayr fawrī, 19
al-Ghazzālī, 134

H

ĥadīth of removal, 171
ĥadjdj, 8, 17
al-ĥaqīqa al-mutasharriʿiyya, 8
al-ĥaqīqa al-sharʿiyya, 8
al-ĥaṣr, 42
ĥilliyya, 74
hint, 44
homonym, 7
ĥudjdja, 2, 105, 106, 107
ĥudjdjiyya al-żawāhir, 139
al-ĥukm al-żāhirī, 1, 2
al-ĥukūma, 163

I

al-'ibāda, 99
al-'ilm al-idjmālī, 72
al-'ilm al-tafṣīlī, 111
Ibn Barrādj, 125
Ibn Idrīs, 125, 131
Ibn Zuhra, 125
al-idjmā', 133
al-idjmā' al-muḥaṣṣal, 136
al-idjtimā', 85, 86
idjtimā'al-amr wa'l nahy, 85
al-idjtimā'al-mawridī, 85
idjtimā'ī, 87
al-idjzā', 69
iḍṭirārī, 69
iḥtirāzī, 41
iḥtiyāṭ, 74
ikhtiyārī, 69
al-'illa, 155, 156
'ilm, 109
'ilmī, 108, 110
impediment, 45, 82, 84, 92, 96, 100, 101, 161, 198
implicative denotation, 31
implicatures of sentences, 31
implicit conveyance, 44
imtinā'ī, 87
incapable ignorant, 72
inclusive, 35, 36, 63, 64, 71, 173, 174
incontrovertible, 72, 73, 74, 83, 112, 115, 160, 167, 178, 181, 183, 185, 186, 187, 188, 189, 190, 191
incorrectness of divesting, 5, 10
independent intellectual proofs, 68
independing, 192
infallible-innocent personality, 121, 122, 123, 124, 133, 135, 136, 141
al-inḥilāl al-ḥukmī, 186
initiation, 26, 27
instrumental obligations, 21
instrumental, 21
intellect, 3, 15, 16, 17, 22, 68, 74, 77, 78, 105, 109, 110, 137, 138, 141, 143, 151, 153, 157, 161, 167, 170, 175, 176, 177, 178, 181, 182, 186, 187, 188, 194
intellectual clearance, 74
intellectual implications, 2, 3, 137, 138
intellectual proof, 1, 68, 133, 134, 135, 137, 138, 141, 175
interference, 162
intervention, 27, 37, 38
al-intifā' 'ind al-intifā', 31
al-iqtiḍā', 44
al-irāda, 15
al-irtibāṭī, 192
ish'ār, 41
al-ishāra, 44
Islamic custom, 151
al-Istibṣār fī-mā Ikhtalaf min al-Akhbār, 125
istikhdām, 56
al-istiqlālī, 192
istiṣḥāb al-kullī, 201
al-istiṣḥāb al-qahqarā, 15, 198
iṭlāq al-maqām, 24, 61

J

joint restrictor, 49
juristic clearance, 74
juristic proof, 2
juristic-literal meaning, 8

K

al-Kāfī, 125
al-khums, 19
al-kifā'ī, 18
al-Kutub al-Arba'a, 125

kaff al-nafs, 29
khabar al-wāĥid, 58, 125
khāṣṣ, 4
Kitāb, 48, 117
knowledge in summary fashion, 72, 111, 167, 178
knowledge-rooted, 110

L

al-laqab, 39, 43
large-scale dubiety, 189
lexical proof, 135
literal, 5, 6, 7, 8, 14, 15, 50, 79, 104, 105, 106, 107, 118, 120, 140, 143, 153, 171, 172
literal principles, 6

M

al-mafāhīm, 31
mafhūm, 31, 32, 33, 34, 35, 36, 37, 39, 40, 41, 42, 43, 44, 57, 58, 64
al-mafhūm al-mukhālif, 32
al-mafhūm al-muwāfiq, 32
major closure proof, 110
making, 3
mandatory, 1, 9, 16, 17, 18, 19, 20, 22, 23, 24, 25, 27, 38, 39, 43, 46, 48, 63, 65, 68, 71, 73, 75, 77, 78, 81, 83, 84, 85, 93, 94, 95, 96, 97, 111, 113, 122, 123, 129, 137, 160, 182, 183, 186, 188, 190, 191, 192, 193, 194, 199, 200
mandūĥa, 88
al-māni', 82
manṭūq, 31, 32, 33, 36, 37, 42, 44
al-marra, 25
mas'ala al-đidd, 79
al-mashrūṭ, 16
massive, 114, 122, 124, 125, 129, 134, 135, 147
al-Ma'ṣūm, 122
mawđū' lah, 4
merely not to do, 29
milākāt al-aĥkām, 172
mode, 21
motive, 155, 156
al-mu'allaq, 17
al-mu'āmala, 100
mu'anwan, 87
al-mubayyan, 65
al-muđayyaq, 19
al-mudjmal, 65
al-Muĥaqqiq al-Iṣfahānī, 2
muĥkam, 117
al-mukhaṣṣiṣ al-munfaṣil, 49
al-mulāzamāt al-'aqliyya, 2
al-munadjdjaz, 17, 72
al-muqaddam, 34
muqaddima, 81
muqaddima al-wādjib, 77
muqaddimāt al-ĥikma, 48, 61, 62
al-muqayyad, 61
al-muqtađī, 82
al-musabbabāt, 38
al-mushtaqq, 13, 14
Muslims' literal meaning, 8
muta'allaq al-mawđu', 40
al-mutabāyinayn, 53
mutawātir, 124, 147
al-muṭlaq, 16, 61
mutual falling, 160
al-muwaqqat, 19
al-muwassa', 19
al-Mużaffar, Muĥammad Riđā, 2

N

nafs an lā taf'al, 29
naskh, 117, 118
naṣṣ, 6, 41, 49, 58, 65, 117, 143
al-naw'ī, 5, 106

al-nawāhī, 29
necessitation, 44
negatively conditioned, 23
non-existence where non-existence, 31, 40, 43
non-inclusion, 47, 164
non-intervention, 37
number, 43

O

object of convention, 4
obligation, 1, 2, 3, 15, 16, 17, 18, 20, 23, 26, 27, 29, 32, 34, 37, 38, 43, 45, 46, 64, 71, 72, 73, 77, 79, 80, 81, 87, 91, 92, 94, 96, 104, 111, 112, 113, 123, 124, 127, 128, 129, 134, 137, 140, 148, 154, 155, 160, 167, 168, 169, 172, 175, 176, 177, 178, 179, 181, 186, 187, 189, 190, 191, 192, 193, 194, 195
obvious implicature in the most particular sense, 31
once, 25
one thing, 8, 17, 26, 85, 89, 91, 187, 190
option, 74, 160, 161, 162, 163, 168, 181, 182, 183, 192, 194
optional, 18
origin, 20, 82, 148, 161, 171, 172, 174, 198

P

particular conjecture, 106, 110
particular opposite, 80
particular, 4, 5, 39, 44, 47, 49, 50, 51, 52, 53, 54, 55, 58, 62, 79, 80, 81, 83, 99, 106, 107, 110, 117, 118, 132, 139, 140, 148, 188, 202
path, 115
penetrative doubt, 201
permanence, 30
personal, 5
persuasive proof, 1, 3, 73
pilgrimage to Mecca, 8, 17, 96, 122
practical celebrity, 147
practical principle, 2, 72, 73, 74, 106, 107, 111, 163, 165, 168, 186, 198, 201
praised opinions, 137, 141
precaution, 2, 3, 10, 74, 111, 115, 149, 161, 167, 169, 172, 174, 175, 176, 177, 178, 181, 183, 187, 190, 193
preceding, 5, 10, 42, 140, 198
preferrer, 160, 161, 162
preliminary, 3, 45, 46, 68, 71, 77, 78, 81, 82, 94, 95, 96, 124, 137, 171, 185, 186, 187, 199
premises of wisdom, 23, 48, 61, 62
primary divisions, 22
primary doubt, 111, 178, 193
principle of absoluteness, 6
principle of appearance, 6, 12
principle of continuity of the previous state, 74, 152, 167, 197
principle of generality, 6
principle of literalness, 6
principle of option, 167
principle, 3, 6, 7, 9, 10, 12, 22, 23, 24, 35, 38, 49, 57, 59, 62, 71, 72, 73, 74, 75, 79, 106, 107, 111, 113, 114, 115, 127, 144, 152, 155, 156, 157, 160, 163, 167, 168, 173, 174, 185, 189, 193, 195, 197, 202
principle of precaution or liability, 167
prohibition, 2, 3, 12, 16, 29, 30, 32, 79, 80, 81, 84, 85, 86, 87, 88, 89, 91, 92, 93, 94, 95, 96, 99, 100, 101, 108, 124, 141, 142, 151, 152, 153, 154, 162, 164, 177

prohibitions, 29
promptitude, 24
proviso, 20, 21, 22, 23, 24, 25, 26

Q

al-qaḍā', 20
qā'ida al-yaqīn, 201
al-qaṭ', 105, 106
al-qaṭṭā', 109
al-Qawānīn al-Muḥkama, 142
qiyās, 105, 110, 111, 130, 137, 155, 156, 157
qualified, 61
qualifier, 39
quasi-reduction, 186
al-Qummī, 142

R

al-raf', 171
real conjunction, 86
relational, 192
religious custom, 151
religiously obligations, 21
religiously, 21
repetition, 25, 30, 71
replacement, 69
reported consensus, 136
restriction, 47, 50, 51, 53, 92, 117, 118, 119, 164
reverse istiṣḥāb, 198
rule of certainty, 201

S

sabab, 115
al-ṣaḥīḥī, 9
ṣalāt, 1, 8, 10
ṣawm, 8
al-Sayyid al-Murtaḍā, 125, 130, 131
secondary divisions, 23
secondary precept, 2, 115
separate restrictor, 49
al-Shaikh al-Anṣārī, 129
al-Shaikh al-Ḥurr al-'Āmilī, 129
al-Shaikh al-Ṭūsī, 125, 130, 131
al-shakhṣī, 5
al-shakk al-badwī, 111
al-shakk al-sārī, 201
al-Shāri',19, 21, 33, 55
al-shubha ghair al-maḥṣūra, 189
al-shubha al-mafhūmiyya, 52
al-shubha al-maḥṣūra, 187
al-shubha al-mawḍū'iyya, 52, 169
al-shuhra al-'amaliyya, 147
al-shuhra al-fatwā'iyya, 147
al-shuhra, 147
shumūlī, 63
single report, 125, 126, 129, 131
single tradition, 58
al-ṣīgha, 21
al-sīra al-Islāmiyya, 151
al-sīra al-shar'iyya, 151
al-sīra, 151
sīra al-mutasharri'a, 151
sīra al-'uqalā', 151
small-scale dubiety, 187
sound, 9
sovereignty, 163
substitutional generality, 48
summary-fashioned knowledge, 177, 178, 181, 182, 183, 185, 186, 187, 188, 189, 190, 191, 193, 194
sunna, 3, 8, 48, 55, 65, 68, 105, 117, 121, 122, 129, 133, 134, 135, 137, 138, 139, 142, 144, 157, 170, 171, 177
suspended, 17

T

al-ta'abbudī, 21

al-ta'abbudiyyāt, 21
al-ta'ādul wa'l tarādjīh, 159
al-ta'āruḍ, 159
al-tabādur, 5, 10
tadākhul al-asbāb, 27, 37, 38
Tafṣīl Wasā'il al-Shī'a, 129
ṭahāra, 74
Tahdhīb al-Aḥkām, 125
al-takhaṣṣuṣ, 47, 164
al-takhṣīṣ, 47, 164
takhṭi'a, 72
takhyīr, 74
al-takhyīrī, 18
ta'kīd, 26, 27
al-takrār, 25, 30
al-ṭalab, 15
al-tālī, 34
al-tanbīh, 44
taqrīr, 121, 124
al-tarākhī, 24
al-ṭarīq, 106, 115
al-tasāquṭ, 160
ta'sīs, 26
taṣwīb, 72, 73
al-tawaṣṣulī, 21
al-tawaṣṣuliyyāt, 21
al-ta'yīnī, 18
al-tazāḥum, 162
termination, 42
the authority, 2, 3, 7, 52, 53, 54, 55, 68, 115, 117, 125, 126, 127, 129, 130, 133, 134, 136, 139, 143, 144, 149, 159, 197, 198, 200, 202
the Book, 55, 58, 59, 68, 105, 117, 126, 133, 137, 139, 142, 144, 145, 148, 157, 169
the caused, 38, 101, 106
the conduct of the wise, 7, 41, 115, 132, 141, 143, 151, 152, 153
the fifth, 19, 190, 199
the least, 53, 54, 55, 97, 192, 193, 194, 195
the least and the most of, 186
the most, 5, 15, 31, 44, 45, 46, 50, 53, 54, 55, 79, 83, 110, 192, 193, 194, 195
the object of the object, 40
the prayers, 1, 8, 10, 16, 17, 18, 19, 21, 23, 26, 27, 29, 36, 44, 45, 75, 80, 81, 85, 86, 87, 93, 94, 96, 97, 100, 112, 113, 168, 183, 193, 195, 200
the preliminary of the mandatory act, 77
the problem of preliminary of the mandatory act, 3
the problem of the opposite, 3, 79, 96
the Qur'ān, 3, 8, 55, 58, 65, 101, 117, 118, 142, 144, 145, 157
thematic proof, 135
timely, 20
total generality, 48
transaction, 100
two divergent things, 53, 186
typical, 5
typical conjecture, 106, 125

U

al-'umūm al-badalī, 48
al-'umūm al-istighrāqī, 47
al-'umūm al-madjmū'ī, 48
unambiguous, 117, 144
unlawfulness, 2, 3, 29, 31, 32, 80, 81, 83, 108, 111, 113, 148, 154, 155, 169, 173, 174, 175, 176, 177, 178, 179, 181, 182, 187, 188, 190, 191, 192, 193, 195, 201, 202
urgent, 19, 163, 173
al-uṣūl al-'amaliyya, 2, 165

al-uṣūl al-lafẓiyya, 6
Uṣūlīs, 2, 4, 5, 6, 9, 13, 14, 15, 16, 18, 19, 20, 24, 25, 27, 29, 30, 32, 33, 42, 44, 50, 57, 58, 61, 65, 77, 79, 82, 83, 85, 88, 91, 106, 108, 113, 125, 128, 133, 134, 135, 136, 151, 167, 168, 169, 170, 171, 174, 175, 176, 177, 178, 179, 199, 202

V

valid conjecture, 106, 107
voluntary-actual, 69

W

al-waḍ', 3
al-waḍ' al-ta'ayyunī, 3
al-waḍ' al-ta'yīnī, 3*al-wādjib*, 18
wāḥid, 124
al-waṣf, 39
way out, 88, 93
what incorporates both, 9
wish, 15, 20, 24, 29, 30, 40, 48, 79, 89, 90, 130, 200
al-wudjūb, 15
al-wurūd, 163

Y

Yūnus b. 'Abd al-Raḥmān, 130

Z

ẓāhir, 6, 41, 65, 69, 117
al-Zamakhsharī, 140
al-ẓann al-ḥudjdja, 106, 110
al-ẓann al-mu'tabar, 106
al-ẓann al-muṭlaq, 110
Zurāra, 130, 199, 200